REVIVAL FIRES 🔥

HISTORY'S MIGHTY REVIVALS

Geoff Waugh

© Geoff Waugh, Flashpoints of Revival
3rd updated and expanded edition, 2009
Reprinted as Revival Fires - History's Mighty Revivals, 2011

This book includes many first person accounts told by those who experienced revival. A Google search provides more information including photographs. The author appreciates reading about other mighty revivals also.
Contact geoffwaugh1@gmail.com

Reprinted with permission by
The Apostolic Network of Global Awakening

ANGA
1451 Clark Street
Mechanicsburg, PA 17055
www.globalawakening.com

ISBN: 978-0-9844-966-6-2

To our children and their children,
a heritage from and for the Lord.
Lucinda & David, Samantha, Jack, Julia,
Jonathan & Melinda, Jemimah, Dante, Ethan,
Melinda & Reuben, Joelle, Dana,
with love and thanks.

Endorsements

God has set off fireworks of revival throughout the history of Christianity, but few of us are aware of the magnitude of his handiwork. In Flashpoints of Revival, Australian author Geoff Waugh walks us through God's gallery of revivals, century by century, to show us that the Holy Spirit can spontaneously ignite at any time, anywhere. You will read details, historically documented facts, and personal accounts of every major move of God for the past three centuries from every corner of the globe. For revival enthusiasts or historians this book is a treasure chest. For those who think God "doesn't do that" this book is a must read.

Outreach Magazine (COC)

Using eye witness accounts, Australian Geoff Waugh takes us on a journey of revivals - beginning with the Moravians in Herrnhut, Germany in 1727 and continuing through the centuries to others in England, America, Canada, Africa, India, Korea, Chile and more, including Brownsville in 1995. This will leave you hungry and thirsty, hopefully crying out to God for revival in Australia. Excellent.

The Australian Evangel (AOG)

What a goldmine of inspiring details! Readers may have heard of some of the revivals described in this book, but Geoff Waugh's comprehensive and up-to-date book provides a global perspective of the unexpected and transforming work of the Holy Spirit around the globe from the 18th century to today. Read, be inspired and encouraged - and open to ways in which the Spirit 'blows where he wills'.

Rev Dr John Olley
former principal Perth Baptist Theological College

The first time I read this book, I couldn't put it down. Not only were the stories researched with clear and concise data, but they provide an account of revivals that blew my mind away. As a person interested in seeing the winds of the Spirit blow in our churches and communities, I was truly impacted reading through history's mighty revivals. Dr. Waugh's simple yet provoking stories of men and women who dared make a difference and in being available for God was used mightily, is but a true story of this humble man of God whom I have had the privilege of working alongside following the revival winds in the Pacific. Once you read this book, you will not want to put it down as the stories comes alive again, showing us the heart of a man who is passionate about revivals and seeing God move especially in our communities. Dr Waugh's book is a must read to all who are passionate about letting the Holy Spirit do his work in their lives, in their church and in their community. An inspirational read.

Romulo Nayacalevu
Fiji lawyer and UN representative

This work of the Rev. Dr. Geoff Waugh is of great significance. In it he has provided a comprehensive overview of the major revivals during the last three centuries. What is particularly important is the way in which we are enabled, through

Dr. Waugh's work, to see how God has acted in all kinds of ways, through unexpected people, in unexpected situations, to bring about revival. Geoff Waugh is respected for his integrity, his communication skills, and his passion for mission and renewal. Churches and Christians around the world will benefit greatly from this timely contribution.

Rev Prof James Haire
Professor of Theology, Charles Sturt University
Executive Director, Australian Centre for Christianity and
Culture

Flashpoints of Revival is a good overview of the major revivals that have taken place in history, especially more recent history. It will be a compendium for historians and others interested in the subject for a long time to come. I doubt if there is a resource quite like it for logical progression and comprehensive treatment.

Rev. Tony Cupit
former Director of Evangelism, Baptist World Alliance

Geoff Waugh has broken new ground by pulling together evidence of divine impacts on people in revival. He emphasises the place of prayer and repentance in our response to God's awesome sovereignty and might. This is a book which will inspire you and help you to persist until the earth is "filled with the knowledge of the glory of the Lord".

Rev Dr Stuart Robinson
Crossway Baptist Church, Melbourne, Australia

I read Flashpoints of Revival with much interest and enjoyment. The Rev. Geoff Waugh has offered us a comprehensive account of spiritual renewal over the centuries. Whilst one of the truly great spiritual renewals has occurred in the latter half of the twentieth century, it finds its genesis in the

Book of Acts. Amazing signs of God's power and love have occurred in the Christian communities which have been open to revival. Those communities have seen increasing membership. The churches which have closed their minds to charismatic renewal have seen decline in membership. I praise God for the Holy Spirit movement in our time.

Bishop Ralph E. Wicks
Anglican Church of Australia

Flashpoints of Revival has brought many hours of interesting reading. It is very informative and up to date concerning revivals both past and present. I am confident that this book will be well received by many scholars and historians.

Rev Dr Naomi Dowdy
Trinity Christian Centre, Singapore

The Rev Dr Geoff Waugh is well able to write about the stories and experiences of revival. He has been a careful and sympathetic student of revival experiences in many parts of the world. In churches that need God's power for great tasks it is important that God's action in other places be studied. Geoff Waugh has made a crucial contribution to that task.

Rev John E Mavor
former President of the Uniting Church in Australia

I love learning about revival and this book adds to that hunger. Geoff Waugh, with great integrity and detailed research draws together much information that will inspire the reader. This is an extension of Geoff's many years of contribution in the area of renewal and revival as editor of the Renewal Journal. Geoff has initiated renewal activities in many denominations in Australia and has participated actively as a member in the growth of Gateway Baptist Church in Brisbane.

Rev Tim Hanna, former Minister, Gateway Baptist Church
Brisbane, Australia

Dr Geoff Waugh's work has a global relevance, which he has applied in the Australian context. As a fellow Australian I am appreciative. My appreciation is greatly enhanced by a deep respect and affection for the author. He is a competent teacher, an excellent communicator, an informed, disciplined renewalist and an experienced educator. All these qualities combine to commend the author and his work.

Rev Dr Lewis Born, former Moderator
Queensland Synod of the Uniting Church

Geoff Waugh places current outpourings of the Holy Spirit in historical context. In 1993 I said that this move of God would go round the world. It has. It is breaking out and touching millions of lives. Geoff's work helps us understand more about God's mighty work in our time.

Pastor Neil Miers
President, Christian Outreach Centre, Australia

Contents

4. Mid-twentieth Century Revival: Healing Evangelism Revival...**115**

5. Late Twentieth Century Revival: Renewal and Revival...**165**

6. Final Decade, Twentieth Century:
River of God Revival...215

7. Twenty First Century:
Transforming Revival...307

Conclusion..389

Geoff Waugh

Foreword

Geoff Waugh and I agree that our generation is likely to be an eye witness to the greatest outpouring of the Holy Spirit that history has ever known. Many others join us in this expectation, some of them sensing that it will come in the next few years.

Here in America, it seems to me that I have heard more reports of revival-like activity in the past three years than in the previous thirty. This has caused revival to be a more frequent topic of Christian conversation than I have ever seen. There is an extraordinary hunger for learning more about how the hand of God works in revival.

That is a major reason why Revival Fires is such a timely book. Christian libraries are well stocked with detailed accounts of certain revivals as well as scholarly analytical histories of revival. But I know of no other book like this one that provides rapid-fire, easy-to-read, factual literary snapshots of virtually every well-known revival since Pentecost.

As I read this book, I was thrilled to see how God has been so mightily at work in so many different times and places. I felt like I had grasped the overall picture of revival for the first time, and I was moved to pray that God, indeed, would allow me not to be just an observer, but rather a literal participant in the worldwide outpouring that will soon come. As you read the book, I am sure you will be saying the same thing.

1st edtion (1998)

By Dr C Peter Wagner, Fuller Theological Seminary, Pasadena

Preface ▆▆▆▆▆▆▆▆▆▆▆▆▆▆▆▆▆▆▆▆▆▆

Bounding across the vivid green ridges and gorges of Papua New Guinea's highlands, I found a gem in Meg, my wonderful wife, now in heaven. We were both Australian missionaries and brought our first child home to our bamboo and grass house in the majestic highlands. We became grateful grandparents, proud of our extended family of three children and their children. Together we have explored dynamic renewal and transforming revival.

My interest in revivals began when I was young. I grew up in a loving family, the son of a Baptist pastor. My earliest memories include drifting off to sleep under a blanket on the pew while my mum played the piano in church and listening to the young people sing around our piano in our home at my bedtime. My parents dedicated me to God, as they did for all their children. They encouraged us to know and love the Bible and the heroes of the faith. I devoured Sunday School books and stories of John Bunyan, John Wesley, John Newton, William Carey, Florence Nightingale, David Livingstone, Mary Slessor, Hudson Taylor and scores more.

I am grateful for that grounding in evangelical faith, especially the truth of the Bible, which I believe now more strongly than ever. However, when I later served the Lord as a minister in Australia and in Papua New Guinea, I soon learned that our way of being the church carries a lot of cultural baggage. That may not be wrong – just limited. I could see the Church in the Pacific, live with fresh faith, grappling with cultural and personal transformation, and dealing with the typical challenges of human relationships, which are part of church life in any culture.

Then the opportunity opened for me to work in the Methodist and the Uniting Church in Australia as a Baptist minister. There I met many compassionate friends who encompassed and encouraged a wide range of views. I am grateful for the experience gained there, mainly in innovative Christian Education ministries and creative theological college teaching, as well as studying fearless missiology with Fuller Theological Seminary in America.

During the 1970's, we encountered – or rather, were encountered by – the wave of renewal and revival. So I gathered reports on revivals. The church publishers produced a series of my study books, including Living in the Spirit and Church on Fire, which examine these vibrant, explosive developments. Our Baptist family was part of Wesley Methodist Church, which from 1977 became Wesley Uniting Church in Kangaroo Point, Brisbane. There I assisted in a team ministry in a traditional morning service and a charismatic evening service that grew rapidly. I worked with dedicated lay leaders of multiplying home groups and community houses to care for the growing congregation. Our home was one of those community houses, with between two and eight others living with us for varying periods. Those lively days of renewal and revival challenged and changed us all.

Then we were part of Gateway Baptist Church in Brisbane which grew from 200 to 1200 in a decade from the mid-eighties, and later with Kenmore Baptist Church, another contemporary and renewed church of over 2,000 in Brisbane. There I told the leaders of the 6 a.m. daily prayer group that I would join them if the Lord woke me. He did. Daily. I was surprised, and not always enthusiastic to jump out of bed in the dark, cold winter mornings.

My work with various church traditions gave me great scope for renewal ministry. Part of that ministry was leading the interdenominational Renewal Fellowship in Brisbane. I deeply appreciate the support and encouragement of that group, especially traveling as teams to various churches and to other countries. I'll always remember the June monsoon rains in Ghana that ceased on the first night of our open-air, combined-churches crusade there and began again the day after our last meeting. I loved teaching inaugural courses on the History of Revivals and on Signs and Wonders at the warmly hospitable Asian Theological Seminary in Manila in the Philippines in their hot summer schools. Our mission teams trekked to dedicated little churches in the cities and villages of Nepal, India and Sri Lanka where a bewildering array of faith-filled Bible Schools inspired us all. They ranged from small local church ones in Nepal and Sri Lanka to the 600-student campus of the indigenous Indian Inland Mission near New Delhi in India.

In the nineties, I began editing the interdenominational Renewal Journal and we published 20 issues in a decade. They are now available on www.renewaljournal.com along with mission and publication news.

I taught at the School of Ministries at Christian Heritage College in Brisbane. The college offers degrees in ministry, education, social sciences, business and arts. Initially they invited me to write the submission for the government accredited Bachelor of Ministry degree, and then I continued teaching there beyond being retired, or re-fired. Their School of Ministries is also the Bible School for Christian Outreach Centre, an Australian revival movement with over 200 churches in Australia and more than 1400 in other nations.

Christians are one in Christ. That is a theological fact and eternal reality. As we rediscover that reality through repentance, reconciliation, unity and love, we also discover revival transformation. God honors his promise in 2 Chronicles 7:14: If my people, who are called by my name, will humble themselves and pray and seek my face and turn from their wicked ways, then will I hear from heaven and will forgive their sin and will heal their land.

Revival Fires, this 3rd revised and expanded edition of Flashpoints of Revival adds many further accounts to the stories in previous editions and includes comprehensive footnotes. These amazing accounts briefly describe God's mighty work in revivals.

Introduction

The Spirit of the Lord is upon me,
because he has anointed me
to bring good news to the poor.
He has sent me to proclaim
release to the captives
and recovery of sight to the blind,
to let the oppressed go free,
to proclaim the year of the Lord's favour
Luke 4:18-19; Isaiah 61:1-2

Jesus, reading from Isaiah's prophecy, claimed its fulfilment in himself. He explained his mission as the Messiah (the Christ, the Anointed One) in terms of being empowered by the anointing of the Spirit of the Lord for his ministry. That ministry, specifically to the poor, captives, blind, and oppressed, demonstrated the liberating good news of the Lord's favour.

That grace and favour met personal and institutional resistance. Jesus illustrated his mandate in his home synagogue with the biblical accounts of the Lord providing for the Gentile Sidon widow and the Syrian army officer. The congregation's rage erupted into one of the many assassination attempts on Jesus' life.[1] His anointed ministry drove him to the cross.

The ministry of Jesus and of his church seen in the 'revivals' of the early church show both the powerful nature of the Spirit's anointing and its power to confront evil.

This book emphasises the importance of these impacts of the Holy Spirit, demonstrated biblically and also historically in revivals. It shows the importance of the Great Commission of Matthew 28:18-20, which declares that Jesus' followers throughout history 'to the end of the age' would obey everything he taught his first disciples. They learned to serve and minister in the power of the Spirit.

Revivals show how different perspectives on Spirit movements find common ground in evangelism, ministry, and in social action.

Different Christian traditions emphasise different dimensions of being baptised in the Spirit. Rather than seeing these perspectives as mutually exclusive, they may be seen as inter-related and integrated. The evangelical emphasis on conversion,[2] the Catholic and Episcopal emphasis on initiation,[3] the Reformed emphasis on covenant,[4] and the Pentecostal emphasis on charismata[5] can be integrated in a dynamic view of Spirit baptism. These perspectives all thrown light on powerful Spirit movements in revival, like facets of a brilliant diamond.

Revival

Revival is God pouring out his Spirit on all people.[6]

Revivals have been thoroughly described and analysed.[7] The Christian term 'revival' may be traced to its earliest use in the phrase "revival of religion."[8]

The Oxford Association for Research in Revival, formed in 1974 through the work of revival historian J. Edwin Orr, distinguished between 'revival' for believers and 'awakening' for the community:

> A spiritual awakening is a movement of the Holy Spirit bringing about a revival of New Testament Christianity in the Church of Christ and its related community. ... The outpouring of the Spirit accomplishes the reviving of the Church, the awakening of the masses and the movements of uninstructed people toward the Christian faith; the revived Church, by many or by few, is moved to engage in evangelism, in teaching and in social action.[9]

The terms 'revival' and 'awakening' have been used interchangeably in revival literature. However, 'revival' now usually refers to local revivals of spiritual life and commitment within the church but also touching the surrounding community through conversions and social transformation. 'Awakening' usually refers to the more widespread influence of revivals across a large area and for a more extended period of time with considerable influence in the community and the nation.

Martin Lloyd-Jones described revival this way:

> It is an experience in the life of the Church when the Holy Spirit does an unusual work. He does that work, primarily, amongst the members of the Church; it is a reviving of the believers. You cannot revive something that has never had life, so revival, by definition, is first of all an enlivening and quickening and awakening of lethargic, sleeping, almost moribund Church members. Suddenly the power of the Spirit comes upon them and they are brought into a new and more profound awareness of the truths that they previously held intel-

lectually, and perhaps at a deeper level too. They are humbled, they are convicted of sin, they are terrified at themselves. Many of them feel they had never been Christians. And they come to see the great salvation of God in all its glory and to feel its power. Then, as the result of their quickening and enlivening, they begin to pray. New power comes into the preaching of ministers, and the result of this is that large numbers who were previously outside the Church are converted and brought in.[10]

Revivals may be examined as sociological phenomena. Revivals occur within a sociological context and usually affect and change that context. The sociological discourses are relevant as significant social explanations, but they often exclude the theological dimensions of divine initiative and intervention, supernatural phenomena, and human repentance and faith.[11] Repentance, renewal and divine intervention feature prominently in revival accounts, adding fuller dimensions to the secular sociological explanations of revival phenomena.

Furthermore, Christian revivals often include mass evangelism meetings, but revival also needs to be distinguished from the use of the term 'revival' for evangelistic meetings. When 'revival' is used for a scheduled revival meeting, such as once a week in a local church, the term is being used in a limited, narrow sense rather than in its historical meaning.

Revival refers to the Lord pouring out his Spirit on everyone.

Biblical witness

The Bible affirms specific, identifiable and profound impacts of the Holy Spirit in the redemptive, liberating action of God in Spirit movements. Biblical terms describing charismatic impacts of the Spirit vary greatly in both the Old and New Testaments. They include the following, with these representative references:

the Spirit was given - Numbers 11:17; John 7:39;
the Spirit came upon - Judges 3:10; Acts 19:5;
the Spirit took control - Judges 6:34; 1 Samuel 11:6; 16:13;
the Spirit poured out - Joel 2:2828; Acts 10:45;
the Spirit came down - Matthew 3:16; Luke 3:22; John 1:33;
the Spirit fell (or came down) Acts 10:44; 11:15;
the Spirit received - Acts 8:1517; 19:2;
baptised in or with the Spirit - Luke 3:16; John 1:33; Acts 1:5;
filled with the Spirit - Acts 2:4; 9:17; Ephesians 5:18.

The specific nature of these charismatic impacts is significant, as is the varied nature of subsequent charismata and ministries resulting from these impacts. Luke's narrative discourses in his gospel and the Acts emphasise the importance of the empowering presence of the Holy Spirit in the ministry of Jesus and his followers, and all the gospel accounts describe the impact of the Holy Spirit upon Jesus at his baptism and in his subsequent ministry.

The Old Testament

The unique Hebrew monotheism involved covenant relationship with God, Yahweh, as supreme. Consequently, any deviation from God's rule required repentance and restoration in personal, communal, national and ultimately in international relationships.

Revival as repentance and return to that covenant relationship is typical of Spirit movements in the Old Testament. However, periods of covenant renewal were not necessarily times of revival, particularly where people merely conformed outwardly to the edicts of their godly rulers. Revival as an outpouring of the Spirit on everyone is foreshadowed, rather than fulfilled, in the Old Testament.[12] The new covenant blessings involve outpourings of the Spirit in the promised messianic era.[13]

The popular, generic biblical 'revival' statement is God's promise to answer the prayers of his repentant people with the restoration of shalom in the healing of the land. This promise, given to Solomon in a night vision at the time of the dedication of the first temple, answered his public national prayer of 2 Chronicles 6 (specifically verses 26-27), with the assurance of God's faithfulness to his covenant: "If my people who are called by my name will humble themselves, and pray and seek my face, and turn from their wicked ways, then I will hear from heaven, and will forgive their sin and heal their land" (2 Chronicles 7:14).

Kaiser[14] notes the significance of 2 Chronicles 7:14, as demonstrated in repentance and reform movements during the reigns of Asa, Jehoshaphat, Hezekiah and Josiah in Judah. Although commentators refer to this passage in terms of the writer's doctrine of retribution, it is also justified exegetically as a pattern for revival as demonstrated in Israel's history and more completely in the messianic era of the Spirit following Pentecost.

Spirit movements in the Old Testament demonstrate God's faithfulness to this covenant promise. Revival or reform always involved returning to theocratic rule, with the prophets as the guardians of the theocracy. Kings were accountable to God, and the true prophets spoke from God.

Where repentance occurred, often in times of crisis and need, the Spirit of the Lord intervened powerfully on the nation and on other nations with glimpses of the blessings of the promised messianic rule.[15]

Examples of 'revival' in Israel's history include movements of reform and repentance under the leadership of:

1. Jacob-Israel (Genesis 35:1-15),
2. Samuel (1 Sameul 7:1-17),
3. Asa (2 Chronicles 15:1-15),
4. Joash (2 Kings 11-12; 2 Chronicles 23-24),
5. Hezekiah (2 Kings 18:18; 2 Chronicles 29-31),
6. Josiah (2 Kings 22-23; 2 Chronicles 34-35),
7. Jonah (Jonah 1-4, involving Ninevah),
8. Haggai and Zechariah with Zerubbabel (Ezra 56)
9. Ezra with Nehemiah (Nehemiah 9:16; 12:44-47).[16]

Although these are not the only occasions of repentance and reform, they were national movements of return to the covenant obligations, and they document the fulfilment of the covenant promises and obligations with typical revival phenomena. Revivals in Israel's history included these characteristics:

1. They occurred in times of moral darkness and national depression;

2. Each began in the heart of a consecrated servant of God who became the energising power behind it;

3. Each revival rested on the Word of God, and most were the result of proclaiming God's Word with power;

4. All resulted in a return to the worship of God;

5. Each witnessed the destruction of idols where they existed;

6. In each revival, there was a recorded separation from sin, especially destruction of idols;

7. In every revival the people returned to obeying God's laws;

8. There was a restoration of great joy and gladness;

9. Each revival was followed by a period of national prosperity.[17]

Revival movements in the Old Testament demonstrated God's faithfulness to his covenant relationship, but the prophets saw such movements as harbingers of the messianic age in which the promise of shalom would be fulfilled, not merely externally upon anointed members of the covenant community, but internally by the outpouring of the Spirit of the Lord upon all people.

The New Testament

Jesus fulfilled and completed the messianic promises in himself. This included the promise of the outpouring of the Spirit. Jesus experienced the empowering of the Spirit at his baptism, which he explained in terms of being anointed for ministry (Luke 4:18-19).

The Spirit-empowered preaching and ministry of the twelve and the seventy also proclaimed and demonstrated the messianic kingdom of God.[18] However, the disciples often failed to understand the significance of the Spirit's liberating presence, and often showed lack of faith and vision, both before and after Pentecost.[19]

Jesus inaugurated the new era of his new blood covenant. His church, filled with his Spirit, still fulfils his mission in the world. The cross and resurrection remain the ultimate and essential victory over evil. Authentic revival demonstrates the triumph of the cross and the presence and power of the risen Lord in his people by his Spirit.

The early church lived in revival. It saw rapid growth in the power of the Holy Spirit from the initial outburst at Pentecost.

Multitudes joined the church, amid turmoil and persecution. As with Pentecost, revivals are often unexpected, sudden, revolutionary, and impact large numbers of people bringing them to repentance and faith in Jesus the Lord.

Characteristics typical of revival can be found in the widely acknowledged prototype of revival in the Pentecost account. These themes recur constantly in accounts of Spirit movements in revival. Stott[20] notes revival characteristics in Acts 2: "Pentecost has been called - and rightly - the first 'revival', using this word to denote one of those altogether unusual visitations of God, in which a whole community becomes vividly aware of his immediate, overpowering presence. It may be, therefore, that not only the physical phenomena (vv 2ff), but the deep conviction of sin (v 37), the 3,000 conversions (v 41) and the widespread sense of awe (v 43) were signs of 'revival.'"

Revivals continually display the characteristics and phenomena of the Pentecost account, including:

1. *Divine sovereignty* (Acts 2:1,2): God chose the day, the time, the place, the people, uniting old covenant promise with new covenant fulfilment. His Spirit came suddenly and people were overwhelmed at the Pentecost harvest festival.

2. *Prayer* (Acts 1:14; 2:1): The believers gathered together to pray and wait on God as instructed by the Jesus at the ascension. All revival literature emphasises the significance of united, earnest, repentant prayer in preparing the way for revival and sustaining it.

3. *Unity* (Acts 2:1): The disparate group meeting 'in one accord' included male and female, old and young, former zealot and former collaborator, most of the twelve and those who joined them. Their differences blended into the diversity of enriched unity .

4. *Obedience to the Spirit* (Acts 2:4): Filled with the Spirit they immediately began using gifts of the Spirit as 'the Spirit gave utterance'.

5. *Preaching* (Acts 2:14): Peter preached with anointed Spirit-empowered boldness, as did the others whose words were heard in many languages.

6. *Repentance* (Acts 2:38-39): Large numbers were convicted and repented. They were instructed to be baptised and to expect to be filled with the Spirit and to live in Spirit-led community, and that succeeding generations should expect this also.

7. *Evangelism* (Acts 2:40-41, 47): The new believers witnessed through changed lives bringing others to faith in the Lord daily.

8. *Charismata* (Acts 2:43): The era of the Spirit inaugurated supernatural phenomena including glossolalia,[21] signs, wonders and miracles, demonstrated powerfully among the leaders, but not limited to them.

9. *Community* (Acts 2:42-47): The outpouring of the Spirit brought the church into being as a charismatic, empowered community which met regularly in homes for discipleship instruction, supportive fellowship, daily informal eucharistic meals, and constant prayer.

10. *Rapid church growth* (Acts 2:47): Typical of revivals, The Lord added to the church those who were being saved. This eventually transformed the community of Judaistic believers into a constantly expanding community embracing all people.

That story of revival declares that "about three thousand persons were added" (Acts 2:41), "many of those who heard the word believed; and they numbered about five thousand" (Acts 4:4), "more than ever believers were added to the Lord, great numbers of both men and women" (Acts 5:14), "The word of God continued to spread; the number of the disciples increased greatly in Jerusalem, and a great many of the priests became obedient to the faith" (Acts 6:7), "the church throughout Judea, Galilee, and Samaria had peace and was built up … it increased in numbers" (Acts 9:31), "a great number became believers" (Acts 11:21), "a great many people were brought to the Lord" (Acts 11:24), "the word of God continued to advance and gain adherents" (Acts 12:24), "the churches were strengthened in the faith and increased in numbers daily" (Acts 16:5).

Those early Christians lived and ministered in the power of the Spirit, facing constant opposition and persecution. They were not faultless, as the epistles indicate, but they were on fire, "people who have been turning the world upside down" (Acts 17:6). Biblical revivals and awakenings return to this normative pattern.

Luke's narrative in Acts is a narrative of revival. Throughout history and still today, revivals continue that story.

Historical witness

Significant impacts of the Spirit of God have continued through history. These Spirit movements were often ignored, minimised or denigrated for many reasons:

1. Some historians wrote for predominantly secular purposes, so ignored significant Spirit movements. Josephus referred only briefly to Jesus and his troublesome sect.[22]

2. Many historians wrote from the perspective of the established church, which often opposed and suppressed revival movements.[23]

3. Strong impacts of the Spirit constantly initiated new movements which criticised and threatened the established order, so these movements were opposed, their writings destroyed and many leaders martyred.[24]

4. Authentic revival movements were often regarded as heretical, and their leaders killed, as happened with Jesus, the leaders in the early church, and throughout history.

5. Some Spirit movements became cults with heretical teachings, and so brought disrepute on the whole movement and suspicion concerning charismata, especially prophecies, so they were opposed and suppressed.

6. Personal and historical accounts of impacts of the Spirit have been systematically destroyed during subsequent historical periods, often burned as heretical.

7. Excessive enthusiasm or fanaticism in revival movements have brought these genuine Spirit movements into disrepute and so generated more opposition.

8. Leaders and adherents of revivals have often been occupied with other pressing priorities such as ensuring their own survival rather than recording their history.

However, records have survived, mostly after the invention of the printing press. Revivals demonstrate biblical patterns of authentic Spirit movements. Evangelical revivals provide evidence of these charismatic encounters that became the empowering force in revival.

Charismatic impacts in Spirit movements are normal in many revivals among masses of people. Throughout history many people led reform and revival movements that powerfully affected the church and the community.

Before Constantine the church spread rapidly in spite of, and even because of, persecution. The witness of the martyrs influenced many people. After Constantine the Holy Spirit continued his work in the church and the world, often causing strong opposition as in the New Testament. He did not take a break during the Middle Ages!

Irenaeus (d 195), a student of the Apostle John's disciple Polycarp, led a considerable spiritual awakening in Lyons in southern Gaul where in addition to his Episcopal responsibilities he learned the local language and his preaching was accompanied by gifts of the Spirit, exorcisms and reports of some raised from the dead.[25]

The Montanists, or the New Prophecy movement, flourished in Asia Minor from the second half of the second century into the fifth century. This movement included a revival of prophecies and of acknowledged prophets including women, a challenge for Christians to forsake worldly attitudes with stricter living standards in Christian communities, and a strong belief in the second coming of Christ with the ideal society soon to be established in the New Jerusalem. Montanus spoke in tongues and began prophesying at his baptism, and taught that the gifts of the Holy Spirit were still available. The lawyer-theologian Tertullian (c 150-223) became the most famous convert to Montanism when he joined that movement early in the third century. The movement came into disrepute because of excesses, particularly in prophecy, but it became a strong challenge to the lax state of the church at that time.

Gregory the Wonderworker (c 213-270), converted through contact with Origen (c 185-254), became bishop of his native Pontus and appears to have led a strong movement of conversion till most of his diocese was Christian.

The church fathers founded monastic orders devoted to serving of God and people, often in protest to laxity and nominal

Christianity in the church. Many of these leaders led strong spiritual movements including various miracles, healings and exorcisms, although caution is needed in distinguishing between fact and subsequent fiction.

Augustine of Hippo in North Africa (354-430), strongly influenced the church and society through his writings. His earlier writings indicated a cessation of the charismata in his time, a position which strongly influenced western theology, even though his later writing acknowledged that miracles occurred in relation to the sacraments, prayer of the relics of the saints, and his work The City of God included a chapter entitled "Concerning Miracles Which Were Wrought in Order that the World Might Believe in Christ and Which Cease Not to Be Wrought Now That the World Does Believe."[26]

Patrick (389-c 461) told of the conversions of thousands of the Irish, initiating active Celtic missionary activity including subsequent evangelism by Columba (521-597) in Scotland and Columban and others in France, Switzerland and northern Italy. By 600 Augustine of Canterbury and his missionaries saw thousands accept Christianity in England and it was reported that they imitated the powers of the apostles in the signs which they displayed.

In the twelfth century Peter Waldo and the Waldensians began reform and revival movements which challenged the church and impacted society. Francis of Assisi in the thirteenth century called people to forsake all and follow Jesus. Many did. They influenced others in society. John Wycliffe and his itinerant preachers, the Lollards, made a powerful impact on England in the fourteenth century. They aroused strong opposition leading to many becoming martyrs.

In the fifteenth century John Hus in Bohemia and Savonarola in Italy led strong reform movements which brought revival but led to their martyrdoms. Hus was known for his unblemished purity of life and uncompromising stand for truth in a decadent society. Savonarola fasted, prayed and preached with prophetic fire which confronted evils of his time, filled the churches, and brought honesty into much of civic and business life.

Gutenburg's printing press invented in 1456 made the Scriptures widely available. This helped spark the sixteenth century Reformation with leaders such as Huldrych Zwingli in Switzerland initially calling for freedom of conscience though later denying this for others, Martin Luther in Germany proclaiming justification by faith alone based on the supreme authority of scripture, and John Calvin in Geneva emphasising the awesome sovereignty and grace of God. Radical reformers, such as Felix Manz the first Anabaptist martyr, were killed by some of the reformers in those days of heated religious conflict. John Knox fearlessly called Scotland to repentance amid the intense political and religious fervour of the times.

Since then many revivals won thousands of people to faith in Jesus Christ and made a powerful impact on society. It still happens.

Revival historian Edwin Orr described the major evangelical awakenings following the Great Awakening of 1727-1745, as the Second Awakening of 1790-1830 (The Eager Feet, fired with missionary commitment), the Third Awakening of 1858-60 (The Fervent Prayer, spread through countless prayer groups) and the Worldwide Awakening from 1900 (The Flaming Tongue, spreading the word around the globe).

Contemporary Witness

Unprecedented revival continues in China especially in house churches, in Africa especially in independent church movements, in Latin America especially in evangelical/pentecostal churches, and in proliferating revival movements throughout the world. All of these now involve powerful impacts of the Spirit of God.

Renewal and evangelism increased throughout the nineties, including revival Spirit movements in the western world. Focal points for renewal and revival have included Toronto in Canada, Brompton in England, and Pensacola in America. Reports continue to multiply of renewed churches, empowered evangelism, and significant social involvement such as crime rates dramatically reduced in Sunderland in England and in Pensacola in America.[27]

We now live through a massive shift in global Christianity, which increasingly acknowledges and rediscovers revival. It holds enormous promise for "the reshaping of religion in the twenty-first century"[28] through transforming revival.

Revival, as described in this book, shows how differing denominational perspectives on Spirit movements may find common ground in evangelism, in equipping Christians for ministry, and in social reform.

Endnotes

[1] Many books have multiple publishers. These endnotes include publishers where page numbers are given.

Introduction
See Matthew 2:16-20 (soldiers); Luke 4:28-30 (cliff); John 8:59 (stones); John 11:53 (plots); Luke 22:1-6 (betrayal).

[2] James Dunn, 1970, Baptism in the Holy Spirit.

[3] Michael Green, 1985, I Believe in the Holy Spirit; Kilian McDonnell and George Montague, 1991, Christian Initiation and Baptism in the Holy Spirit.

[4] Rodman Williams, 1992, Renewal Theology.

[5] Derek Prince, 1995, Baptism in the Holy Spirit.

[6] Joel 2:28; Acts 2:17.

[7] J. Edwin Orr provides the most detailed and comprehensive study of revival history, particularly in his books on evangelical awakenings: The Eager Feet: Evangelical Awakenings, 1792 & 1830; The Fervent Prayer: Evangelical Awakenings, 1858-1860; and The Flaming Tongue: Evangelical Awakenings, 1900.

[8] The Oxford English Dictionary notes that the New England Puritan preacher and writer Cotton Mather in his Magnalia Christi Americana (1702), referred to the seventeenth century Puritan preacher Francis Higginson in Leicester describing "a notable revival of religion among them".

[9] Edwin Orr, 1973, The Eager Feet, Moody, p. vii.

[10] Martyn Lloyd-Jones, 1959, "Revival: An Historical and Theological Survey" in How Shall they Hear? the compiled papers from the Puritan and Reformed Studies Conference of 1959 in London. Reproduced in R E Davies, 1992, I will Pour out My Spirit, Monarch, p. 17.

[11] William McLoughlin, for example, examines the Great Awakening and American revivals sociologically. He describes American revivals in terms of anthropologist Anthony Wallace's (1956) five stages of a revitalisation movement. McLoughlin (1978, Revivals, Awakening and Reform, University of Chicago Press, pp. 2, 10) concludes: "Great awakenings (and the revivals that are part of them) are the results ... of critical disjunctions in our self-understanding. ... Awakenings begin in periods of cultural distortion and grave personal stress, when we lose faith in the legitimacy of our norms, the viability of our institutions, and the authority of our leaders in church and state. ... They are times of revitalization. They are therapeutic and cathartic, not pathological. They restore our natural verve and our self-confidence, helping us to maintain faith in ourselves, our ideals, and our 'covenant with God' even while they compel us to reinterpret that covenant in the light of new experience. ... In short, great awakenings are periods when the culture system has had to be revitalized in order to overcome jarring disjunctions between norms and experience, old beliefs and new realities, dying patterns and emerging patterns of behavior."

[12] Cf. Joel 2:28-32; Isaiah 44:3; Ezekiel 36:27; 39:29.

[13] Cf. Jeremiah 31:31-34; Hebrews 8:8-12.

[14] Walter Kaiser, 1986, Quest for Renewal: Personal Revival in the Old Testament.

[15] Cf. 2 Chronicles 15, 2930; 2 Kings 23; Nehemiah 89; also a more detailed discussion of this phenomena in Scripture in Brian Mills, 1990, Preparing for Revival, Kingsway, pp. 26-27.

[16] These are representative examples. Many accounts detail other Old Testament Spirit movements ranging beyond the scope of this preliminary survey.

[17] Adapted from Winkie Pratney, 1994, Revivals, Whitaker, p. 13, citing Wilbur Smith.

[18] Matthew 10:1-8; Mark 6:7-13; Luke 9:1-6; 10:1-20.

[19] Peter provides examples of 'failure' as in failing to walk on water, opposing Jesus' intention to go to Jerusalem, his denial of Jesus, and his conflict with Paul at Antioch. Jesus constantly chided his disciples for their lack of faith and vision, including during the post-resurrection encounters (as in Mark 16:14), and most of the New Testament epistles address similar 'failures' in the early church.

[20] John Stott, 1990, The Message of Acts, InterVasity Press, p. 61.

[21] The Pentecost account may have included akolalia. Pentecostal theologian Harold Hunter (1983, "Spirit Baptism and the 1896 Revival in Cherokee County, North Carolina," in Pneuma: The Journal of the Society for Pentecostal Studies, Vol. 5, No. 2. Fall., p. 13) notes, "Glossolalia is a form of speech which does not directly correspond to any known language, while akolalia can be used to describe that phenomenon in which the speaker uses one language and the audience 'hears' the words in a different language." Room must be given for the presence of akolalia at Pentecost, particularly as the text indicates that the crowds 'heard' in their own languages. Australian Alan Walker (1969, Breakthrough, Fontana, pp. 51-52) gives an example of this from his preaching to over 12,000 people from the first meeting at Albert Park in Suva, Fiji in a nine day mission. After the first afternoon when an interpreter was used the people said they could understand without that interruption, even though most of them did not know English. Walker commented, "For the rest of the mission I spoke in English without an interpreter. There was no complaint from the people. The crowds grew as the week passed. All seemed to gasp the meaning of the Gospel. The mission came to a wonderful climax on the second Sunday night in that city park, with the power of God obviously resting upon us."

[22] Jopsephus gives one brief paragraph reference to Jesus (including later Christian editing) in his section on Pilate within his voluminous accounts of The Antiquities of the Jews: "There was about this time a wise man named Jesus - if it is lawful to call him a man, for he was a doer of wonderful works - a teacher of the type of men who enjoy hearing the truth. He drew many of the Jews and Gentiles to him; he was the Christ. When Pi-

late, at the suggestion of the Jewish leaders, condemned him to the cross, those that loved him at first did not forsake him, for he appeared to them alive the third day, as the divine prophets had foretold, along with many other wonderful things concerning him. The tribe of Christians named for him still exists today" (1988, Josephus, Barbour, p. 61).

[23] The excesses of Montanism, for example, brought it into disrepute and for centuries it was regarded as heretical. Wesley acknowledged the Montanists' authenticity, as do recent historians, while also noting their fanatical and schismatic tendencies.

[24] The Reformation period provides many examples, such as the burning of the works of Hus, Savonarola, Wycliffe, and the reformers, many of them suffering martyrdom.

[25] Iranaeus "Against Heresies" in A Roberts and J Donaldson, eds., 1979, The Ante-Nicene Fathers. Eerdmans, 2.32.4, 2.31.2 and Richard Riss, 1988, A Survey of 20th Century Revival Movements in North America, Hendrickson, p. 8.

[26] Augustine, "The City of God", in Philip Schaff and Henry Wace, eds., 1979, Nicene and Post-Nicene Fathers of the Christian Church, Vol. 2., Eerdmans, pp. 485-489.

[27] For example, regional statistics indicated that Sunderland's car theft rate, the highest in Europe in 1995, had decreased by 40% two years later. A youth group of 60 former criminals led by a converted convicted criminal met at the church by 1998 (Ken and Lois Gott, 1995, The Sunderland Refreshing, and 1998, Anointed or Annoying?). Individual accounts of revival describe these revival phenomena and sociological results more fully.

[28] Harvey Cox, 1995, sub-title to Fire from Heaven.

Chapter 1

Eighteenth Century Revival:
The Great Awakening and Evangelical Revival

The powerful revivals of the eighteenth century spread through Europe, especially England, and to North America. They became known as the Evangelical Revivals in England and the Great Awakening in America. They grew out of the outpouring of the Spirit of God on small communities of refugees which has suffered severe persecution in Europe.

1727 - August: Herrnhut, Saxony (Nicholas Zinzendorf)

No one present could tell exactly what happened on the Wednesday morning of the specially called communion service. The glory of the Lord came upon them so powerfully that they hardly knew if they were on earth or in heaven. The Spirit of God moved powerfully on those three hundred refugees in Saxony in 1727. One of their historians wrote:

[Church history] abounds in records of special outpourings of the Holy Ghost, and verily the thirteenth of August, 1727, was a day of the outpouring of the Holy Spirit. We saw the hand of

God and his wonders, and we were all under the cloud of our fathers baptized with their Spirit. The Holy Ghost came upon us and in those days great signs and wonders took place in our midst. From that time scarcely a day passed but what we beheld his almighty workings amongst us. A great hunger after the Word of God took possession of us so that we had to have three services every day, at 5:00 and 7.30 a.m. and 9:00 p.m. Every one desired above everything else that the Holy Spirit might have full control. Selflove and selfwill, as well as all disobedience, disappeared and an overwhelming flood of grace swept us all out into the great ocean of Divine Love.[1]

Count Nicholas Ludwig von Zinzendorf (1700-1760), the benefactor and 27 year old leader of that community, gave this account at a meeting in London in 1752:

We needed to come to the Communion with a sense of the loving nearness of the Saviour. This was the great comfort which has made this day a generation ago to be a festival, because on this day twentyseven years ago the Congregation of Herrnhut, assembled for communion (at the Berthelsdorf church) were all dissatisfied with themselves. They had quit judging each other because they had become convinced, each one, of his lack of worth in the sight of God and each felt himself at this Communion to be in view of the noble countenance of the Saviour. ...

In this view of the man of sorrows and acquainted with grief, their hearts told them that he would be their patron and their priest who was at once changing their tears into oil of gladness and their misery into happiness. This firm confidence changed them in a single moment into a happy people which they are to this day, and into their happiness they have since led many thousands of others through the memory and help which the heavenly grace once given to themselves, so many thousand times confirmed to them since then.[2]

Zinzendorf described it as "a sense of the nearness of Christ" given to everyone present, and also simultaneously to two members of their community working twenty miles away.

The Moravian brethren had grown from the work and martyrdom of the Bohemian Reformer, John Hus. They suffered centuries of persecution. Many had been killed, imprisoned, tortured or banished from their homeland. This group had fled for refuge to Germany where the young Christian nobleman, Count Zinzendorf, offered them asylum on his estates in Saxony. They named their new home Herrnhut, 'the Lord's Watch'. From there, after their baptism of fire, they became pioneering evangelists and missionaries.

Fifty years before the beginning of modern missions with William Carey, the Moravian Church had sent out over 100 missionaries. Their English missionary magazine, *Periodical Accounts*, inspired Carey. He threw a copy of the paper on a table at a Baptist meeting, saying, "See what the Moravians have done! Cannot we follow their example and in obedience to our Heavenly Master go out into the world, and preach the Gospel to the heathen?"[3]

That missionary zeal began with the outpouring of the Holy Spirit. Zinzendorf observed: "The Saviour permitted to come upon us a Spirit of whom we had hitherto not had any experience or knowledge. ... Hitherto we had been the leaders and helpers. Now the Holy Spirit himself took full control of everything and everybody."[4]

Converted in early childhood, at four years of age Zinzendorf composed and signed a covenant: "Dear Saviour, be mine, and I will be Thine." His life motto was, "Jesus only".

Zinzendorf learned the secret of prevailing prayer. He actively established prayer groups as a teenager, and on finishing college at Halle at sixteen he gave Professor Francke a list of seven praying societies he had established.

The disgruntled community at Herrnhut early in 1727 criticised one another. Heated controversies threatened to disrupt the community. The majority belonged to the ancient Moravian Church of the Brethren. Other believers attracted to Herrnhut included Lutherans, Reformed, and Anabaptists. They argued about predestination, holiness, and baptism.

Zinzendorf, pleaded for unity, love and repentance. At Herrnhut, Zinzendorf visited all the adult members of the deeply divided community. He drew up a covenant calling upon them to seek out and emphasise the points in which they agreed rather than stressing their differences.

On 12 May, 1727, they all signed the 'Brotherly Covenant'[5] dedicating their lives, as Zinzendorf had dedicated his, to the service of the Lord Jesus Christ. The Moravian revival of 1727 was preceded and then sustained by extraordinary personal and communal, united prayer. A spirit of grace, unity and supplications grew among them.

On 16 July, Zinzendorf poured out his soul in a prayer accompanied with a flood of tears. This prayer produced an extraordinary effect. The whole community began praying as never before.

On 22 July, many of the community covenanted together on their own accord to meet often to pour out their hearts in prayers and hymns.

On 5 August, Zinzendorf spent the whole night in prayer with about twelve or fourteen others following a large meeting for prayer at midnight where great emotion prevailed.

On Sunday, 10 August, Pastor Johann Rothe, a Pietist friend of Zinzendorf and minister of the Berthelsdorf parish church, was overwhelmed by the Spirit about noon. He sank down into the dust before God. So did the whole congregation. They continued till midnight in prayer and singing, weeping and praying.

On Wednesday, 13 August, the Holy Spirit was poured out on them all at the specially arranged communion service in the Berthelsdorf church. Their prayers were answered in ways far beyond anyone's expectations. Many of them decided to set aside certain times for continued earnest prayer.

On Tuesday, 26 August, twentyfour men and twentyfour women covenanted together to continue praying in intervals of one hour each, day and night, each hour allocated by lots to different people.

On Wednesday, 27 August, this new regulation began. Others joined the intercessors and the number involved increased to seventyseven. They all carefully observed the hour which had been appointed for them. The intercessors had a weekly meeting where prayer needs were given to them.

The children began a similar plan among themselves. Those who heard their infant supplications were deeply moved. The children's prayers and supplications had a powerful effect on the whole community.

That astonishing prayer meeting beginning in 1727 lasted a century. Known as the Hourly Intercession, it involved relays of men and women in prayer without ceasing made to God. That prayer also led to action, especially evangelism. More than 100 missionaries left that village community in the next twentyfive years, all constantly supported in prayer.

One result of their baptism in the Holy Spirit was a joyful assurance of their pardon and salvation. This made a strong impact on people in many countries, including the Wesleys. Their prayers and witness profoundly affected the eighteenth century evangelical awakening.

1735 - January: New England, North America (Jonathan Edwards)

Jonathan Edwards (170301758), the preacher and scholar who later became a President of Princeton University, was a prominent leader in a revival movement which came to be called the Great Awakening as it spread through the communities of New England and the pioneering settlements in America. Converts to Christianity reached 50,000 out of a total of 250,000 colonists. Early in 1735 an unusually powerful move of God's Spirit brought revival to Northampton, which then spread through New England in the north east of America. Edwards noted that:

> a great and earnest concern about the great things of religion and the eternal world, became universal in all parts of the town, and among persons of all degrees and all ages; the noise among the dry bones waxed louder and louder; all other talk but about spiritual and eternal things, was soon thrown by....

> The minds of people were wonderfully taken off from the world; it was treated among us as a thing of very little consequence. They seemed to follow their worldly business, more as a part of their duty, than from any disposition they had to it....

> And the work of conversion was carried on in a most astonishing manner, and increased more and more;

souls did as it were come by flocks to Jesus Christ. From day to day, for many months together, might be seen evident instances of sinners brought out of darkness into marvellous light ... with a new song of praise to God in their mouths....

Our public assemblies were then beautiful: the congregation was alive in God's service, every one earnestly intent on the public worship, every hearer eager to drink in the words of the minister as they came from his mouth; the assembly in general were, from time to time, in tears while the word was preached; some weeping with sorrow and distress, others with joy and love, others with pity and concern for the souls of their neighbours....

Those amongst us who had been formerly converted, were greatly enlivened, and renewed with fresh and extraordinary incomes of the Spirit of God; though some much more than others, according to the measure of the gift of Christ. Many who before had laboured under difficulties about their own state, had now their doubts removed by more satisfying experience, and more clear discoveries of God's love.[6]

Describing the characteristics of the revival, Edwards said that it gave people:

an extraordinary sense of the awful majesty, greatness and holiness of God, so as sometimes to overwhelm soul and body; a sense of the piercing, all seeing eye of God, so as sometimes to take away the bodily strength; and an extraordinary view of the infinite terribleness of the wrath of God, together with a sense of the ineffable misery of sinners exposed to this wrath. ... and ... longings after more love to Christ, and greater conformity to him; especially longing after these two things, to be more perfect in humility and adoration. The flesh and the heart seem often to cry out, lying low before God and adoring him with greater love and humility. ... The person felt a great delight in singing praises to God and Jesus Christ, and longing that this present life may be as it were one continued song of praise to God. ... Together with living by faith to a great degree, there was a constant and extraordinary distrust of our own strength and wisdom; a great dependence on God for his help ... and being restrained from the most horrid sins.[7]

1739 - January: London, England (John Wesley, George Whitefield)

When the New England revival was strongest, George Whitefield (1714-1770) in England and Howell Harris (1714-1773) in Wales were both converted at 21 in 1735. Both ignited revival fires, seeing thousands converted and communities changed. By 1736 Harris began forming his converts into societies and by 1739 there were nearly thirty such societies. Whitefield travelled extensively, visiting Georgia in 1738 (the first of seven journeys to America), then ministering powerfully with Howell Harris in Wales 1739 and with Jonathan Edwards in New England in 1740, all in his early twenties.

At the end of 1735, John Wesley (1703-1791) sailed to Georgia, an American colony. A company of Moravian immigrants travelled on that vessel. During a storm they faced the danger of shipwreck. John Wesley wrote in his journal for Sunday 25 January 1736:

At seven I went to the Germans. I had long before observed the great seriousness of their behaviour. Of their humility they had given a continual proof by performing those servile offices for the other passengers which none of the English would undertake; for which they desired and would receive no pay, saying, "It was good for their proud hearts," and "their loving Saviour had done more for them." And every day had given them occasion of showing a meekness, which no injury could move. If they were pushed, struck or thrown down, they rose again and went away; but no complaint was found in their mouth. Here was now an opportunity of trying whether they were delivered from the spirit of fear, as well as from that of pride, anger and revenge. In the midst of the Psalm wherewith their service began, the sea broke over, split the mainsail in pieces, covered the ship and poured in between the decks, as if the great deep had already swallowed us up. A terrible screaming began among the English. The Germans calmly sung on. I asked one of them afterwards: "Were you not afraid?" He answered, "I thank God, no." I asked: "But were not your women and children afraid?" He replied mildly: "No, our women and children are not afraid to die."[8]

Back in England in 1738 after John Wesley's brief and frustrating missionary career, the Wesleys were challenged by the Moravian missionary Peter Bohler. In March 1738 John Wesley wrote:

Saturday, 4 March, I found my brother at Oxford, recovering from his pleurisy; and with him Peter Bohler, by whom (in the hand of the great God) I was, on Sunday the 5th, clearly convinced of unbelief, of the want of that faith whereby alone we are saved.

Immediately it struck into my mind, "Leave off preaching. How can you preach to others, who have not faith yourself?" I asked Bohler whether he thought I should leave it off or not. He answered, "By no means." I asked, "But what can I preach?" He said, "Preach faith *till* you have it; and then, *because* you have it, you *will* preach faith."

Monday, 6 March I began preaching this new doctrine, though my soul started back from the work. The first person to whom I offered salvation by faith alone was a prisoner under sentence of death. His name was Clifford. Peter Bohler had many times desired me to speak to him before. But I could not prevail on myself so to do; being still a zealous assertor of the impossibility of a deathbed repentance.[9]

Both John and Charles were converted in May 1738, Charles first, and John three days later on Wednesday 24 May. He wrote his famous testimony in his Journal:

In the evening I went very unwillingly to a society in Aldersgate Street, where one was reading Luther's preface to the *Epistle to the Romans*. About a quarter before nine, while he was describing the change which God works in the heart through faith in Christ, I felt my heart strangely warmed. I felt I did trust in Christ, Christ alone, for salvation; and an assurance was given me, that he had taken away my sins, even mine, and saved me from the law of sin and death.[10]

Later that year John Wesley visited the Moravian community at Herrnhut. He admired their zeal and love for the Lord, and he prayed that their kind of Christianity, full of the Holy Spirit, would spread through the earth. Back in England he preached evangelically, gathered converts into religious societies (which were nicknamed Methodists because of his methodical procedures), and continued to relate warmly with the Moravians. Evangelical revival fires began to stir in England and burst into flame the following year.

1739 saw astonishing expansion of revival in England. On the evening of 1 January the Wesleys and Whitefield (recently back from America) and four others from their former Holy Club at Oxford University, along with 60 others, met in London for prayer and a love feast. The Spirit of God moved powerfully on them all. Many fell down, overwhelmed. The meeting went all night and they realised they had been empowered in a fresh visitation from God.

> Mr Hall, Kinchin, Ingham, Whitefield, Hitchins, and my brother Charles were present at our lovefeast in Fetter Lane, with about sixty of our brethren. About three in the morning, as we were continuing instant in prayer, the power of God came mightily upon us, insomuch that many cried out for exceeding joy, and many fell to the ground. As soon as we were recovered a little from that awe and amazement at the presence of his majesty, we broke out with one voice, "We praise Thee, O God, we acknowledge Thee to be the Lord."[11]

This Pentecost on New Year's Day launched the revival known later as the Great Awakening. Revival spread rapidly. In February 1739 Whitefield started preaching to the Kingswood coal miners in the open fields near Bristol because many churches opposed him, accusing him and other evangelicals of 'enthusiasm'. In February about 200 attended. By March 20,000 attended. Whitefield invited Wesley to take over then and so in April Wesley reluctantly began his famous open air preaching, which continued for 50 years.

He described that first weekend in his Journal:

> Saturday, 31 March In the evening I reached Bristol, and met Mr Whitefield. I could scarce reconcile myself at first to this strange way of preaching in the fields, of which he set me an example on Sunday; having been all my life (till very lately) so tenacious of every point re-

lating to decency and order, that I should have thought the saving of souls almost a sin if it had not been done in a church.

Sunday, 1 April In the evening, I begun expounding our Lord's Sermon on the Mount (one pretty remarkable precedent of fieldpreaching) to a little society in Nicholas Street.

Monday, 2 April At four in the afternoon I submitted to be more vile, and proclaimed in the highways the glad tidings of salvation, speaking from a little eminence in a ground adjoining to the city, to almost three thousand people. The scripture on which I spoke was "The Spirit of the Lord is upon me, because he has anointed me to preach the gospel to the poor."[12]

Sometimes strange manifestations accompanied revival preaching. Wesley wrote in his Journal of 26 April 1739 that during his preaching at Newgate, Bristol, "One, and another, and another sunk to the earth; they dropped on every side as thunderstruck."[13]

He returned to London in June reporting on the amazing move of God's Spirit with many conversions and many people falling prostrate, a phenomenon he never encouraged. Features of this revival were enthusiastic singing, powerful preaching, and the gathering of converts into small societies called weekly Class Meetings.

Initially, leaders such as George Whitefield criticised some manifestations in Wesley's meetings, but this changed. Wesley wrote on 7 July 1739,
I had opportunity to talk with Mr Whitefield about those outward signs which had so often accompanied the inward work of God. I found his objections were chiefly grounded on gross

misrepresentations of matter of fact. But the next day he had opportunity of informing himself better: for no sooner had he begun (in the application of his sermon) to invite all sinners to believe in Christ, than four persons sank down, close to him, almost in the same moment. One of them lay without either sense or motion; a second trembled exceedingly; the third had strong convulsions all over his body, but made no noise, unless by groans; the fourth, equally convulsed, called upon God, with strong cried and tears. From this time, I trust, we shall all suffer God to carry on His own work in the way that pleaseth Him.[14]

Both John Wesley and George Whitefield continued preaching outdoors as well as in churches which welcomed them. Whitefield's seven visits to America continued to fan the flames of revival there.

Revival caught fire in Scotland also. After returning again from America in 1741, Whitefield visited Glasgow. Two ministers in villages nearby invited him to return in 1742 because revival had already begun in their area. Conversions and prayer groups multiplied. Whitefield preached there at Cambuslang about four miles from Glasgow. The opening meetings on a Sunday saw the great crowds on the hillside gripped with conviction, repentance and weeping more than he had seen elsewhere. The next weekend 20,000 gathered on the Saturday and up to 50,000 on the Sunday for the quarterly communion. The visit was charged with Pentecostal power which even amazed Whitefield.

1745 - August: Crossweeksung, North America (David Brainerd)

Jonathan Edwards published the journal of David Brainerd (1718-1747), a missionary to the North American Indians from 1743 to his death at 29 in 1747. Brainerd tells of revival breaking out among Indians at Crossweeksung in August 1745 when the power of God seemed to come like a rushing mighty wind. The Indians were overwhelmed by God. The revival had greatest impact when Brainerd emphasised the compassion of the Saviour, the provisions of the gospel, and the free offer of divine grace. Idolatry was abandoned, marriages repaired, drunkenness practically disappeared, honesty and repayments of debts prevailed. Money once wasted on excessive drinking was used for family and communal needs. Their communities were filled with love.

Part of his journal for Thursday 8 August reads:

> The power of God seemed to descend on the assembly "like a rushing mighty wind" and with an astonishing energy bore all down before it. I stood amazed at the influence that seized the audience almost universally and could compare it to nothing more aptly than the irresistible force of a mighty torrent... Almost all persons of all ages were bowed down with concern together and scarce was able to withstand the shock of astonishing operation.[15]

On November 20, he described the revival at Crossweeksung in his general comments about that year in which he had ridden his horse more than 3,000 miles to reach Indian tribes in New England:

> I might now justly make many remarks on a work of grace so very remarkable as this has been in divers respects; but shall confine myself to a few general hints only.

> 1. It is remarkable that God began this work among the Indians at a time when I had least hope and, to my apprehension, the least rational prospect of seeing a work of grace propagated amongst them. ...

2. It is remarkable how God providentially, and in a manner almost unaccountable, called these Indians together to be instructed in the great things that concerned their souls; how He seized their minds with the most solemn and weighty concern for their eternal salvation, as fast as they came to the place where His Word was preached...

3. It is likewise remarkable how God preserved these poor ignorant Indians from being prejudiced against me and the truths I taught them...

4. Nor is it less wonderful how God was pleased to provide a remedy for my want of skill and freedom in the Indian language by remarkably fitting my interpreter for, and assisting him in, the performance of his work...

5. It is further remarkable that God has carried on His work here by such means, and in such manner, as tended to obviate and leave no room for those prejudices and objections that have often been raised against such a work ... [because] this great awakening, this surprising concern, was never excited by any harangues of terror, but always appeared most remarkable when I insisted upon the compassions of a dying Saviour, the plentiful provisions of the gospel, and the free offers of divine grace to needy distressed sinners.

6. The effects of this work have likewise been very remarkable. ... Their pagan notions and idolatrous practices seem to be entirely abandoned in these parts. They are regulated and appear regularly disposed in the affairs of marriage. They seem generally divorced from drunkenness ... although before it was common for some or other of them to be drunk almost every

day. ... A principle of honesty and justice appears in many of them, and they seem concerned to discharge their old debts. ... Their manner of living is much more decent and comfortable than formerly, having now the benefit of that money which they used to consume upon strong drink. Love seems to reign among them, especially those who have given evidence of a saving change.[16]

1781 - December: Cornwall, England

Forty years after the Great Awakening began the fires of revival had died out in many places. Concerned leaders called the church to pray.

Jonathan Edwards in America had written a treatise called, *A Humble Attempt to Promote Explicit Agreement and Visible Union of God's People in Extraordinary Prayer for the Revival of Religion and the Advancement of Christ's Kingdom*. It was reprinted in both England and Scotland and circulated widely.

John Erskine of Edinburgh persisted in urging prayer for revival through extensive correspondence around the world. He instigated widespread combined churches monthly prayer meetings for revival called Concerts of Prayer.

An example of the prayer movement was the effect in Cornwall in the 1780s. On Sunday, Christmas Day 1781, at St. Just Church in Cornwall, at 3 a.m., intercessors met to sing and ray. The Spirit moved among them and they prayed until 9 a.m. and regathered on Christmas evening. By March 1782 they were praying each evening until midnight.

Two years later in 1784, when 83year old John Wesley visited that area, he wrote, "This country is all on fire and the flame is spreading from village to village."[17]

The chapel which George Whitefield had built decades previously in Tottenham Court Road, London, had to be enlarged to seat 5,000 people, the largest in the world at that time. Baptist churches in North Hampton, Leicester, and the Midlands, set aside regular nights for prayer for revival. Methodists and Anglicans joined them. Converts were being won at the prayer meetings. Some were held at 5 a.m., some at midnight. Some unbelievers were drawn by dreams and visions. Some came to scoff but were thrown to the ground under the power of the Holy Spirit. Sometimes there was noise and confusion; sometimes stillness and solemnity. But always there was that ceaseless outpouring of the Holy Spirit. Whole denominations doubled, tripled and quadrupled in the next few years. The number of dissenting churches increased from 27 in 1739 to 900 in 1800, 5,000 by 1810 and 10,000 by 1820.[18] It swept out from England to Wales, Scotland, United States, Canada, and to some Third World countries.[19]

That eighteenth century revival of holiness brought about a spiritual awakening in England and America, established the Methodists with 140,000 members by the end of the century, and renewed other churches and Christians. It impacted the nation with social change and created the climate for political reform such as the abolition of slavery through the reforms of William Wilberforce, William Buxton and others. John Howard and Elizabeth Fry led prison reform. Florence Nightingale founded modern nursing. Ashley Cooper, the Earl of Shaftesbury, reformed labour conditions.

The movement grew. William Carey, Andrew Fuller, John Sutcliffe and other leaders began the Union of Prayer, calling Christians to pray together regularly for revival. By 1792, the year after John Wesley died, this Second Great Awakening (1792-1830) began to sweep Great Britain and America.

Endnotes

[1] John Greenfield, 1927, *Power from on High,* Christian Literature Crusade (Reprint), p. 14.

[2] Greenfield, p. 15.

[3] Greenfield, p. 19.

[4] Greenfield, p. 21.

[5] Zinzendorf's 'Brotherly Covenant' became in essence the 'Brotherly Agreement' still followed by Moravian Brethren. American Moravian evangelist John Greenfield summarised the progress of that covenant relationship at Herrnhut (1927, *Power from on High,* pp. 26-30).

[6] Jonathan Edwards, 1835, *The Works of Jonathan Edwards,* Vol. 1, 1974 edition, Banner of Truth, p.348.

[7] Edwards, p. 377.

[8] Greenfield, p. 35,36.

[9] Christopher Idle, 1986, *The Journal of John Wesley,* Lion, p. 43.

[10] Idle, p. 46.

[11] Idle, p. 55.

[12] Idle, pp. 56,57.

[13] Robert Backhouse, ed., 1996, *The Classics on Revival,* Hodder and Stoughton, p. 212.

[14] Backhouse, p. 212.

[15] Edwards, pp. 142-143.

[16] Phillip Howard, 1949, *The Life and Diary of David Brainerd, edited by Jonathan Edwards,* Baker, pp. 239-251.

[17] Stuart Robinson, 1993, "Praying the Price", *Renewal Journal,* Vol. 1, Brisbane, p. 9.

[18] Edwin Orr, 1973, *The Eager Feet: Evangelical Awakenings, 1792 & 1830,* Moody, p. 19.

[19] Robinson, pp. 89.

Chapter 2

Nineteenth Century Revival:
Frontier and Missionary Revival

Edwin Orr's research identified two major awakenings in Europe and North America in the nineteenth century following the first Great Awakening of the eighteenth century. His earlier writings identified a second general awakening in 1798-1812 and a third general awakening in the 1830s, with another strong resurgence of revival in 1858-1860. However, his later writings identified the second general awakening as covering 1798 to the 1830s, interrupted by the British-American War of 1812-15, and producing a wave of missionary societies early in the nineteenth century. Orr then identified the third general awakening as 1858-1860, preceding the American Civil War (1861-1865).[1]

John Erskine's eighteenth century voluminous correspondence from Edinburgh urging prayer for revival struck a chord in New England. In 1794 a score of New England ministers, led by Baptists Isaac Backus and Stephen Gano, issued a circular letter inviting ministers and churches of all denominations to engage in and promote a Concert of Prayer for spiritual awakening commencing on the first Tuesday in January, Epiphany, 6 January 1795. The response was immediate, cordial and earnest. Presbyterian Synods in New York and

New Jersey recommended the call to all their churches, as did the Methodist Episcopal Church. Congregational and Baptist associations joined in, and the Moravian and Reformed communities co-operated. Some met quarterly; most met monthly.

Stirrings of revival affected Connecticut from October 1798 in West Simsbury with Jeremiah Hallock where the congregation experienced deep conviction of sin and many leading infidels became strong converts. Late in October similar movements of repentance spread in the state including in New Hartford. "On a Sunday in November, the Spirit of God manifested Himself in the public service, and a general work of revival began in earnest. Meetings were commenced in various parts of the town, attended by deeply affected crowds, though without convulsions or outcries."[2] Soon over 50 families became involved. In Plymouth, in February 1799 "'like a mighty wind' the Spirit came upon the people." Revival spread through he United States at the turn of the century as it was affecting churches in Britain. Orr argues that prayer for revival was being answered in the face of growing 'revolution and infidelity' in the wake of the French Revolution.[3]

1800 - June: Red and Gasper Rivers, America (James McGready)

James McGready (1763-1817), a Presbyterian minister in Kentucky, promoted the Concert of Prayer every first Monday of the month, and urged his people to pray for him at sunset on Saturday evening and sunrise Sunday morning. Revival swept Kentucky in the summer of 1800.

McGready had three small congregations in Muddy River, Red River and Gasper River in Logan County in the southwest of the state. Most of the people were refugees from all states in the Union who fled from justice or punishment. They included murderers, horse thieves, highway robbers, and counterfeiters. The area was nicknamed Rogues Harbour.

The first real manifestations of God's power came, however, in June 1800. Four to fivehundred members of McGready's three congregations, plus five ministers, had gathered at Red River for a "camp meeting" lasting several days. On the final day, "a mighty effusion of [God's] Spirit" came upon the people, "and the floor was soon covered with the slain; their screams for mercy pierced the heavens."

Convinced that God was moving, McGready and his colleagues planned another camp meeting to be held in late July 1800 at Gasper River. They had not anticipated what occurred. An enormous crowd as many as 8,000 began arriving at the appointed date, many from distances as great as 100 miles. ... Although the term *camp meeting* was not used till 1802, this was the first true camp meeting where a continuous outdoor service was combined with camping out. ...

At a huge evening meeting lighted by flaming torches ... a Presbyterian pastor gave a throbbing message ... McGready recalled: "The power of God seemed to shake the whole assembly. Toward the close of the sermon, the cries of the distressed arose almost as loud as his voice. After the congregation was dismissed the solemnity increased, till the greater part of the multitude seemed engaged in the most solemn manner. No person seemed to wish to go home hunger and sleep seemed to affect nobody eternal things were the vast concern. Here awakening and converting work was to be found in every part of the multitude; and even some things strangely and wonderfully new to me."[4]

These frontier revivals became an increasing emphasis in American revivalism. One unfortunate result was the identification of revival in America with 'revivalism' identified as crusades or campaigns called revivals and tending to emphasise emotionalism, hell-fire preaching, and the sawdust trail - used in nineteenth century revivals to lay the dust or soak up the moisture on the ground of the revival meetings.

1801 - August: Cane Ridge, North America (Barton Stone)

Impressed by the revivals in 1800, Barton Stone (1772-1844), a Presbyterian minister, organised similar meetings in 1801 in his area at Cane Ridge, northeast of Lexington. A huge crowd of around 12,500 attended in over 125 wagons including people from Ohio and Tennessee. At that time Lexington, the largest town in Kentucky, had less than 1,800 citizens. Presbyterian, Methodist and Baptist preachers and circuit riders formed preaching teams, speaking simultaneously in different parts of the camp grounds, all aiming for conversions.

James Finley, later a Methodist circuit rider, described it:

> The noise was like the roar of Niagara. The vast sea of human being seemed to be agitated as if by a storm. I counted seven ministers, all preaching at one time, some on stumps, others in wagons and one standing on a tree which had, in falling, lodged against another. ... I stepped up on a log where I could have a better view of the surging sea of humanity. The scene that then presented itself to my mind was indescribable.

At one time I saw at least *five hundred* swept down in a moment as if a battery of a thousand guns had been opened upon them, and then immediately followed shrieks and shouts that rent the very heavens.[5]

A Presbyterian minister, the Rev. Moses Hoge, wrote,

The careless fall down, cry out, tremble, and not infrequently are affected with convulsive twitchings ... Nothing that imagination can paint, can make a stronger impression upon the mind, than one of those scenes. Sinners dropping down on every hand, shrieking, groaning, crying for mercy, convulsed; professors praying, agonizing, fainting, falling down in distress for sinners or in raptures of joy! ... As to the work in general there can be no question but it is of God. The subject of it, for the most part, are deeply wounded for their sins, and can give a clear and rational account of their conversion.[6]

Revival early in the nineteenth century not only impacted the American frontier, but also towns and especially colleges. One widespread result in America, as in England, was the formation of missionary societies to train and direct the large numbers of converts filled with missionary zeal.

That Second Great Awakening produced the modern missionary movement and it's societies, Bible societies, saw the abolition of slavery, and many other social reforms. The Napoleonic Wars in Europe (1803-15) and the American War of 1812 (1812-15) dampened revival zeal, but caused many to cry out to God for help, and fresh stirrings of revival continued after that, especially with Charles G. Finney.

1821 - October: Adams, North America (Charles Finney)

Charles Finney (1792-1875) became well known in revivals in the nineteenth century. A keen sportsman and young lawyer, he had a mighty empowering by God's Spirit on the night of his conversion on Wednesday 10 October 1821. That morning the Holy Spirit convicted him on his way to work. So he spent the morning in the woods near his small town of Adams in New York State, praying. There he surrendered fully to God. He walked to his law office that afternoon profoundly changed and in the afternoon assisted his employer Squire Wright to set up a new office. That night he was filled with the Spirit. He describes that momentous night in his autobiography:

> By evening we had the books and furniture adjusted, and I made a good fire in an open fireplace, hoping to spend the evening alone. Just at dark Squire W, seeing that everything was adjusted, told me good night and went to his home. I had accompanied him to the door, and as I closed the door and turned around my heart seemed to be liquid within me. All my feelings seemed to rise and flow out and the thought of my heart was, "I want to pour my whole soul out to God." The rising of my soul was so great that I rushed into the room back of the front office to pray.

> There was no fire and no light in this back room; nevertheless it appeared to me as if it were perfectly light. As I went in and shut the door after me, it seemed to me as if I met the Lord Jesus Christ face to face. It seemed to me that I saw him as I would see any other man. He said nothing, but looked at me in such a manner as to break me right down at his feet. It

seemed to me a reality that he stood before me, and I fell down at his feet and poured out my soul to him. I wept aloud like a child and made such confession as I could with my choked words. It seemed to me that I bathed his feet with my tears, and yet I had no distinct impression that I touched him.

I must have continued in this state for a good while, but my mind was too much absorbed with the interview to remember anything that I said. As soon as my mind became calm enough I returned to the front office and found that the fire I had made of large wood was nearly burned out. But as I turned and was about to take a seat by the fire, I received a mighty baptism of the Holy Spirit. Without any expectation of it, without ever having the thought in my mind that there was any such thing for me, without any memory of ever hearing the thing mentioned by any person in the world, the Holy Spirit descended upon me in a manner that seemed to go through me, body and soul. I could feel the impression, like a wave of electricity, going through and through me. Indeed it seemed to come in waves of liquid love, for I could not express it in any other way. It seemed like the very breath of God. I can remember distinctly that it seemed to fan me, like immense wings.

No words can express the wonderful love that was spread abroad in my heart. I wept aloud with joy and love. I literally bellowed out the unspeakable overflow of my heart. These waves came over me, and over me, and over me, one after another, until I remember crying out, "I shall die if these waves continue to pass over me." I said, "Lord, I cannot bear any more," yet I had no fear of death.[7]

That night a member of the church choir which Finney led called in at his office, amazed to find the former sceptic in a "state of loud weeping" and unable to talk to him for some time. That young friend left and soon returned with an elder from the church who was usually serious and rarely laughed. "When he came in," Finney observed, "I was very much in the state in which I was when the young man went out to call him. He asked me how I felt and I began to tell him. Instead of saying anything he fell into a most spasmodic laughter. It seemed as if it was impossible for him to keep from laughing from the very bottom of his heart."[8]

Next morning, with "the renewal of these mighty waves of love and salvation" flowing through him, Finney witnessed to his employer who was strongly convicted and later made his peace with God.

That morning a deacon from the church came to see Finney about a court case due to be tried at ten o'clock. Finney told him he would have to find another lawyer, saying, "I have a retainer from the Lord Jesus Christ to plead his cause and I cannot plead yours." The astonished deacon later became more serious about God and settled his case privately.

Finney described the immediate change in his own life and work:

> I soon sallied forth from the office to converse with those whom I might meet about their souls. I had the impression, which has never left my mind, that God wanted me to preach the Gospel, and that I must begin immediately. ...
>
> I spoke with many persons that day, and I believe the Spirit of God made lasting impressions upon every one of them. I cannot remember one whom I spoke

with, who was not soon after converted. ...

In the course of the day a good deal of excitement was created in the village because of what the Lord had done for my soul. Some thought one thing and some another. At evening, without any appointment having been made, I observed that the people were going to the place where they usually held their conference and prayer meetings. ...

I went there myself. The minister was there, and nearly all the principal people in the village. No one seemed ready to open the meeting, but the house was packed to its utmost capacity. I did not wait for anybody, but rose and began by saying that I then knew that religion was from God. I went on and told such parts of my experience as it seemed important for me to tell. ...

We had a wonderful meeting that evening, and from that day we had a meeting every evening for a long time. The work spread on every side.

As I had been a leader among the young people I immediately appointed a meeting for them, which they all attended. ... They were converted one after another with great rapidity, and the work continued among them until only one of their number was left unconverted.

The work spread among all classes, and extended itself not only through the village but also out of the village in every direction.[9]

Finney continued for the rest of his life in evangelism and revival. During the height of the revivals he often saw the awesome holiness of God come upon people, not only in meetings but also in the community, bringing multitudes to repentance and conversion. Wherever he travelled, instead of bringing a song leader he brought someone to pray. Often Father Nash, his companion, was not even in the meetings but in the woods praying. Finney founded and taught theology at Oberlin College which pioneered coeducation and enrolled both blacks and whites. His *Lectures on Revival* were widely read and helped to fan revival fire in America and England.

Finney emphasised Hosea 10:12, "Break up your fallow ground: for it is time to seek the Lord till He comes and rains righteousness on you." He believed that if we do our part in repentance and prayer, God would do his in sending revival.

He preached in Boston for over a year during the of the revival in 1858. Many reports tell of the power of God producing conviction in people not even in the meetings. At times people would repent as they sailed into Boston harbour, convicted by the Holy Spirit.

Various revival movements influenced society in the nineteenth century but 1858 in America and 1859 in Britain were outstanding. Typically, it followed a low ebb of spiritual life. Concerned Christians began praying earnestly and anticipating a new move of God's Spirit.

1857 - October: Hamilton, Canada (Phoebe Palmer)

Revival broke out at evangelistic meetings during October 1857 in Hamilton, Canada, led by the talented Phoebe Palmer (1807-1874), assisted by her physician husband Walter. They had been leading camp meetings in Ontario and Quebec from June with crowds of 5,000. Stopping over in Hamilton for a train connection back to New York, they spoke at a Methodist Church. Many were converted, so they stayed for several weeks. Attendances reached 6,000, and 600 professed conversion, including many civic leaders. Newspapers reported it widely.

The Third Great Awakening (1857-59) had begun. Prayer meetings began to proliferate across North America and in Great Britain. Prayer and repentance accelerated with the stock market crash of October 1957 and the threatening clouds of the civil war over slavery (1861-65). The Palmers travelled widely, fanning the flames of revival and seeing thousands converted.

Phoebe, a firebrand preacher, impacted North America and England with her speaking and writing. She wrote influential books, and edited of *The Guide to Holiness*, the most significant magazine on holiness at that time. Her teaching on the baptism of the Holy Ghost and endowment of power spread far and wide.

1857 - October: New York, North America (Jeremiah Lanphier)

Jeremiah Lanphier (1809-1894), a city missioner, began a weekly noon prayer meeting upstairs in the Old Dutch North Church, a Dutch Reformed Church in Fulton Street, New York on September 23, 1857. He began alone, then six men joined him for that first noon prayer meeting. In October it became a daily prayer meeting attended by many businessmen. Anticipation of revival grew, especially with the financial collapse that October after a year of depression. Lanphier continued to lead that Fulton Street prayer meeting till 1894.

At the beginning of 1858 the Fulton Street prayer meeting had grown so much they were holding three simultaneous prayer meetings in the building and other prayer groups were starting in the city. By March newspapers carried front page reports of over 6,000 attending daily prayer meetings in New York, 6,000 attending them in Pittsburgh, and daily prayer meetings were held in Washington at five different times to accommodate the crowds.

Other cities followed the pattern. Soon a common midday sign on business premises read: *Will reopen at the close of the prayer meeting.*

By May, 50,000 of New York's 800,000 people were new converts. A newspaper reported that New England was profoundly changed by the revival and in several towns no unconverted adults could be found!

> Similar stories could be told of the 1858 American Revival. Ships as they drew near the American ports came within a definite zone of heavenly influence. Ship after ship arrived with the same tale of sudden conviction and conversion. In one ship a captain and the entire crew of thirty men found Christ out at sea and entered the harbour rejoicing. Revival broke out on the battleship "North Carolina" through four Christian men who had been meeting in the bowels of the ship for prayer. One evening they were filled with the Spirit and bunt into song. Ungodly shipmates who came down to mock were gripped by the power of God, and the laugh of the scornful was soon changed into the cry of the penitent. Many were smitten down, and a gracious work broke out that continued night after night, till they had to send ashore for ministers to help, and the battleship became a Bethel. This overwhelming sense of God, bringing deep conviction of sin, is perhaps the outstanding feature of true revival.[10]

In 1858 a leading Methodist paper reported these features of the revival: few sermons were needed, lay people witnessed, seekers flocked to the altar, nearly all seekers were blessed, experiences remained clear, converts had holy boldness, religion became a social topic, family altars were strengthened, testimony given nightly was abundant, and conversations were marked with seriousness.

Edwin Orr's research (1974) indicated that 1858-59 saw a million Americans become converted in a population of thirty million and at least a million Christians were renewed, with lasting results in church attendances and moral reform in society.

1859 - March: Ulster, Ireland (James McQuilkin)

Revival swept Great Britain also, including the Ulster revival of 1859. During September 1857, the same month the Fulton Street meetings began, James McQuilkin commenced a weekly prayer meeting in a village schoolhouse near Kells with three other young Irishmen. This is generally seen as the start of the Ulster revival. The first conversions in answer to their prayer came in December 1857. Through 1858 innumerable prayer meetings started, and revival was a common theme of preachers.

On 14 March 1859, James McQuilkin and his praying friends organised a great prayer meeting at the Ahoghill Presbyterian Church. Such a large crowd gathered that the building was cleared in case the galleries collapsed. Outside in the chilling rain as a layman preached with great power hundreds knelt in repentance. This was the first of many movements of mass conviction of sin.

No town in Ulster was more deeply stirred during the 1859 Revival than Coleraine. It was there that a boy was so troubled about his soul that the schoolmaster sent him home. An older boy, a Christian, accompanied him, and before they had gone far led him to Christ. Returning at once to the school, this latest convert testified to the master, "Oh, I am so happy! I have the Lord Jesus in my heart." The effect of these artless words was very great. Boy after boy rose and silently left the room. On investigation the master found these boys ranged alongside the wall a the playground, everyone apart and on his knees! Very soon their silent prayer became a bitter cry. It was heard by those within and pierced their hearts. They cast themselves upon their knees, and their cry for mercy was heard in the girls' schoolroom above. In a few moments the whole school was upon its knees, and its wail of distress was heard in the street outside. Neighbours and passers-by came flocking in, and all, as they crossed the threshold, came under the same convicting power. Every room was filled with men, women, and children seeking God.[11]

The revival of 1859 brought 100,000 converts into the churches of Ireland. God's Spirit moved powerfully in small and large gatherings bringing great conviction of sin, deep repentance, and lasting moral change. Prostrations were common people lying prostrate in conviction and repentance, unable to rise for some time. By 1860 crime was reduced, judges in Ulster several times had no cases to try. At one time in County Antrim no crime was reported to the police and no prisoners were held in police custody.

This revival made a greater impact on Ireland than anything known since Patrick brought Christianity there. By the end of 1860 the effects of the Ulster revival were listed as thronged services, unprecedented numbers of communicants, abundant prayer meetings, increased family prayers, unmatched scripture reading, prosperous Sunday Schools, converts remaining steadfast, increased giving, vice abated, and crime reduced.

Revival fire ignites fire. Throughout 1859 the same deep conviction and lasting conversions revived thousands of people in Wales, Scotland and England.

Revival in Wales found expression in glorious praise including harmonies unique to the Welsh which involved preacher and people in turn. There too, 100,000 converts (one tenth of the total population) were added to the church and crime was greatly reduced. Scotland and England were similarly visited with revival. Again, prayer increased enormously and preaching caught fire with many anointed evangelists seeing thousands converted.

Charles Haddon Spurgeon, a Baptist minister known as the prince of preachers, saw 1859 as the high water mark although he had already been preaching in his Metropolitan Tabernacle in London for five years with great blessing and huge crowds.

1859 - May: Natal, South Africa (Zulus)

The wave of revival in 1857-1859 included countries around the globe. Missionaries and travellers told of thousands being converted, and others began crying out to God to send revival to their nations.

It happened in South Africa. Revival began among the Zulu tribes before it spilled over into the Dutch Reformed Church. Tribal people gathered in large numbers on the frontier mission stations and then took revival fire, African style, into their villages.

On Sunday night, 22 May, the Spirit of God fell on a service of the Zulus in Natal so powerfully that they prayed all night. News spread rapidly. This revival among the Zulus of Natal on the east coast ignited missions and tribal churches. It produced deep conviction of sin, immediate repentance and conversions, extraordinary praying and vigorous evangelism.

In April 1860 at a combined missions conference of over 370 leaders of Dutch Reformed, Methodist and Presbyterian missions meeting at Worcester, South Africa, discussed revival. Andrew Murray Sr., moved to tears, had to stop speaking. His son, Andrew Murray Jr., now well known through his books, led in prayer so powerfully that many saw that as the beginning of revival in those churches.

By June revival had so impacted the Methodist Church in Montague village, near Worcester, that they held prayer meetings every night and three mornings a week, sometimes as early as 3 am. The Dutch Reformed people joined together with the Methodists with great conviction of sin to seek God in repentance, worship and intercession. Reports reached Worcester, and ignited similar prayer meetings there.

As an African servant girl sang and prayed one Sunday night at Worcester, the Holy Spirit fell on the group and a roaring sound like approaching thunder surrounded the hall which began to shake. Instantly everyone burst out praying! Their pastor, Andrew Murray Jr., had been speaking in the main sanctuary. When told of this he ran to their meeting calling for order! No one noticed. They kept crying loudly to God for forgiveness.

All week the prayer meetings continued, beginning in silence, but "as soon as several prayers had arisen the place was shaken as before and the whole company of people engaged in simultaneous petition to the throne of grace."[12] On the

Saturday, Andrew Murray Jr. led the prayer meeting. After preaching he prayed and invited others to pray. Again the sound of thunder approached and everyone prayed aloud, loudly. At first Andrew Murray tried to quieten the people, but a stranger reminded him that God was at work, and he learned to accept this noisy revival praying. People were converted. The revival spread.

Fifty men from that congregation went into full time ministry, and the revival launched Andrew Murray Jr. into a worldwide ministry of speaking and writing.

1871 - October: New York, North America (Dwight L Moody)

D. L. Moody (1837-1899), converted in 1855, later led powerful evangelistic campaigns in America and England. Two women in his church prayed constantly that he would be filled with the Spirit, and his yearning for God continued to increase. While visiting New York in 1871 to raise funds for churches and orphanages destroyed in the Chicago fire of October that year, in which his home, church sanctuary and the YMCA buildings were destroyed, he had a deep encounter with God. He wrote,

> I was crying all the time God would fill me with his Spirit. Well, one day in the city of New York oh, what a day! I cannot describe it, I seldom refer to it; it is almost too sacred an experience to name. Paul had an experience of which he never spoke for fourteen years. I can only say that God revealed Himself to me, and I had such an experience of His love that I had to ask him to stay his hand. I went to preaching again. The sermons were not different; I did not present any new truths; and yet hundreds were converted. I would

not be placed back where I was before that blessed experience for all the world it would be as the small dust of the balance.[13]

On a visit to Britain he heard Henry Varley say, "The world has yet to see what God will do
with a man fully consecrated to him." He resolved to be that man.

Moody worked vigorously to establish the Young Men's Christian Association (YMCA) in America and England as a means of converting and discipling youth. A Baptist minister in London, the Rev. R. Boyd, went to a meeting where Moody had just spoken and observed, "When I got to the rooms of the Young Men's Christian Association, Victoria Hall, London, I found the meeting on fire. The young men were speaking with tongues, prophesying. What on earth did it mean? Only that Moody had addressed them that afternoon."[14]

God's Spirit powerfully impacted people through Moody's ministry, especially in conversion and in deep commitment to God. Among thousands converted through Moody's ministry were the famous Cambridge Seven, who were students at Cambridge University and also national sportsmen, including international cricketer C. T. Studd. They all eventually served the Lord in foreign missions.

Endnotes

[1] J Edwin Orr, 1975, *The Flaming Tongue: Evangelical Awakenings, 1900,* Moody, pp. i-vxiii.

[2] J Edwin Orr, 1973, *The Eager Feet: Evangelical Awakenings, 1792 & 1830,* Moody, p. 53, citing S B Halliday and D S Gregory, 1896, *The Church in America and its Baptisms of Fire*, p. 91. Orr gives detailed accounts of 'the second awakening', 1792-1830.

[3] Orr, 1973, p. 1. Orr sees the fall of the Bastille on July 14, 1789, and the French National Assembly's declaration of the Rights of Man on August 27, 1789 as the signals for revolution far and wide. Roman Catholic persecution of the Huguenots had produced free-thinking skepticism and infidelity among perjuring Huguenots antagonistic to forced religion, and Voltaire denounced a 'L'Infame' the whole system of ecclesiastico-political oppression.

[4] *Christian History*, No. 23, p. 25.

[5] Winkie Pratney, 1994, *Revival,* p. 104, citing Taylor.

[6] *Christian History*, No. 23, p. 26.

[7] Helen Wessel,1977, *The Autobiography of Charles Finney,* Bethany, pp. 20-22.

[8] Wessel, p. 22.

[9] Wessel, pp. 26-31.

[10] Orr, 1974, *The Fervent Prayer: Evangelical Awakenings, 1858.* Moody, p. 44.

[11] Orr, 1974, p. 44.

[12] Orr, 1975, p. 58.

[13] W R Moody, 1900, *The Life of D. L. Moody,* Revell, p. 149.

[14] Eddie Hyatt, 1998, *2000 Years of Charismatic Christianity,* Revival and Renewal Resources, p. 141, citing Gordon Lindsay, "The Speaking in Tongues in Church History", *Voice of Healing,* August 1964, p. 3.

Chapter 3

Early Twentieth Century Revival:
Worldwide Spirit Movements

Revival in the twentieth century had its roots in the eighteenth century Wesleyan concept of sanctification and the subsequent nineteenth century holiness churches emphasising an experience of 'entire sanctification'. From within these movements with their promotion of a 'second blessing' grew acceptance and promotion of a specific, empowering work of God's grace.

1901 - January: Topeka, Kansas, North America (Charles Parham)

Holiness preacher Charles Fox Parham (1873-1929), established Bethel Bible College as a missionary training school at Topeka, Kansas, from October 1900 in an old stone mansion rented from the American Bible Society on the outskirts of town. After prolonged periods of prayer and study the 34 students would meet in plenary sessions to discuss their findings. The final topic for discussion that year was the question: What is the Bible evidence whereby a person may know that he or she has been baptised in the Holy Spirit? On 31 December, after three days of personal study the students agreed unanimously that speaking in tongues was that evidence. Parham concurred.

The school emphasised personal and communal prayer, with staff and students continually using an upper room for prayer. They met there for their New Year's Eve watchnight service which continued into the early hours of the new year. On the next evening of 1 January, 1901,[1] Agnes Ozman (1870-1937), a Holiness preacher and inner city missioner studying at the school asked for prayer with laying on hands to receive the baptism in the Spirit with the gift of tongues. Parham and the leaders prayed for her and she experienced a strong encounter of the Spirit with tongues. Parham and half of the students also spoke in tongues during the next three days in which there was constant prayer, praise and worship. Initially they believed that these tongues were gifts of other languages (xenolalia[2]) to be used in missionary evangelism. Those events have been seen as the beginning of Pentecostalism in America, being the first recorded time that the doctrine of speaking in tongues as the initial evidence of the baptism in the Holy Spirit was articulated, taught and experienced.[3]

Parham established his Apostolic Faith movement among holiness groups, itinerated widely and ran various Bible Schools including a short term Bible School in Houston, Texas, in 1905-1906 where William Seymour, a Negro holiness preacher and son of Baptist slaves, attended.[4] Seymour accepted Parham's teaching on tongues as the initial evidence of baptism in the Spirit and adopted the Apostolic Faith title for his independent mission at Azusa Street in Los Angeles from April 1906.

Seymour invited Parham to speak at Azusa Street in October 1906, but Parham objected to the style and freedom of the meetings, so Seymour broke fellowship with him. Parham promoted the theological foundations of Pentecostalism from his experience of the Spirit at Topeka, but Seymour became the apostle of Pentecostalism through the Azusa Street revival.

1904 - October: Loughor, Wales (Evan Roberts)

Beginning with thousands of small prayer groups worldwide, the first years of the twentieth century saw revival break out in unprecedented measure.[5] An Australian example was the preparation for the evangelistic meetings of Reuben A. Torrey with Charles M. Alexander in Australia in 1902.[6] In preparation for their visit to Melbourne, 1,700 home prayer groups met to pray for the mission and revival. The Australian campaign registered over 20,000 enquirers, 8,642 in Melbourne, and many churches were filled early this century. Torrey reported on the large numbers of Melbourne home 'prayer circles' when he spoke at the annual Keswick Convention in England in July 1902. The 5,000 people attending Keswick responded with enthusiasm, committing themselves to pray for worldwide revival in ever increasing 'prayer circles'. Volunteers gathered names of additional thousands committed to join in united, constant prayer for revival.[7]

The Welsh Revival of 1904-1905 became the most powerful expression of that revival, and it, in turn, impacted the world. As news of the revival spread in print and as missionaries sailed from Great Britain, fervent prayer for revival increased across the world. Powerful revivals touched India, Korea, and China, and stirred revivals in South Africa and Japan, along with fresh awakenings in Africa, Latin America, and the Pacific.[8]

From November 1904 in Wales, thousands were converted in a few months and 100,000 within a year. That number did not include nominal members converted in the Anglican and Free Churches. Five years later 80,000 converts remained active in the churches.[9] During the revival, crime dropped dramatically, with some judges left without any cases to try. Convictions for drunkenness were halved in the Principality, and many taverns went bankrupt. At times so many miners were converted that it caused slowdowns in the mines because the pit ponies hauling coal stopped, confused, not understanding instructions without profanity.[10]

Early in 1904, touches of revival stirred New Quay, Cardiganshire, on the west coast of Wales where Joseph Jenkins was minister. At a testimony meeting at Jenkin's Methodist Church, a recent teenage convert, Florrie Evans, announced, "If no one else will, I must say that I do love my Lord Jesus with all my heart."[11] The Holy Spirit instantly moved powerfully on the meeting with strong conviction. Many wept. One after another stood and acknowledged their submission God. Jenkins led teams of revived young people conducting testimony meetings throughout the area.

The evangelist, Seth Joshua, arrived at New Quay in September 1904 to find remarkable moves of the Spirit in his meetings. On Sunday 18, he reported that he had "never seen the power of the Holy Spirit so powerfully manifested among the people as at this place just now." His meetings lasted far into the night. His diary continued:

> Monday 19. Revival is breaking out here in greater power ... the young people receiving the greatest measure of blessing. They break out into prayer, praise, testimony and exhortation.

> Tuesday 20. I cannot leave the building until 12 and even 1 o'clock in the morning I closed the service several times and yet it would break out again quite beyond control of human power.

Wednesday 21. Yes, several souls ... they are not drunkards or open sinners, but are members of the visible church not grafted into the true Vine ... the joy is intense.

Thursday 22. We held another remarkable meeting tonight. Group after group came out to the front, seeking the "full assurance of faith."

Friday 23. I am of the opinion that forty conversions took place this week. I also think that those seeking assurance may be fairly counted as converts, for they had never received Jesus as personal Saviour before."[12]

Seth Joshua, alarmed by the inroads of liberalism in the churches, had prayed that God would use a zealous young Christian to bring revival to Wales. One such young man, converted through his own ministry was Evan Roberts (1978-1951).

Born in Loughor in Glamorgan, between Swansea and Llanelly, Evan Roberts (1878-1951) was an exemplary school pupil. At twelve he began working in the mine with his father. He founded a Sunday school for the children of miners, and decided to become a preacher. Constantly he read the Bible, even in the mine. He published poems in the *Cardiff Times* under the pseudonym of Bwlchydd, learned shorthand, and taught himself to be a blacksmith. He describes his encounters with the Spirit as follows:

For thirteen years I prayed that I might receive the Spirit. I had been led to pray by a remark of William Davies, one of the deacons: 'Be faithful! Supposing the Spirit were to come down and you were not there. Remember Thomas, and how much he lost from not being present on the evening of the Resurrection.'

So I said to myself: 'I want to receive the Spirit at any price.' And I continually went to meetings despite all difficulties. Often, as I saw the other boys putting out to sea in their boats, I was tempted to turn round and join them. But no. I said to myself, 'Remember your resolution to be faithful', and I would go to the meeting. Prayer meeting on Monday evening at the chapel, prayer meeting for the Sunday school on Tuesday evening at 'Pisgah', meeting at the church on Wednesday evening, and of Hope meeting on Thursday evening. I supported all these faithfully for years. For ten or eleven years I prayed for revival. I spent whole nights reading accounts of revivals or talking about them. It was the Spirit who in this way was driving me to think about revival.

One Friday evening that spring (1904), as I was praying at my bedside before going to bed, I was taken up into a great expanse - without time or space. It was communion with God. Up to that time I had only had a God who was far off. That evening I was afraid, but that fear has never come back. I trembled so violently that the bed shook, and my brother was awakened and took hold of me, thinking I was ill.

After this experience I woke each night about one o'clock in the morning. It was the more strange, as usually I slept like a log and no noise in my room was enough to wake me. From one o'clock I was taken up into communion with God for about four hours. What it was I cannot tell you, except that it was of God. About five o'clock I was again allowed to sleep until about nine o'clock. I was then taken up again and carried away in the same experience as in the early hours of the morning, until about midday or one o'clock.

At home they questioned me, and asked why I got up so late ... but these things are too holy to speak of. This experience went on for about three months.[13]

He entered the Calvanistic Methodist Academy at Newcasle Emlyn in midSeptember 1904. He was convinced revival would touch all Wales and eventually he led a small band all over the country praying and preaching.

Seth Joshua held meetings at Newcastle Emlyn, following his meetings at New Quay. Students from the Methodist Academy attended. Among them was Sidney Evans a room mate of Evan Roberts. The students, including Evan Roberts, attended the next Joshua meetings in Blaenannerch.

There on Thursday 29 September, Seth Joshua closed the 7 a.m. meeting before breakfast crying out in Welsh, "Lord ... bend us." Evan Roberts remembered, "It was the Spirit that put the emphasis for me on 'Bend us.' 'That is what you need,' said the Spirit to me. And as I went out I prayed, O Lord, bend me" (Evans 1969, 70). During the 9 a.m. meeting, Evan Roberts eventually prayed aloud after others had prayed. He knelt with his arms over the seat in front, bathed in perspiration as he agonised in prayer. He regarded that encounter with the Spirit as crucial in launching him into his revival ministry which began one month later.

A motto of the revival became "Bend the church and save the world." Soon after the impact of the Spirit on him at Seth Joshua's meetings, he took leave from the Academy to return home to challenge his friends, especially the young people.

Arriving home by train at his village of Loughor on the south coast of Wales on Monday, 31 October, Evan Roberts obtained permission to speak at meetings from Daniel Jones, minister at Moriah Church in Loughor and its chapel Pisgah, and from Thomas Francis minister at Moriah's daughter church in Gorseinon. Roberts spoke after the usual Monday night prayer meeting at Moriah to 17 young people. The Holy Spirit moved on them all in that two hour session, and they all publicly confessed Christ as their personal Saviour, including Evan Roberts' three sisters and his brother Dan, all of whom later a took leading part in many revival meetings. Meetings followed at Pisgah and Gorseinon. He then spoke every night to increasing crowds at Moriah Church where he began emphasising four points which became his constant theme. People were convicted as Evan Roberts repeatedly emphasised four requirements, that they must:

1. put away any unconfessed sin,
2. forsake any doubtful habit,
3. obey the Spirit promptly,
4. confess Christ publicly.

He believed that a baptism in the Spirit was the essence of revival and that the primary condition of revival is that individuals should experience such a baptism in the Spirit.[14] By the weekend the church was packed. Roberts spoke to a crowded church on Saturday night on 'Be filled with the Spirit'. An after meeting with Roberts followed Sunday night service at Libanus Chapel, Gorseinon. Evan Roberts described the response on the Sunday evening, 6 November, when by midnight the congregation was overwhelmed with tears.

> Then the people came down from the gallery, and sat close to one another. "Now," said I, "we must believe that the Spirit will come; not think He will come; not hope He will come; but firmly believe that He will come." Then I read the promises of God, and pointed out how definite they were. (Remember, I a.m. doing all under the guidance of the Holy Spirit, and praise be to Him.) After this, the Spirit said that everyone was to

pray. Pray now, not confess, not sing, not give experience, but pray and believe, and wait. And this is the prayer, "Send the Spirit now, for Jesus Christ's sake."

The people were sitting, and only closed their eyes. The prayer began with me. Then it went from seat to seat boys and girls young men and maidens. Some asking in silence, some aloud, some coldly, some with warmth, some formally, some in tears, some with difficulty, some adding to it, boys and girls, strong voices, then tender voices. Oh, wonderful! I never thought of such an effect. I felt the place beginning to be filled, and before the prayer had gone half way through the chapel, I could hear some brother weeping, sobbing, and saying, "Oh, dear! dear! well! well! Oh, dear! dear!" On went the prayer, the feeling becoming more intense; the place being filled more and more (with the Spirit's presence)."[15]

The crowded Monday evening meeting went till 3 a.m. Meetings continued every night. The Cardiff newspaper *The Western Mail* published this report on Thursday 10 November, the first of many daily reports on the progress of the revival:

Great Crowds of People Drawn to Loughor

Congregation Stays till 2:30 in the Morning

A remarkable religious revival is now taking place in Loughor. For some days a young man named Evan Roberts, a native of Loughor, has been causing great surprise at Moriah Chapel. The place has been besieged by dense crowds of people unable to obtain admission. Such excitement has prevailed that the road on which the chapel is situated has been lined with people from end to end. Roberts, who speaks in Welsh, opens his discourse by saying that he does not know what he is going to say but that when he is in communion with the Holy Spirit, the Holy Spirit will speak, and he will simply be the medium of His wisdom. The preacher soon after launches into a fervent and at times impassioned oration. His statements have had the most stirring effects upon his listeners. Many who have disbelieved Christianity for years are returning to the fold of their younger days. One night, so great was the enthusiasm invoked by the young revivalist that, after his sermon which lasted two hours, the vast congregation remained praying and singing until two-thirty in the morning. Shopkeepers are closing early in order to get a place in the chapel, and tin and steel workers throng the place in working clothes.[16]

Revival meetings began to multiply rapidly, the early ones in South Wales being led by Evan Roberts, Sydney Evans, Seth Joshua and Joseph Jenkins with teams of young people. Rev. R. B. Jones began a ten day mission on Tuesday, 8 November in Rhos in North Wales during which revival broke out and rapidly spread through the north as well as the south.

Many of the 800 attending the Moriah meeting on Friday, 11 November were on their knees repenting for a long time. The *Western Mail* report of that meeting circulated widely in Wales and throughout the rest of Britain:

> Instead of the set order of proceedings … everything was left to the spontaneous impulse of the moment … at 4:25 a.m., the gathering dispersed. But even at that hour, the people did not make their way home. When I left to walk back to Llanelly, I left dozens of them about the road discussing the chief subject of their lives. … I felt that this was no ordinary gathering.[17]

Newspaper reports generated intense interest in the meetings. Crowds arrived in Loughor on Saturday 12 November filling the streets with wagons and carts. Shops emptied of food supplies. Roberts' college room mate preached at one chapel and Roberts at the other on Saturday, both meetings lasting till after dawn Sunday. Hundreds of coalminers and tin plate workers were converted, filled with the Spirit, and radically transformed. Swearing, drunkenness, immorality and crime began to diminish.

From Sunday 13 November, Evan Roberts and his teams conducted meetings by invitation, first at Aberdare and then throughout the towns and hamlets of Wales. He usually took a small team with him to pray, witness and sing. November 1904 saw revival spread throughout Wales. Newspapers described the crowded meetings. Churches and chapels sent statistics of conversions to the papers. By the end of January 1905 the papers had reported 70,000 converted in three months.[18]

As with other evangelists and ministers, Evan Roberts travelled the Welsh valleys, often never preaching but earnestly praying. In Neath he spent a week in prayer without leaving his rooms while the revival continued to pack the churches. Characteristics of the meetings were singing Welsh hymns in harmony for over an hour, the decline of the sermon, emphasis on baptism in the Spirit and the guidance of the Spirit, public repentance and the *hywl,* a half sung, half spoken harmony ending in a hymn, or a cry of thanksgiving or repentance.[19]

Churches filled. The revival spread. Meetings continued all day as well as each night, often late into the night or through to morning. Crowds were getting right with God and with one another in confession, repentance and restitution of wrongs done. People prayed fervently and worshipped God with great joy. Police had so little to do they joined the crowds in the churches, sometimes forming singing groups. The impact of the Spirit across the churches produced new levels of unity, joy, boldness, power to witness, changed lives, and enthusiasm explained as being "fervent in spirit" (Romans 12:11).

Roberts, prophetically gifted, was unusually sensitive to the responses in the congregation. Public criticism of Evan Roberts and some revival phenomena included the usual objections to enthusiasm or fanaticism, emotionalism and confusion.[20] At age 27, he lacked maturity and theological balance and fell too easily into nervous exhaustion, as did other young leaders in the revival.[21] More experienced ministers avoided these errors and contributed significantly to revival leadership. Defenders of revival phenomena pointed to thousands of changed lives and the spiritual zeal generated.[22]

Roberts believed his unusual prophetic and intuitive charismatic abilities came from his 'baptism in the Spirit' and urged everyone to actively seek such a baptism. Revival historians trace a direct link from the Welsh revival to increased worldwide fervent prayer, increased expectation of revival, increased evangelism and the emergence of Pentecostalism, even though many evangelicals regarded Pentecostalism as an aberration of revival.[23]

On Sunday, 20 November 1904, the brothers Stephen and George Jeffreys were converted in Siloh Chapel in Maesteg, their home church in the Welsh Independent (Congregational) church. Although initially opposed to Pentecostalism which emerged in Wales in 1908, they became involved from 1911. Both were powerful evangelists in Great Britain and abroad, preaching to huge crowds and seeing hundreds healed and thousands converted. They often travelled and ministered together and established many churches. George Jeffreys' campaigns included a crusade in Birmingham with 10,000 converted and powerful ministry in Europe such as 14,000 converted in Switzerland in 1934-1936, and he became the founder and leader of the Elim Foursquare Alliance (Elim Pentecostal Church). Stephen Jeffreys also pioneered many Elim churches and worked actively with the newly formed Assemblies of God of Britain and Ireland as an independent evangelist.

The Pentecostal movement in Great Britain has direct personal and theological roots in the Welsh Revival. The Jeffrey brothers were converted in the revival. Donald Gee, the leading Pentecostal apologist, was converted through Seth Joshua. Anglican priest, Alexander A. Boddy, 'the father of the British Pentecostal movement' participated in the revival, worked with Evan Roberts, and was convinced that the Pentecostal movement was a direct continuation of the revival.[24] Smith Wigglesworth, a leading healing evangelist, and Stanley Frodsham, prolific writer and leader, were baptised in the Spirit, including glossolalia, at Boddy's Anglican Church in Sunderland.

Welsh revival phenomena, including the emphasis on being baptised in the Spirit, being led by the Spirit, discerning spiritual influences, receiving prophetic insights, and encouraging spontaneous participation in the meetings and well as involving lay people including women, men and children in personal and public ministry, became widely characteristic of Pentecostalism.

The Welsh Revival emphasised the importance of a baptism in the Spirit. Specific impacts of the Spirit in New Quay, Newcastle Emlyn, Blaenannerch and Moriah both prepared the way for revival in those involved and set the pattern of seeking and responding to the Spirit in the revival. Reports of the 'influx' of the Spirit, and the testimony of thousands involved, generated new interest in Spirit movements, in revival, and eventually in the emerging Pentecostal and charismatic movements.

1905 - Mukti, India (Pandita Ramabai)

Honoured with the title Pandita by the Sanskrit scholars of Calcutta University, Ramabai (1858-1922), became a Christian by the turn of the century, mastered seven languages, translated the Bible into Marathi and published books including *A Life of Christ*. The Indian government issued a postage stamp in her honour in 1989, recognising her social impact on the nation, especially in rescuing young widows from death or degradation.

She established a compound for widows and orphan girls during severe famine in her area near Pune (Poona) just south of Bombay, and called it Mukti (salvation). By 1901, she had 2,000 girls and women and from January 1905, she began teaching about the need for revival. Soon over 500 people met twice daily to pray for revival, mostly women and girls.

Ramabai heard about early moves of the Spirit in north east India and challenged her women to leave secular studies for a time to go into the villages to preach in teams. Thirty volunteered. They met daily to pray for the endowment of the Holy Spirit. Then on Thursday, 29 June the Spirit moved on many of the girls. The girls saw flames engulfing one of the girls, so another girl raced to get a bucket of water, only to discover she was not being burned.

Then on Friday, 30 June, while Ramabai taught from John 8, the Holy Spirit fell on them all suddenly with great power. Everyone there began to weep and pray aloud, crying out to be baptised with the Holy Spirit and fire. One twelve year old girl, though very plain, became radiantly beautiful and laughed constantly. Others had visions of Jesus.

Revival spread through their mission, and into many surrounding areas. Regular school activities gave way to confession, repentance, and great joy with much praise and dancing. Many were baptised in the Spirit, spoke in tongues, and were filled with zeal for evangelism and social care. A missionary, Albert Norton, visited the mission where Minnie Abrams, a teacher, invited him to observe a revival prayer group in the school. He reported,

> One week ago I visited the Mukti Mission. Miss Abrams asked me if I should like to go into a room where about twenty girls were praying. After entering, I knelt with closed eyes by a table on one side. Presently I heard someone praying near me very distinctly in English. Among the petitions were, "O Lord, open the mouth; O Lord, open the mouth; O Lord, open the heart; O Lord, open the eyes! O Lord, open the eyes! Oh, the blood of Jesus, the blood of Jesus! Oh, give complete victory! Oh, such a blessing! Oh, such glory!"

> I was struck with astonishment, as I knew that there was no one in the room who could speak English, beside Miss Abrams. I opened my eyes and within three feet of me, on her knees, with closed eyes and raised hands was a woman, whom I had baptised at Kedgaon in 1899, and whom my wife and I had known intimately since as a devoted Christian worker. Her mother tongue was Marathi, and she could speak a little Hindustani. But she was unable to speak or understand English such as she was using. But when I heard her speak English idiomatically, distinctly, and fluently, I was impressed as I should have been had I seen one, whom I knew to be dead, raised to life.

A few other illiterate Marathi women and girls were speaking in English and some were speaking in other languages with none at Kedagaon understood. This was not gibberish, but it closely resembled the speaking of foreign languages to which I had listened but did not understand. ...

I have an idea that it is in mercy to us poor missionaries from Europe and America who, as a class, seem to be Doubting Thomases, in regard to gifts and workings of the Spirit, and not receiving the power of the Spirit as we ought.[25]

That powerful revival spread throughout many areas of India, with Christians and unbelievers repenting in large numbers and being filled with the Holy Spirit and the fire of God. It provides another example of the poor and despised discovering propagating the immeasurable grace of God especially among the 'common people'.

1905 - October: Dohnavur, South India (Amy Carmichael)

Revival spread to south India where Amy Carmichael (1867-1951) at Dohnavur among the Tamils had been praying and longing for a visitation of the Spirit of God. In October the Spirit moved upon them so powerfully they could neither preach nor pray aloud. They broke down weeping.

It was so startling and so awful. I can use no other word ... It was at the close of the morning service that the break came. The one who was speaking was obliged to stop, overwhelmed by the sudden realisation of the inner force of things. It was impossible even to pray. One of the older lads in the boys' school began to try to pray, but he broke down, then another, then all together, the older lads chiefly at first. Soon many among the younger ones began to cry bitterly, and pray for forgiveness. It spread to the women ... Soon the whole upper half of the church was on its face on the floor crying to God, each boy and girl, man and woman, oblivious of all others. The sound was like the sound of waves of strong wind in the trees. No separate voice could be heard. I had never heard of such a thing as this among Tamil people. Up in the north, of course, one knew that it had happened, but our Tamils are so stolid, so unemotional I had never imagined such a thing as this occurring. Nothing disturbed those who were praying, and that hurricane of prayer continued with one short break of a few minutes for over four hours.[26]

Effects during the next seven months in particular included the professed conversion of all the school pupils, revival among the Christians, restoration among the lapsed, successful evangelism in the surrounding areas, and a remarkable spirit of unity among everyone. That unity transcended personal and doctrinal differences among Christians, another sign of the Spirit's transforming presence.

1906 - March: Assam, North East India

Revival stirred in Assam before the Mukti revival, but took much longer to ignite and did not spread with the intensity of the western fires. From the beginning of 1905 the Khasi hill tribe Christians met every night to pray for revival for over eighteen months. Their Welsh Presbyterian missionaries brought news of revival in Wales which stirred them to earnest prayer. Those nightly meetings often went past 10 p.m.

The Bible teaching on Sunday 4 March 1906 concerning the baptism of the Spirit stirred the prayers deeply. The Christians felt an unusual sense of the Spirit's presence which produced prolonged prayer, weeping and praise. Gradually revival spread through the presbytery with powerful messages from Khasi preachers and widespread repentance.

The Baptists also reported remarkable awakenings along the wide Brahmaputra River valley. Revival spread throughout 1907 into all the churches of the Brahmaputra, then south into the Naga hills and then on to the Mizo people further south. A pagan antirevival movement flared in 1911-12, but when a plague of rats invaded the area demolishing their food, the people suffered terribly. Refugees poured down into the plains where Christians shared their food and cared for them. So the pagan revival died out and in 1913 and then again in 1919 greater revivals of Christianity ignited the hills again.

The Spirit's movement in revival and the teaching on baptism in the Spirit had transcended denominational, national and racial boundaries, and continued to spread rapidly among the humble and spiritually hungry.

1906 - April: Los Angeles, North America (William Seymour)

Early in 1906 William J. Seymour (1870-1922), the Negro Holiness pastor, studied briefly at Charles Parham's short term Bible School in Houston, Texas. Segregation laws in that state prohibited Negoes from joining the classes. Most reports indicate that he sat in the hall and listened through the doorway.

Julia Hutchins, the pastor of a small holiness church in Los Angeles, heard of Seymour from a friend, Luci Farrow, who had visited Houston. Hutchins invited William Seymour to preach in her church with the possibility of becoming pastor of the church. His first sermon there, from Acts 2:4, emphasised being filled with the Spirit and speaking in tongues. He soon found himself locked out of the building.

Seymour then began cottage meetings in the home of Richard Asbery at 214 Bonnie Brae Street, which still exists as a Pentecostal landmark. Many there, including Seymour, fell to the floor and began speaking in tongues at the prayer meeting on Monday, April 9. Numbers grew until the weight of the crowd broke the front verandah, so they had to move. They found an old two storey weatherboard stable and warehouse at 312 Azusa Street which had previously been an African Episcopal Methodist church.

So Seymour, now leader of The Apostolic Faith Mission, began meetings there on Easter Saturday, April 14, 1906. About 100 attended including blacks and whites. The Spirit of God moved powerfully on that little mission. Many were baptised in the Spirit with speaking in tongues and prophecies. Four days later on Wednesday, April 18, the day of the San Fanscisco earthquake, the *Los Angeles Times* began carrying articles about the weird babble of tongues and wild scenes at Azusa Street.[27]

Not only was the racial mixture unusual, but the newspaper reports, usually critical of those noisy Pentecostal meetings, drew both Christians and unbelievers, poor and rich, to investigate. Soon crowds crammed into the building to investigate or mock. Hundreds were saved, baptised in the Spirit and ignited for apostolic style mission which included prayers for healing and outreach in evangelism and overseas mission.

Frank Bartleman, an independent holiness preacher, reported regularly on 'Azusa Street' for holiness periodicals. He gathered his autobiographical accounts into his 1925 book *How Pentecost Came to Los Angeles: How it was in the Beginning,*[28] reprinted in 1980. He wrote:

In the beginning in "Azusa" we had no musical instruments. In fact we felt no need of them. There was no place for them in our worship. All was spontaneous. We did not even sing from hymn books. All the old well known hymns were sung from memory, quickened by the Spirit of God. ...But the "new song" was altogether different, not of human composition. It cannot be successfully counterfeited. The crow cannot imitate the dove. But they finally began to despise this "gift," when the human spirit asserted itself again. They drove it out by hymn books and selected songs by leaders. It was like murdering the Spirit ... The spirit of song given from God in the beginning was like the Aeolian harp, in its spontaneity and sweetness. In fact it was the very breath of God, playing on human heart strings, or human vocal chords. The notes were wonderful in sweetness, volume and duration. If fact they were oftentimes humanly impossible. It was "singing in the Spirit."

Brother Seymour was recognized as the nominal leader in charge. But we had no pope or hierarchy. We were "brethren." We had no human programme. The Lord Himself was leading. We had no priest class, nor priest craft. These things have come in later, with the apostatising of the movement. We did not even have a platform or pulpit in the beginning. All were on a level. The ministers were servants, according to the true meaning of the word. We did not honor men for their advantage, in means or education, but rather for their God-given "gifts." He set the members in the "body." ...

Brother Seymour generally sat behind two empty shoe boxes, one on top of the other. He usually kept his head inside the top one during the meeting, in prayer. There was no pride there. The services ran almost continuously. Seeking souls could be found under the power almost any hour, night and day. The place was never closed nor empty. The people came to meet God. He was always there. Hence a continuous meeting. The meeting did not depend on the human leader. God's presence became more and more wonderful. In that old building, with its low rafters and bare floors, God took strong men and women to pieces, and put them together again, for His glory. It was a tremendous overhauling process. Pride and self-assertion, self-importance and self-esteem, could not survive there. The religious ego preached its own funeral sermon quickly.

No subjects or sermons were announced ahead of time, and no special speakers for such an hour. No one knew what might be coming, what God would do. All was spontaneous, ordered of the Spirit. We wanted to hear from God, through whoever he might speak. We had no "respect of persons." The rich and educated were the same as the poor and ignorant, and found a much harder death to die. We only recognized God. All were equal. No flesh might glory in His presence. He could not use the self-opinionated. Those were Holy Ghost meetings, led of the Lord. It had to start in poor surroundings, to keep out the selfish, human element. All came down in humility together, at His feet. They all looked alike, and had all things in common in that sense at least. The rafters were low, the tall must come down. By the time they got to "Azusa" they were humbled, ready for the blessing. The fodder was thus placed for the lambs, not for giraffes. All could reach it.

We were delivered right there from ecclesiastical hier-archism and abuse. We wanted God. When we first reached the meeting we avoided as much as possible human contact and greeting. We wanted to meet God first. We got our head under some bench in the cor-ner in prayer, and met men only in the Spirit, knowing them "after the flesh" no more. The meetings started themselves, spontaneously, in testimony, praise and worship. The testimonies were never hurried by a call for "popcorn." We had no prearranged programme to be jammed through on time. Our time was the Lord's. We had real testimonies, from fresh heart-experience. Otherwise, the shorter the testimonies, the better. A dozen might be on their feet at one time, trembling under the mighty power of God. We did not have to get our cue from some leader. And we were free from lawlessness. We were shut up to God in prayer in the meetings, our minds on Him. All obeyed God, in meekness and humility. In honor we "preferred one another." The Lord was liable to burst through any one. We prayed for this continually. Some one would finally get up anointed for the message. All seemed to recognize this and gave way. It might be a child, a woman, or a man. It might be from the back seat, or from the front. It made no difference. We rejoiced that God was working. No one wished to show himself. We thought only of obeying God. In fact there was an atmosphere of God there that forbade any one but a fool attempting to put himself forward without the real anointing. And such did not last long. The meetings were controlled by the Spirit, from the throne. Those were truly wonderful days. I often said that I would rather live six months at that time than fifty years of ordinary life. But God is just the same today. Only we have changed.

Some one might be speaking. Suddenly the Spirit would fall upon the congregation. God himself would give the altar call. Men would fall all over the house, like the slain in battle, or rush for the altar *en masse*, to seek God. The scene often resembled a forest of fallen trees. Such a scene cannot be imitated. I never saw an altar call given in those early days. God himself would call them. And the preacher knew when to quit. When He spoke we all obeyed. It seemed a fearful thing to hinder or grieve the Spirit. The whole place was steeped in prayer. God was in His holy temple. It was for man to keep silent. The Shekinah glory rested there. In fact some claim to have seen the glory by night over the building. I do not doubt it. I have stopped more than once within two blocks of the place and prayed for strength before I dared go on. The presence of the Lord was so real.

Presumptuous men would sometimes come among us. Especially preachers who would try to spread themselves, in self-opinionation. But their effort was short lived. The breath would be taken from them. Their minds would wander, their brains reel. Things would turn black before their eyes. They could not go on. I never saw one get by with it in those days. They were up against God. No one cut them off. We simply prayed. The Holy Spirit did the rest. We wanted the Spirit to control. He wound them up in short order. They were carried out dead, spiritually speaking. They generally bit the dust in humility, going through the process we had all gone through. In other words they died out, came to see themselves in all their weakness, then in childlike humility and confession were taken up of God, transformed through the mighty "baptism" in the Spirit. The "old man" died with all his pride, arrogancy and good works. In my own case I came to abhor myself. I begged the Lord to drop a curtain so close behind me on my past that it would hit my heels. He told me to forget every good deed as though it had never occurred, as soon as it was accomplished, and go forward again as though I had never accomplished anything for Him, lest my good works become a snare to me. We saw some wonderful things in those days. Even very good men came to abhor themselves in the clearer light of God. The preachers died the hardest. They had so much to die to. So much reputation and good works. But when God got through with them they gladly turned a new page and chapter. That was one reason they fought so hard. Death is not at all a pleasant experience. And strong men die hard.[29]

Bartleman's account, before the benefit of hindsight through the twentieth century, identified many of the key elements of strong impacts of the Spirit. These included spontaneous Spirit inspired worship mingled with prayer and current testimony; acknowledged leadership which facilitated response to the Spirit; repentance and humility in the awesome present of God; mutual honour and respect for everyone whether poor or rich, black or white, female or male, unknown or known; constant use of spiritual gifts including the controversial glossolalia, prayer for the sick and testimonies of answered prayer; large numbers of locals and visitors 'baptised in the Spirit' and taking that blessing across America and the globe with a strong, humbling anointing.

The exploding Pentecostal movement around the world traces its origins to Azusa Street, from which fire spread across the globe.[30] For example, John G. Lake had visited the mission at Azusa Street. In 1908 he pioneered Pentecostal missions in South Africa where, after five years he had established 500 black and 125 white congregations. Later he established healing rooms where thousands were healed through medicine and prayer at Spokane, Washington, which soon became known as the healthiest city in America at that time.

Cox, quoting Bartleman, begins his chapter on Azusa Street[31] announcing, "Pentecost has come to Los Angeles, the American Jerusalem. Every sect, creed and doctrine under heaven ... as well as every nation is represented."[32] He argues that Los Angeles provided a place of new hopes and dreams, and for Seymour in segregated Jim Crow America, God was assembling and pouring his inclusive Spirit on a radically inclusive people. A southern white preacher, at first offended, then inspired, noted that at Azusa Street "the colour line was washed away by the blood."[33]

Press hostility to this radical, racial mixture and its 'wild scenes' drew crowds, many of whom "came to scorn and stayed to pray."[34] The San Franscisco earthquake and fire, in which 10,000 died, sent geological and spiritual tremors through Los Angeles, provoking many apocalyptic interpretations and warnings.

Perhaps the most significant reason the impact of the Spirit in Azusa Street ignited such powerful global mission was its literal fulfilment of the messianic charter announced in Nazareth. These despised and rejected people were also powerfully anointed by the Spirit as the beneficiaries and heralds of the new era of the Spirit.

Bartleman prophetically concluded his book on Azusa Street with his final chapter being "A Plea for Unity." Looking beyond the fragmenting Holiness and Pentecostal churches a decade after the Azusa Street revival, and sensing that doctrinal unity is neither possible nor desirable, he wrote:

The Spirit is labouring for the unity of believers today, for the "one body" that the prayer of Jesus may be answered, "that they may all be one, that the world may believe." But the saints are ever too ready to serve a system or party, to contend for religious, selfish, party interests. ... "Error always leads to militant exclusion. Truth evermore stoops to wash the saints' feet." One feels even in visiting many Pentecostal missions today that they do not belong there, simply because they have not lined up officially with that particular brand or variety. These things ought not to be. "In one Spirit are we all baptized, into one body." - 1 Cor. 12:13. We should be as one family, which we are, at home in God's house anywhere.

> We belong to the whole body of Christ, both in Heaven and on earth. God's church is one.[35]

Cox concludes his chapter on Azusa Street noting the absence of a physical memorial to Seymour's mission in Azusa Street today, he declares that, "the Azusa Street memorial is something they could never have foreseen. It is a spiritual hurricane that has already touched nearly half a billion people, and an alternative vision of the human future whose impact may only be in its earliest stages today."[36]

1907 - January: Pyongyang, Korea

Revival in Korea broke in the nation in 1907. Presbyterian missionaries, hearing of revival in Wales, and of a similar revival among Welsh Presbyterian work in Assam, prayed earnestly for the same in Korea. From Wednesday 2 January, church representatives gathered for ten days at the annual New Year Bible study course at Pyongyang, then the capital of Korea. A spirit of prayer broke out. The meetings carried on day after day, with confessions of sins, weeping and trembling.

Then on Monday night 7 January, so many wanted to pray that the leaders called all 1500 of them to pray aloud together. Their prayers mingled with public confession, much weeping, and many dropping prostrate on the floor in agonies of repentance.

It astounded observers. The delegates of the New Year gathering returned to their churches taking with them this spirit of prayer which strongly impacted the churches of the nation with revival. That pattern of simultaneous prayer became a feature of Korean church life. Everywhere conviction of sin, confession and restitution were common. Within two months 2,000 were converted, and 30,000 had become Christians by the middle of 1907.

Persecution at the hands of the Japanese and then the Russian and Chinese communists saw thousands killed, but still the church grew in fervent prayer. Prior to the Russian invasion thousands of North Koreans gathered every morning at 5 am. Sometimes 10,000 were gathered in one place for prayer each morning.

Early morning daily prayer meetings became common, as did nights of prayer throughout Korea. Now over a million gather every morning around 5 a.m. for prayer in the churches. Prayer and fasting is normal. Churches have over 100 prayer retreats in the hills called Prayer Mountains to which thousands go to pray, often with fasting. Healings and supernatural manifestations continue. Koreans have sent over 10,000 missionaries into other Asian countries. Korea now has the largest Presbyterian and Methodist churches in the world, and has four of the world's seven largest Sunday church attendances.

David Yonggi Cho has amazing growth in Seoul where he is senior pastor of a Full Gospel church of 800,000 with over 25,000 home cell groups, and sustained church growth. During the week over 3,000 a day and over 5,000 at weekends pray at their prayer mountain.

1908 - February: China (Jonathan Goforth)

"You must go forward on your knees," Hudson Taylor advised a young Canadian missionary named Jonathan Goforth (1859-1936). While a student at Knox College in Toronto, Canada, Goforth was profoundly moved during three days of meetings with D L Moody in 1988 just before he and his wife Rosalyn left for north Henan province in China that year. Yet, after thirteen years of faithful praying and preaching, and what most would consider a very successful ministry, Goforth became restless and dissatisfied.

In 1900, the Goforths had to excape across China during the Boxer Rebellion. Jonathan was attacked and injured with a sword, but they both survived and escaped to the safety a "Treaty Port" and went back to Canada for a year. After returning to Henan in 1901, Jonathan Goforth felt increasingly restless. In 1904 and 1905, he was inspired by news of the great Welsh Revival and read Finney's "Lectures on Revivals". People from England began sending him pamphlets on the Welsh revival of 1904. Goforth was deeply stirred as he read these accounts. "A new thought, a new conception seemed to come to him of God the Holy Spirit." He then gave himself to much more prayer and Bible study. Goforth now found himself being driven by a fresh vision, a vision for a mighty outpouring of the Holy Spirit.

Soon he began to meet daily with other missionaries to pray for revival. These men vowed to God and to one another that they would pray until revival came to China. In 1907 he witnessed revival in Korea. As he returned to China through

Manchuria from February 1908, the Manchurian Revival broke out. In 1908, Jonathan Goforth's prayers and dreams began to be realized.

Goforth began going to different missionary stations and simply led his fellow missionaries in prayer. Then suddenly earnest prayer gave way to the open confession of sin. As the Christians confessed and forsook their secret sin the Holy Spirit rushed in like a mighty wind. This open and honest confession of sin was the most striking feature of the revival. Everywhere Goforth went revival would spread, and almost always in the same way.

First prayer was encouraged among the Christians, which then spontaneously led to heart- breaking confessions of sin. And then like a flood, the lost were brought into the kingdom by the thousands. One after another broken-hearted believers emptied themselves through the uncovering of all secret sin. Goforth clearly identified unconfessed sin among Christians as a major hindrance to God-sent revival.

Walter Phillips describes one of Goforth's revival meetings:

> At once, on entering the church one was conscious of something unusual. The place was crowded to the door and tense, reverent attention sat on every face. The people knelt for prayer, silent at first, but soon one here and another there began to pray aloud. The voices grew and gathered volume and blended into a great wave of united supplication that swelled until it was almost a roar. Now I understood why the floor was so wet - the very air was electric and strange thrills coursed up and down ones body.[37]

When Goforth preached, "The cross burned like a living fire in the heart of every address." The person of Jesus Christ was exalted throughout the entire revival as a King and Saviour who must be reckoned with. In this great revival Jonathan Goforth clearly saw that all of his previous sweating and striving had reaped only frustration. He came to the firm conviction that revival is only born through humility, faith, prayer and the power of the Holy Spirit. Goforth writes,

> If revival is being withheld from us it is because some idol remains still enthroned; because we still insist in placing our reliance in human schemes; because we still refuse to face the unchangeable truth that "It is not by might, but by My Spirit."[38]

1909 - July: Valparaiso, Chile (Willis Hoover)

Minnie Abrams, who worked at Mukti in India during the 1905 revival there, sent an account of it in 1907 to her friend Mary Hoover, wife of Willis Hoover (1856-1936), Methodist missionaries in Chile. They began praying with their congregation for a similar revival in Chile. Often groups prayed all night. Many confessed sins openly and made restitution for wrongs done. That prepared the way for the revival which burst on them on Sunday July 4. Willis Hoover wrote:

> Saturday night was an all night of prayer, during which four vain young ladies (three of them were in the choir) fell to the floor under the power of the Spirit. One of them, after praying a long time, began to exhort saying, "The Lord is coming soon and commands us to get ready." The effect produced was indescribable. The following morning in Sunday School, at ten o'clock, a daze seemed to rest upon the people. Some were unable to rise after the opening prayer which had been like 'the sound of many waters,' and all were filled with

wonder. From that time on the atmosphere seemed charged by the Holy Spirit, and people fell on the floor, or broke out in other tongues, or singing in the Spirit, in a way impossible in their natural condition. On one occasion a woman, a young lady, and a girl of twelve were lying on the floor in different parts of the prayer room, with eyes closed and silent. Suddenly, as with one voice, they burst forth into a song in a familiar tune but in unknown tongues, all speaking the same words. After a verse or two they became silent; then again suddenly, another tune, a verse or two, and silence. This was repeated until they had sung ten tunes, always using the same words and keeping in perfect time together as if led by some invisible chorister.[39]

Within two months the congregation grew from 300 to 1,000 and the revival spread to other cities. Willis Hoover had to leave the denomination, but established the Pentecostal Methodist Church which now has over 600,000 members in Chile.

1914: Belgian Congo, Africa (Charles T Studd)

Africa has seen many powerful revivals, such as the Belgian Congo outpouring with C T Studd (1860-1931) in 1914. Charles T Studd played cricket for England in the famous 1882 match won by Australia which was the beginning of the Ashes. He was one of the famous "Cambridge Seven" who served God in pioneering mission work in China from 1885 in Hudson Taylor's China Inland Mission. He wrote,

Some want to live within the sound of church or chapel bell; I want to run a rescue shop within a yard of hell.

He was a pastor in India (1900-1906) and then from 1910 pioneered mission in Africa, founding the Heart of Africa Mission which later became the Worldwide Evangelical Crusade (WEC). His daughter married Norman Grubb who led WEC after Studd died in Africa. He saw revival in the Congo in 1914.

"The whole place was charged as if with an electric current. Men were falling, jumping, laughing, crying, singing, confessing and some shaking terribly," he reported. "As I led in prayer the Spirit came down in mighty power sweeping the congregation. My whole body trembled with the power. We saw a marvellous sight, people literally filled and drunk with the Spirit."[40]

Accounts like that are typical of the continuing moves of God's Spirit in Africa this century. Early this century an estimated 10% of the population was Christian. The Christian population reached 50% of Africa south of the Sahara. By the end of the twentieth century the number of African Christians exceeded 400 million. The majority of this growth is with the African independent churches characterised by strong Spirit movements

Local revivals are a continuing characteristic of revivals in Africa and of the worldwide growth of the church this century.

1915 - October: Gazaland, South Africa (Rees Howells)

A further example of strong sprit movements spreading in revival from Wales is told by Rees Howells (1879-1950) who founded the Bible College of Wales following his return from missionary work in South Africa. Converted while working in America in 1904 for three years, he returned to Wales and participated actively in the revival. In 1906 at the Llandrindod Convention, he made a total surrender of his life to God and was filled with the Spirit. This led him to offer for missionary work in Africa.

In 1915, he joined the South Africa General Mission founded by Andrew Murray, which then had 170 European and African worker in 25 stations, north as far as Belgian Congo. He was sent to Rusity Mission Station in Gazaland near the border of Portugese East Africa. There he reported on the Welsh Revival.

Within six weeks the Spirit began to move upon the Christians. On a Friday evening the Spirit moved on the group meeting in the Howell's home as they sang, and they continued the singing the next days in their gardens and elsewhere. Howells recognized a sound he had heard in the Welsh Revival. "You know it when you hear it," he said, "but you can't make it; and by the following Thursday, I was singing it too. There was something about it which changed you, and brought you into the stillness of God."[41] The following Sunday revival broke out as the Spirit moved on them all. Rees Howells reported:

> The Sunday was October 10 - my birthday - and as I preached in the morning, you could feel the Spirit coming on the congregation. In the evening, down He came. I shall never forget it. He came upon a young girl, Kufase by name, who had fasted for three days under conviction that she was not ready for the Lord's coming. As she prayed she broke down crying, and within five minutes the whole congregation were on their faces crying to God. Like lightning and thunder the power came down. I had never seen this, even in the Welsh Revival. I had only heard about it with Finney and others. Heaven had opened, and there was no room to contain the blessing.

I lost myself in the Spirit and prayed as much as they did. All I could say was, "He has come!" We went on until late in the night; we couldn't stop the meeting. What He told me before I went to Africa was actually taking place, and that within six weeks. You can never describe those meetings when the Holy Spirit comes down. I shall never forget the sound in the district that night - praying in every kraal.

The next day He came again, and people were on their knees till 6 p.m. This went on for six days and people began to confess their sins and come free as the Holy Spirit brought them through. They had forgiveness of sins, and met the Savior as only the Holy Spirit can reveal Him. Everyone who came near would go under the power of the Spirit. People stood up to give their testimonies, and it was nothing to see twenty-five on their feet at the same time.

At the end of one week nearly all were through. We had two revival meetings every day for fifteen months without a single break, and meetings all day on Fridays. Hundreds were converted - but we were looking for more - for the ten thousand, upon whom He had told us we had a claim.[42]

The revival spread through all the mission stations within a year. The Howells visited many of the stations and spoke at the annual conference. The mission reported over 10,000 converts during the three year revival, which included a lot of public confession and great joy.

1921 - March: Lowestoft, England (Douglas Brown)

Douglas Brown, a Baptist minister in South London, saw conversions in his church every Sunday until he began he began itinerant evangelism in 1921. Within eighteen months he then addressed over 1700 meetings, and saw revival in his evangelistic ministry. The Lord had convicted him about leaving his pastorate for mission work. Although reluctant, he finally surrendered. He described it this way:

God laid hold of me in the midst of a Sunday evening service, and he nearly broke my heart while I was preaching. I went back to my vestry and locked the door, and threw myself down on the hearthrug in front of the vestry fireplace brokenhearted. Why? I do not know. My church was filled. I loved my people, and I believe my people loved me. I do not say they ought to, but they did. I was as happy there as I could be. I had never known a Sunday there for fifteen years without conversions. That night I went home and went straight up to my study. ... I had no supper that night. Christ laid his hand on a proud minister, and told him that he had not gone far enough, that there were reservations in his surrender, and he wanted him to do a piece of work that he had been trying to evade. I knew what he meant. All November that struggle went on, but I would not give way; I knew God was right, and I knew I was wrong. I knew what it would mean for me, and I was not prepared to pay the price. ...

All through January God wrestled with me. There is a love that will not let us go. Glory be to God! ...

It was in February 1921, after four months of struggle that there came the crisis. Oh, how patient God is! On the Saturday night I wrote out my resignation to my church, and it was marked with my own tears. I loved the church, but I felt that if I could not be holy I would be honest; I felt that I could not go on preaching while I had a contention with God. That night the resignation lay on my blotter, and I went to bed but not to sleep. As I went out of my bedroom door in the early hours of the morning I stumbled over my dog. If ever I thanked God for my dog I did that night. As I knelt at my study table, the dog licked his master's face; he thought I was ill; when Mike was doing that I felt I did not deserve anybody to love me; I felt an outcast.

Then something happened. I found myself in the loving embrace of Christ for ever and ever; and all power and joy and blessedness rolled in like a deluge. How did it come? I cannot tell you. Perhaps I may when I get to heaven. All explanations are there, but the experience is here. That was two o'clock in the morning. God had waited four months for a man like me; and I said, "Lord Jesus, I know what you want; You want me to go into mission work. I love Thee more than I dislike that." I did not hear any rustling of angels' wings. I did not see any sudden light.[43]

Hugh Ferguson, the Baptist minister at London Road Baptist Church in Lowestoft on the East Anglia coast had invited Douglas Brown to preach at a mission there from Monday 7th to Friday 11th March. The missioner arrived by train, ill. However, he spoke on Monday night and at meetings on Tuesday morning, afternoon and night. The power of the Holy Spirit moved among the people from the beginning. On Wednesday night 'inquirers' packed the adjacent schoolroom for counselling and prayer. Sixty to seventy young people were converted that night, along with older people. Each night more packed the 'inquiry room' after the service. So the mission was extended indefinitely. Douglas Brown returned to his church for the weekend and continued with the mission the next Monday. By the end of March the meetings were moved from the 700 seating Baptist Church and other nearby churches to the 1100 seating capacity of St John's Anglican Church.

March saw the beginning of revival in the area. Although Douglas Brown was the main speaker in many places, ministers of most denominations found they too were evangelising. Revival meetings multiplied in the fishing centre of Yarmouth as well in Ipswich, Norwich, Cambridge and elsewhere. Scottish fishermen working out of Yarmouth in the winter were strongly impacted, and took revival fire to Scottish fishing towns and villages in the summer. Jock Troup, a Scottish evangelist, has visited East Anglia during the revival and ministered powerfully in Scotland.

At the same time, the spirit of God moved strongly in Ireland, especially in Ulster in 1921 through the work of W. P. (William Patteson) Nicholson a fiery Irish evangelist. This was at the time when Northern Ireland received parliamentary autonomy accompanied by tension and bloodshed. Edwin Orr was converted then, although not through W. P. Nicholson. Orr reported that "Nicholson's missions were the evangelistic focus of the movement: 12,409 people were counselled in the inquiry rooms; many churches gained additions, some a hundred, some double; ... prayer meetings, Bible classes and missionary meetings all increased in strength. ... Ministerial candidates doubled."[44]

1927 - February: Shanghai, China (John Sung)

John Sung (1901-1944), from Hinghwa of the Fukien province in southeast China, son of a Methodist minister, was converted at nine and studied in America from 1920 at Wesleyan

University of Ohio, Ohio State University where he gained his Doctor of Philisophy degree in chemistry, and at Union Theological Seminary.

On 10 February, 1927, when a decade of revival was starting to break out in China, John Sung recommitted himself to Christ after a period of scepticism and was suddenly filled with the Holy Spirit and an inexpressible joy. Seminary authorities, concerned at his sudden fanaticism had him committed to an asylum where he had only his Bible and a fountain pen for six months. During that time he read the Bible forty times.

He returned to China in October, 1927, married, and soon became the field evangelist of the Bethel Bible School of Shanghai. He allied himself with Andrew Gih and other graduates from the school to form the Bethel Evangelistic Band. This apostolic team spread revival all over China. Although reserved, when preaching Sung was fervent with and intense emotion, denouncing sin and emphasising repentance and restitution. His prophetic gifting often revealed specific sins or obstructions to faith. He laid hands on the sick and hundreds were healed in his meetings. Like other revivalists he prayed long and earnestly.

God used this apostolic team mightily to spread the fires of revival all over China as they went out preaching and singing the gospel. When John Sung was not behind the pulpit, he was reserved and even subdued. However, when preaching he was a man of fervency and intense emotions.

He always emphasized repentance and the need for complete restitution where it was at all possible. He fearlessly denounced all sin and hypocrisy wherever he found it, especially among hardened ministers. Yet he also moved audiences with the message of Christ's tender and unfailing love, like few others could. Sung's meetings were always accompanied by a tremendous amount of conviction and brokenness over sin. It was not uncommon for hundreds of people to be seen with tears streaming down their faces and crying out for mercy. Convicted sinners frequently would rush forward to openly confess their sins before the whole congregation. On several occasions he pointed out the sins of some backslidden pastor with an incredible and fearful accuracy.

When John Sung was not actively preaching or organizing a new evangelistic team, he usually could be found writing in his diary or adding to his ever growing prayer list. He carefully prayed over an extensive list of people's needs, with dozens of small photographs. John Sung was a faithful intercessor and always requested a small picture of those desiring prayer in order to help him intercede with a deeper burden. Everywhere he went, he urged the people to give themselves to prayer.

John Sung made it his regular habit to be up every morning at 5 a.m. to pray for two or three hours. He believed that prayer was the most important work of the believer. He defined faith as watching God work while on your knees.

Because it was evident that John Sung was a man of great power in prayer, the sick and crippled increasingly came to him to receive prayer for their bodies. John Sung always made time to tenderly pray for their needs. Sometimes he would personally lay hands on and pray for as many as 500-600 people at one time. In spite of the fact that so many marvellous healings followed his ministry, he suffered for years from intestinal tuberculosis. This disease consistently plagued him with painful and infected bleeding ulcers in his colon. Nevertheless he still continued to fervently preach, sometimes in a kneeling position to lesson the terrible pain. Finally after years of suffering with this affliction, he died at only 43, on August 18, 1944.

Estimates of conversions in that decade of revival run to hundreds of thousands in China and South East Asia, with thousands of churches established throughout the whole region.[45]

1936 - June: Gahini, Rwanda (East African Revival)

Evangelical Anglican missionaries of the Church Missionary Society working in the east central Africa countries of Rwanda, Burundi and Uganda, emphasised the Keswick teaching of new birth, being filled with the Holy Spirit and living in victory. This teaching undergirded the East African Revival which continued for fifty years from the 1930s.

The Rwanda mission, founded in 1920, experienced local revivals in the late 1920s and early 1930s. Increasingly people prayed. By 1936 thousands were praying.

Then powerful revival broke out at the mission station at Ghini in Rwanda on Wednesday, 24 June 1936. "It seemed as though the Holy Spirit with His unseen hand gathered together the hospital staff, men from the nearby village, and others in a room with the hospital. They prayed and sang, and some were smitten down under a tremendous conviction of sin. Revival swept into the girl's school, and similar manifestations came from five different centers across the mission. Everywhere the mysterious power of the Holy Spirit was at work."[46]

The revival spread to the theological college where 50 students caught fire. During the midyear holiday period 70 evangelists travelled in revival teams of two or three into the villages.

The African Rwanda Mission had 20,000 converts by 1942 in 700 village congregations with 1,400 trained workers including five ordained priests.

The famous East African revival which began in Rwanda in June 1936 rapidly spread to the neighbouring countries of Burundi, Uganda and the Congo, then further around. The Holy Spirit moved upon mission schools, spread to churches and to whole communities, producing deep repentance and changed lives. Anglican Archdeacon Arthur Pitts wrote in September, "I have been to all the stations where this Revival is going on, and they all have the same story to tell. The fire was alight in all of them before the middle of June, but during the last week in June, it burst into a wild flame which, like the African grass fire before the wind, cannot be put out."[47]

That East African revival continued for forty to fifty years and helped to establish a new zeal for enthusiastic holiness in African Christianity. It confronted demonic strongholds, and began to prepare churches to cope with the horrors of massacres and warfare of later years.

Now revival is again transforming whole communities in East Africa.[48]

Endnotes

1 Many writers merge this event with the watch night service. Lyle Murphy (1974, "Beginning at Topeka," *Calvary Review,* 13:1, Spring, Kansas City, p. 4), investigating original sources in Topeka, wrote, "The mercury hovered near the zero mark that Monday evening as the faithful gathered to pray in the new year. Mr Parham would later recall that there were about 115 in attendance. These included the Parham family, the Bethel students, and the Apostolic congregation. There was even a contingent from Kansas City. At seven the next evening, January 1, 1901, Miss Agnes Ozman experienced "the touch felt round the world." Mr Parham recalled, "I laid my hands upon her and prayed. I had scarcely repeated three dozen sentences when a glory fell upon her, a halo seemed to surround her head and face, and she began speaking the Chinese language…"

2 Xenolalia (from the prefix *xeno-* foreign, alien), tongues in a language unknown to the speaker but known to hearers, has been present and debated among Pentecostals from the beginning. For Parham and other Pentecostal pioneers it was closely related to missionary zeal and regarded as a supernatural gift for mission. Agnes Ozman wrote, "The next night after I received the Holy Ghost … I with others went to a mission downtown in Topeka and my heart was full of glory and blessings. I began to pray in English and then in tongues. At the close of the services a man who is a Bohemian said he understood what I said in his own language" (Grant McClung, 1986, *Azusa Street and Beyond,* Bridge, p. 12). Experience soon revealed that this was rare; the exception, not the rule. Stanley Frodsham (1946, *With Signs Following: The Story of the Latter-Day Pentecostal Revival,* Gospel Publishing House, pp. 229-252) gives a full chapter to recorded examples of xenolalia, including many in missionary contexts, and Ralph Harris (1973, *Spoken by the Spirit*) collected reports of xenolalia. Some discussions use other related terms such as *xenoglassolalia* (Harris, 1973, p. 6), *xenoglossia* (William Samarin, 1972, *Tongues of Men and of Angels,* Macmillan, p. 109), and even *heteroglossolalia* (Harold Hunter, 1983, "Spirit Baptism and the 1896 Revival in Cherokee County, North Carolina," *Pneuma: The Journal of the Society for Pentecostal Studies,* Vol. 5, No. 2, p. 13). Another significant related term is

akolalia (Hunter 1983, p. 13) for those who 'hear' and understand although the speaker is using another language unknown to the hearer. Australian Alan Walker (1969, Breakthrough, Fontana, p. 51) noted this phenomenon in Suva, Fiji when he preached in English to 12,000 people in a nine day mission and the audience said they did not need an interpreter because they 'heard' and understood in their own languages.

[3] Pentecostal historian Vinson Synan, 1971, *The HolinessPentecostal Movement in the United States,* Eerdmans, p. 122, notes, "It was precisely this settlement, that tongues were the only initial evidence of the reception of the Holy Spirit, that gave Pentecost its greatest impetus."

[4] Most accounts repeat that Seymour had to sit outside the classroom in the hall because of segregation laws in Texas, but Parham's grand-daughter denied this.

[5] J Edwin Orr (1975, *The Flaming Tongue: Evangelical Awakenings, 1900,* Moody, pp. 191-200) gives detailed accounts of widespread worldwide prayer for revival at the turn of the century, including in Australia.

[6] Reuben A Torrey, successor to D. L. Moody at Moody Church in Chicago accompanied by song leader Charles Alexander, compiler of the *Alexander Hymnal* widely used in evangelical churches for 50 years, conducted evangelistic campaigns in Australia and New Zealand in 1902, including Melbourne, Sydney and country centres.

[7] Orr, 1975, pp. 107-109.

[8] Orr, 1975, pp. 107-109. In England 30 bishops promoted the revival after one bishop told of confirming 950 new coverts in a rural parish church. Other Protestant denominations in England increased by 300,000 (10%) in 1903-1906. In 1905 American Methodists in Philadelphia had over 6,100 converts; one church in New York received 364 into membership, 217 of them new converts; Southern Baptists increased by 25% in one year, and First Baptist Church in Paducah, Kentucky added 1,000 in two months, their old pastor, Dr J. Cheek, dying of exhaustion, which

the Southern Baptists called 'a glorious end to a devoted ministry'; 180,000 attended united meetings in Los Angeles; USA Methodist churches reported the 'greatest revivals in their history'; church membership in seven Protestant denominations in the USA increased by more than two million in five years, not including the rapid growth of the Pentecostals from 1906. The Methodist Church in South Africa increased by 30% in three years after 1905. In Burma, 1905 "brought ingathering quite surpassing anything known in the history of the [American Baptist] mission" with 2,000 Karens baptised that year. Revivals came in three waves in Korea in 1903, 1905, and 1907 with the churches quadrupling and the national church created. Protestant communicants doubled in China in the decade after the Boxer Rebellion of 1900 to 250,000. Evangelicals in Indonesia trebled to 300,000 in that decade. Protestant communicants in African missions increased by 200,000 to 500,000 in 1903-1910.

[9] Orr, 1993, *Renewal Journal,* No. 1, pp.13-18; 1975, pp.194.

[10] Orr, 1975, pp. 15-28, includes a full chapter on the social effects of the revival. That included Registrar-General's statistics on illegitimate births declining in every Welsh county in 1905 by up to 40% as in Radnor and Merioneth; police in Cardiff reported a 60% decrease in drunkenness and 40% fewer people in jail at the beginning January 1905; convictions for drunkenness in populous Glamorgan dropped from 10,528 in 1903 and 11,282 in 1904 to 8,164 in 1905, 5,490 in 1906 and 5,615 in 1907; convictions of drunkenness in Wales dropped by 33% in 1905-1907; magistrates in several places had no cases to try in 1905.

[11] Walter Hollenweger, 1972, *The Pentecostals,* SCM, pp. 177, 179. His chapter on the significance of the Welsh Revival for the origin of Pentecostalism in Great Britain, draws strongly on Henri Bois, 1905, *Le réveil au pays de Galles,* Société des Publications Morales et Religieuses (163 pages), a professor of theology and analyser of religious phenomena who was sympathetic to the revival, because Bois' account "is an example of how it is possible to describe an irrational revival in a way which is both discriminating in its judgment and rational in both human and theological terms."

[12] Orr, 1975, p. 3.

[13] Hollenweger, 1972, pp. 179-180.

[14] Penn-Lewis, 1905, *The Awakening in Wales,* in collaboration with Even Roberts, discussed the significance and implications of baptism in the Spirit. However, the work lacks theological depth, confuses some charismata with delusion, and ultimately denies much of the valid prophetic and charismatic gifts demonstrated in Robert's ministry in the revival and subsequently in the emerging Pentecostal groups in Wales and throughout Great Britain.

[15] Duewel, 1995, *Revival Fire,* Zondervan, p. 190.

[16] Orr, 1975, p. 8.

[17] Orr, 1975, p. 9.

[18] *The Western Mail*, Cardiff, 25 January, 1906, carried headlines about the revival indicating over 70,000 conversions were reported since the beginning of November, 1905.

[19] Hollenweger, 1972, p. 177.

[20] Congregational minister Peter Price aroused heated debate in the papers by publishing criticism of Evan Roberts at the end of January 1905, claiming genuine revival in his church but false revival with Roberts and his "singing ladies". Roberts refrained from involvement in the dispute and was strongly supported by clergy, magistrates and converts. Hollenweger (1972, p. 182) notes, "Every journal of the German Evangelical movement spoke of him in terms of the highest enthusiasm."

[21] Orr, 1975, p. 25, comments on the effects of strain from revival leaders working 16-20 hours a day. Sidney Evans and Samuel Jenkins also suffered exhaustion. Four doctors signed a medical examination report of Evan Roberts declaring him mentally and physically quite sound but suffering from the effects of overwork and needing rest.

[22] Hollenweger, 1972, p. 183: "Every observer agrees that the up-heaval caused by the revival overcame the craze for gambling, drunkenness, idleness and prostitution over wide areas for at least half a generation."

[23] Hollenweger, 1972, p. 178, notes that in Germany as well as in Great Britain, many evangelical writers who affirmed the Welsh revival and its phenomena later condemned Pentecostalism as diabolical.

[24] Hollenweger, 1972, p. 184.

[25] Stanley Frodsham, 1946, *With Signs Following: The Story of the Latter-Day Pentecostal Revival.* Gospel Publishing House, pp. 107108.

[26] Frank Houghton 1955, *Amy Charmichael of Dohnavur,* Christian Literature Crusade, pp. 146-148.

[27] The full article from page one of the *Los Angeles Times*, 18 April, 1906, is included in Bartleman 1980, *Azusa Street: The Roots of Modern-day Pentecost,* Bridge, pp. 174-177. It follows the bi-lines, "Weird Babel of Tongues - New Sect of Fanatics is Breaking Loose - Wild Scene Last Night on Azusa Street - Gurgle of Wordless Talk by a Sister" and begins, "Breathing strange utterances and mouthing a creed which it would seem no sane mortal could understand, the newest religious sect has started in Los Angeles."

[28] Reprinted in abridged form in Bartleman, 1955, *Another Wave Rolls In*, and in full in Bartleman, 1980.

[29] Bartleman, 1980, pp. 57-61.

[30] Other Pentecostal movements preceded Azusa Street, but did not have the worldwide influence of the Azusa Street revival. These included various groups using the charismata.
(1) The 'Irvingites' led by Edward Irving (1792-1834), a Scottish Presbyterian minister who taught on the charismata in London from 1822, from 1830 used tongues, prophecies and healing first in prayer groups, then in church services. Censured by the

London Presbytery in 1832 for violating liturgical regulations by allowing women and men not properly ordained to speak in the services, Irving founded the Catholic Apostolic Church in 1833 but died in 1834. The church died out later that century (Burgess & McGee, eds., 1988, *Dictionary of Pentecostal and Charismatic Movements,* Zondervan, p. 470).

(2) The Church of God (Cleveland), one of the oldest and largest Pentecostal churches in America, grew out of a Pentecostal revival from 1896 in North Carolina among the Christian Union of Tennessee formed in 1886. They established their headquarters in Cleveland, Tennessee, in 1907 and included baptism in the Spirit in their constitution in 1908, through the influence of the Azusa Street revival (Burgess & McGee, 1988, pp. 197-202).

(3) Russian and Armenian Pentecostals migrated to California from Armenia in 1905 and linked with the Apostolic Faith Mission from 1906 (John Sherrill, 1975, *The Happiest People on Earth,* Hodder & Stoughton, pp. 13-26).

[31] Cox 1995, *Fire from Heaven,* Addison-Wesley, pp. 45-65, Chapter 2, "The Fire Falls in Los Angeles."

[32] Cox, p. 45.

[33] Cox, p. 58.

[34] Cox, p. 59.

[35] Bartleman 1980, p. 173.

[36] Cox, 1995, p. 65.

[37] From "Jonathan Goforth" by David Smithers, www.watchword.org

[38] Smithers, www.watchword.org

[39] Frodsham, 1946, pp. 177-178.

[40] Worldwide Evangelism Crusade, 1954, *This is That,* pp. 12-15.

[41] Norman Grubb, 1952, *Rees Howells, Intercessor,* Christina Literature Crusade, p. 156.

[42] Grubb, pp. 156-157.

[43] S C Griffin, 1992, *Forgotten Revival,* One Day Publications, pp. 17-18.

[44] Griffin, p. 87.

[45] David Smithers on http//www.watchword.org/articles/Smithers/ww51a.html drawn from *John Sung* by Leslie T. Lyall, *The Diaries of John Sung* translated by Stephen L. Sheng, *The Revival in Indonesia* by Kurt Koch, *The Shantung Revival* by Mary K. Crawford, and *The Awakening, Revival in China 1927-1937* by Marie Monsen.

[46] Duewel, 1995, p. 300.

[47] H H Osborn, 1991, *Fire in the Hills,* Highland, p. 21.

[48] See Transformation 2, with George Otis Jr. Video/DVD, The Sentinal Group.

Chapter 4

Mid-twentieth Century Revival:
Healing Evangelism Revival

Following the devastation and deaths of World War II, 1939-1945, including the genocide of six million Jews, revival again exploded across the world. Jews returned to their homeland with the State of Israel proclaimed in 1948. Healing evangelism spread worldwide, in spite of resistance and opposition from many traditional churches. Revival spilled out from the churches into the community bringing to birth many revival movements and independent networks.

1946 - June: North America (Healing Evangelism)

Following World War II, especially in 1947-48 significant ministries in healing and evangelism emerged in America, led by people who later had worldwide impact. These included William Branham, Kathryn Kuhlman, Oral Roberts, Billy Graham, and T. L. and Daisy Osborn.

William Branham (1909-1965) began his full time healing evangelism ministry in St Louis, Missouri in June, 1946.

"Branham's sensational healing services, which began in 1946, are well documented and he was the pacesetter for those who followed."[1] Historians mark his full time ministry as inaugurating the healing evangelism revival of the mid-twentieth century. Branham reported that on Tuesday, May 7, 1946, an angel spoke to him saying, "Fear not, I am sent from the presence of Almighty God to tell you that your peculiar life and your misunderstood ways have been to indicate that God has sent you to take a gift of divine healing to the people of the world. If you will be sincere, and can get the people to believe you, nothing shall stand before your prayer, not even cancer."[2] He became renowned for accurate words of knowledge and amazing healings.

On Sunday, April 27, 1947, when **Kathryn Kuhlman** (1907-1976) began a teaching series on the Holy Spirit in Franklin, Pennsylvania a woman in the audience was healed of a tumour, and testified about it the following night. That marked the beginning of Kathryn Kuhlman's thirty years of incredible healing evangelism. Based at Pittsburgh, Pennsylvania from 1948 she held regular services in Carnegie Hall and the First Presbyterian Church, developed a daily radio ministry, and produced over 500 telecasts for the CBS network. For ten years she regularly filled the 7,000 seating Shrine Auditorium in Los Angeles at her monthly miracle services there.

On Wednesday, May 14, 1947, following seven months of intensive prayer including fasting, **Oral Roberts** (1918-2009) received direction from God about beginning his now famous healing evangelistic ministry. He had himself been healed through prayer at 17 after being bed ridden with tuberculosis for five months. From 1948, he used a tent seating 2,000 people and from 1953 he had a tent seating 12,500. By 1956 his monthly magazine *Abundant Life* had a circulation of over a million. In 1965, he opened a college which later became Oral Roberts University now with 4,500 students. By the eighties 15 million copies of his books had been sold, and thousands of people continue the healing and evangelistic ministry he began.

On Tuesday, June 24, 1947, Henrietta Mears, Christian Education Director at First Presbyterian Church of Hollywood, spoke at a teachers and leaders conference at Forest Home in the nearby mountains. A group of young leaders including the newly converted Bill Bright (later founder of Campus Crusade for Christ) met late that night for prayer with Henrietta Mears, confessing sin with much weeping and crying out to God. "Then, the fire fell. However it can be explained, God answered their prayer with a vision. They saw before them the college campuses of the world teeming with unsaved students, who held in their hands the power to change the world. The college campuses - they were the key to world leadership, to world revival"[3]. Annual College Briefing Conferences were then held at Forest Home. **Billy Graham** (1918-) and Edwin Orr (1912-1987) spoke at the 1949 conference there, where Billy Graham also experienced a deep infilling of the Holy Spirit as the presence of God engulfed him while he prayed alone on a mountain. His Los Angeles crusade later that year attracted wide press coverage and launched him into an international ministry.

In July, 1947, **Tommy** (1923-) and **Daisy Osborn** (1924-1995), Pentecostal pastors in Oregon, were deeply moved at a camp meeting by a message on seeing Jesus. They had returned to America after an unsuccessful time as missionaries in India in 1945-46 where sickness plagued them. Following the Oregon meeting T. L. Osborn wrote:

> The next morning at six o'clock, I was awakened by a vision of Jesus Christ as he came into our room. I looked upon him. I saw Him like I see anyone. No tongue can tell of His splendour and beauty. No lan-

guage can express the magnificence and power of His person.

I lay there as one that was dead, unable to move a finger or toe, awe-stricken by His presence. Water poured from my eyes, though I was not conscious of weeping, so mighty was His presence.

Of all I had heard and read about Him, the half had never been told me. His hands were beautiful; they seemed to vibrate with creative ability. His eyes were as streams of love, pouring forth into my innermost being. His feet, standing amidst clouds of transparent glory, seemed to be as pillars of justice and integrity. His robes were white as the light. His presence, en-hanced with love and power, drew me to Him.

After perhaps thirty minutes of utter helplessness, I was able to get out of bed to the floor, where I crawled into my little study and lay on my face on the floor in full surrender of my entire life to Him whom I had come to know as LORD.

I lay there on my fact until the afternoon. When I came out of that room, I was a new man. Jesus had become the Master of my life. I knew the truth; *He is alive; He is more than a dead religion*.

My life was changed. I would never be the same. Old traditional values began to fade away, and I felt im-pressed daily by a new and increasing sense of rever-ence and serenity. Everything was different. I wanted to please *Him. That is all that mattered since that un-forgettable morning.*[4]

In September, 1947, the Osborns attended a meeting where William Branham healed he sick and cast out demons, including deliverance of a deaf-mute girl who then heard and spoke perfectly. T. L. Osborn reported:

> When I witnessed that and many other miracles, there seemed to be a thousand voices whirling over my head, saying over and over, "You can do that! That's the Bible way! Peter and Paul did it that way! That's the way Jesus did it. That proves that the Bible way works today! You can do that! That's what God wants you to do!"

> We went home in total awe and reverent exuberance. We had witnessed the Bible in action. It was the thing I had always longed for. At last, I had seen God do what He promised to do through a human person. Our entire lives were changed that very night.[5]

After that the Osborns ministered to millions, preached to crowds of 20,000 to 250,000 in crusades in 76 countries, and led hundreds of thousands of people to Jesus Christ. Vast numbers were healed, including the deaf, blind, and crippled. Body organs have been recreated and restored, cancers died and vanished, lepers were healed and the dead raised.

Most of their powerful evangelism and healing ministry was huge crowds in developing nations. They regularly established 400 churches a year in these nations.

1948 – February: Saskatchewan, Canada (Sharon Schools)

A revival movement which came to be called the Latter Rain revival (from Joel 2:28) began suddenly in the Sharon Orphan-

age and Schools including the Bible School in North Battl-
eford, Saskatchewan, Canada. Previously, teachers from the
Bible School had been deeply impressed by the words of
knowledge and healings at meetings conducted by William
Branham in 1947 in Vancouver. They and the students began
praying and fasting and studying the Scriptures with new intensity from November that year.

The staff and most of the 70 students had gathered in the
largest classroom for devotions on Thursday, February 12,
1948, when the Holy Spirit fell on their gathering. Ern Hawtin, a teacher there described it in their magazine the *Sharon
Star*:

> Some students were under the power of God on the
> floor, others were kneeling in adoration and worship
> before the Lord. The anointing deepened until the awe
> was upon everyone. The Lord spoke to one of the
> brethren, 'Go and lay hands upon a certain student
> and pray for him.' While he was in doubt and con-
> templation one of the sisters who had been under the
> power of God went to the brother saying the same
> words, and naming the identical student he was to
> pray for. He went in obedience and a revelation was
> given concerning the student's life and future ministry.
> After this a long prophecy was given with minute de-
> tails concerning the great thing God was about to do.
> The pattern for the revival and many details concern-
> ing it were given.[6]

They spent Friday studying the Scriptures for insight into
these events, and then Ern Hawtin reported that on Saturday,
February 14, "It seemed that all Heaven broke loose upon our
souls, and heaven came down to greet us." Visible manifestation of gifts was evident when candidates were prayed over,
and many were healed. Hawtin continued, "Day after day the

glory and power of God came among us. Great repentance, humbling, fasting and prayer prevailed in everyone." [7]

Through their publications, camp meetings, conventions and visits of pastors and teachers from Sharon to churches and meetings across Canada and America thousands were touched by God in this fresh outpouring of his Spirit. Stanley Frodsham, then editor of the Assemblies of God magazine *Pentecostal Evangel*, visited churches touched by this revival and gave it strong support.

Many Pentecostal denominations rejected this move which emphasised laying on of hands for the impartation of spiritual gifts, the recognition of apostles and prophets in the church, and the gift of prophecy for directing and commissioning ministerial candidates and for church government. However, the Latter Rain revival and the healing revivals through the fifties had a strong influence on the charismatic renewal of the sixties and seventies.

1949 - October: Hebrides Islands, Scotland (Duncan Campbell)

Following the trauma of World War II, spiritual life reached a low ebb in the Scottish Hebrides. By 1949 Peggy and Christine Smith (84 and 82) had prayed constantly for revival in their cottage near Barvas village on the Isle of Lewis, the largest of the Hebrides Islands in the bleak north west of Scotland. God showed Peggy in a dream that revival was coming. Months later, early one winter's morning as the sisters were praying, God give them an unshakeable conviction that revival was near.

Peggy asked her minister James Murray Mackay to call the church leaders to prayer. Three nights a week the leaders prayed together for months. One night, having begun to pray at 10 pm, a young deacon from the Free Church read Psalm 24 and challenged everyone to be clean before God. As they waited on God his awesome presence swept over them in the barn at 4 am Mackay invited Duncan Campbell (1898-1972) to come and lead meetings. Within two weeks he came. God had intervened and changed Duncan's plans and commitments. At the close of his first meeting in the Presbyterian Church in Barvas the travel weary preacher was invited to join an all night prayer meeting. Thirty people gathered for prayer in a nearby cottage. Duncan Campbell described it:

> God was beginning to move, the heavens were opening, we were there on our faces before God. Three o'clock in the morning came, and God swept in. About a dozen men and women lay prostrate on the floor, speechless. Something had happened; we knew that the forces of darkness were going to be driven back, and men were going to be delivered. We left the cottage at 3 am to discover men and women seeking God. I walked along a country road, and found three men on their faces, crying to God for mercy. There was a light in every home, no one seemed to think of sleep.[8]

When Duncan and his friends arrived at the church that morning it was already crowded. People had gathered from all over the island, some coming in buses and vans. No one discovered who told them to come. God led them. Large numbers were converted as God's Spirit convicted multitudes of sin, many lying prostrate, many weeping. After that amazing day in the church, Duncan pronounced the benediction, but then a young man began to pray aloud. He prayed for 45 minutes. Once more the church filled with people repenting and the service continued till 4 am the next morning before Duncan could pronounce the benediction again.

Even then he was unable to go home to bed. As he was leaving the church a messenger told him, "Mr. Campbell, people are gathered at the police station, from the other end of the parish; they are in great spiritual distress. Can anyone here come along and pray with them?"

Campbell went and what a sight met him. Under the still starlit sky he found men and women on the road, others by the side of a cottage, and some behind a peat stack all crying to God for mercy. The revival had come.

His mission continued for five weeks. Services were held from early morning until late at night and into the early hours of the morning. The revival spread to the neighbouring parishes from Barvas with similar scenes of repentance, prayer and preaching. People sensed the awesome presence of God everywhere.

That move of God in answer to prevailing prayer continued in the area into the fifties and peaked again on the previously resistant island of North Uist in 1957. Meetings were again crowded and night after night people cried out to God for salvation.

The Hebrides revival, experienced in a Presbyterian context, illustrates how the impact of the Sprit floods and transcends any context. Campbell emphasised the importance of a baptism in the Spirit, as had been a common theme in the Welsh revival.

1951 - June: City Bell, Argentina (Edward Miller)

Edward Miller, a Pentecostal missionary, tells of revival breaking out in Argentina after God told him to call his small church to pray every night from 8 pm to midnight beginning on a Monday. Their little group prayed for three nights, mostly silently except for their missionary Ed Miller. No one seemed to have any leading, except one lady felt she was told to hit the table, but she wouldn't do anything so strange. On the fourth night, Ed Miller led the group in singing around the table, and hit it as they sang. Eventually others did the same. Then the lady did. Immediately the Spirit of God fell. They were baptised powerfully in the Spirit. They heard the sound of strong wind. Their little church filled. People were convicted, weeping, and praying.

By Saturday, teams were going out in powerful evangelism. Two teenage girls were weeping in the street. Two doctors mocked them, but listened to their testimonies and were convicted. They knelt there in the street and asked for prayer.

Two church members visited a lady whose mother was paralysed, in bed for 5 years. They prayed for her, and she got up and drank tea with them. Two elderly people visited man in coma, a cripple with a liver damaged from drink. When they prayed for him he was healed.

A young man, Alexander and his band of rebels sat in the front row of a revival meeting aiming to disrupt it. God convicted him and he repented. His gang began to leave but fell under the Spirit on the way out. All were converted. Two of them went to the Bible School.

Ed Miller taught at the Bible Training Institute in 1951 in the little town of City Bell, near Buenos Aires. In June he was led to cancel lectures so the whole Bible School could pray every day. He announced this on the first Sunday in June. That night Alexander, the former rebel leader, a teenager of Polish descent, was praying long after midnight out in the fields when he sensed something pressing down on him, an intense light surrounding him and a heavenly being enfolding him. Terrified he ran back to the Institute.

The heavenly visitor entered the Institute with him, and in a few moments all the students were awake with the fear of God upon them. They began to cry out in repentance as God by his Spirit dealt with them. The next day the Spirit of God came again upon Alexander as he was given prophecies of God's moving in far off countries. The following day Alexander again saw the Lord in the Spirit, but this time he began to speak slowly and distinctly the words he heard from the angel of God. No one could understand what he was saying, however, until another lad named Celsio (with even less education than Alexander), overcome with the Spirit of God markedly upon him, began to interpret... These communications (written because he choked up when he tried to talk) were a challenge from God to pray and indeed the Institute became a centre of prayer till the vacation time, when teams went out to preach the kingdom. It was the beginning of new stirrings of the Spirit across the land.[9]

The Bible Institute continued in prayer for four months from that initial outpouring of the glory of God on Monday 4 June. They prayed 8-10 hours a day, with constant weeping. Bricks became saturated with their tears. One student prayed against a plaster wall daily, weeping. After six hours his tear stains reached floor. After eight hours his tears began to form a puddle on floor.

Two students went to a town, wept and prayed for three to four weeks. Then the Holy Spirit led them to hold tent meetings which filled the tent. The Lord moved on the crowds powerfully.

Prophecies given to the Bible School told of God filling the largest auditoriums and stadiums in Argentina and in other countries.

Edwin Orr visited each of the 25 states and territories in neighbouring Brazil in 1952 seeing powerful moves of the spirit in his meetings which were supported by all denominations. The evangelical church council declared that the year of 1952 saw the first of such a general spiritual awakening in the country's history. Many meetings had to be moved into soccer stadiums, some churches increased in numbers by 50% in one week, and the revival movement continued in local churches in Brazil.

Also in 1952, Tommy Hicks was conducting a series of meetings in California when God showed him a vision. While he was praying he saw a map of South America covered with a vast field of golden wheat ripe for harvesting. The wheat turned into human beings calling him to come and help them.

He wrote a prophecy in his Bible about going by air to that land before two summers would pass. Three months later, after an evangelistic crusade, a pastor's wife in California gave that same prophecy to him that he had written down. He was invited to Argentina in 1954 and had enough money to buy a one way air ticket to Buenos Aires.

On his way there after meetings in Chile, the word Peron came to his mind. He asked the air stewardess if she knew what it meant. She told him Peron was the President of Argentina. After he made an appointment with the Minister of Religion, wanting to see the President, he prayed for the Minister's secretary who was limping. He was healed. So the Minister made an appointment for Hicks to see the President. Through prayer the President was healed of an ugly eczema and gave Hicks the use of a stadium and free access to the state radio and press.

The revival campaign shifted into the Argentina's largest arena, the Hurricane Football Stadium, seating 110,000 which overflowed. During nightly meetings over two months 300,000 registered decisions for Christ and many were healed at every meeting.

1954 - April: Nagaland, India (Rikum)

Nagas are a Mongalite tribal people hailing from Manchuria via China and Thailand to Burma, finally settling down in the Patkai Hill regions. They were animists by religion. Each village was independent. They had a self government system of government. Each tribe had its own language and costume peculiar to the tribe. Each tribe had its own typical social customs.

The Nagas do not have their own script and their history has been transferred to the succeeding generations orally. The British people conquered village after village and appointed Gaum Buras to rule over the village. They had absolute power to inflict even the death penalty. It was the Britishers who introduced the Roman script system.

Each village fought against another village. Whoever defeated the other village became its ruler. This was the manner in which the Naga people lived for centuries till the British overcame them and brought them under the Indian Union. But right from the beginning the Nagas demanded an Independent Sovereign State. After a long struggle they got separate fully fledged Statehood in 1964.

The Nagas converted into Christianity. By 1976, almost 95 % of the Nagas became Christian. It started with the coming of the first missionary, William Clarke. He was an American Baptist. He first came to Molung Yimtsen in 1872. The villagers opposed him by throwing stones and spears at him. But a miracle took place which led to the unopposed preaching of the gospel. At one time he was preaching the gospel outside. The people threw spears at him but the spears, instead of hurting him, landed all around him and became a barrier. This amazed the villagers, and they began to listen to what he said. This miracle led to the conversion of many Nagas. Tribe after tribe became Christian.

In 1952, one Naga named Rikum was converted at Allahabad Bible Seminary. In 1954, the Lotha Baptist Association invited him for revival meetings. The meetings were held from April 11 to 18, 1954. The churches joined together and a great revival broke out as a result.[10]

In this revival people forgot about food. They were praying day and night. Many miracles took place. Some of the miracles were as follows.

They went into procession singing revival and salvation songs with great joy and happiness. Angels used to lead them; two angels - one on the left side and the other on the right aide. Wherever the angel stopped they would stop and sing joyful hymns. The singing was a non-stop phenomenon. During the evenings Satan used to visit in the homes of people who did not go to the church. So they were afraid and sat outside around a fire.

Once they were sitting around a fire. A cow came near and said, "Jesus is coming. What are you doing?" They were so frightened that they all went to the church. And they felt at the church that the church was literally lifted up. The people knew that it was God visiting them. They became converted to Christianity because they not only saw the miracle but also heard the messages and experienced God's touch in their bodies. The gospel spread without much opposition.

Some Nepalese used to live in the forest. They cut timber. They heard a beautiful sound of singing coming from the trees.

As they were following the singing they reached the church where the people were singing under the mighty anointing of the Spirit of God. Some of them could understand the messages of God. This was the means by which the gospel spread among the Nepalese also. Now thousands of Nepalese are becoming Christians.

In the year 1976, a revival meeting was convened at Mokohung and Rev. Bikum was invited as the speaker. It was here that the great revival explosion took place. Many were filled with the Spirit and spoke in tongues. This resulted in mass conversions throughout Nagaland. Some of the astounding miracles were raising of the dead and many people were reported missing. No one has any clue to what happened to those missing, but all assume that they were taken to heaven alive.

1960 -April: Van Nuys, North America (Dennis Bennett)

The outbreak of charismatic renewal in denominational churches in America is usually identified with the ministry of Dennis Bennett (1917-1991) at St Mark's Episcopal Church in Van Nuys, California, because of the national press coverage generated there, Bennett's subsequent national and international ministry in renewal, and the huge sales of Bennett's 1970 autobiographical book *Nine O'clock in the Morning,* and his subsequent teaching books, especially *The Holy Spirit and You.*

During Bennett's ministry as senior priest at St Mark's from 1953 to 1960 the church had grown with the population in the area and maintained a staff of four priests and office assistants. Respected lay people had been baptized in the Spirit and began holding home meetings for those interested,

Bennett and his wife Elberta among them. Soon many were experiencing this renewal, including many of the youth. Renewal meetings introduced increasing numbers to this experience, and people learned to pray naturally for one another for all needs, including healing.

Bennett was cautious, sensing possible problems in the parish, but initially received wide support from parishioners, even those not directly involved. Bennett reports how a neurosurgeon, the husband of the Altar Guild directoress who was involved in the renewal, commented favourably:

> "Oh, by the way, I see what's happening to my wife, and I like it!"
> I did a "double-take": "You *do?*"
> "Yes," he replied. "You're going to have a hard time explaining this 'speaking in tongues' to some people, though." He paused a moment and then added casually: "Of course, I understand it."
> I was so surprised that I simply said again: "You do?"
> "Sure! You see, the speech centers dominate the brain. If they were yielded to God, then every other area would be affected, too. Besides," he continued, "I think about God sometimes, and I run out of words. I don't see why He shouldn't give me some additional words to use."[11]

Others disagreed, and found it threatening or inappropriate. Bennett's second assistant publicly threw his vestments on the altar at the end of the second of the three morning services on Passion Sunday, 3 April, 1960, saying "I can no longer work with this man!" That Sunday Bennett had told his testimony of being baptized in the Spirit five months previously and urged openness and acceptance of this transforming experience now common in the parish. A small but volatile group erupted in open opposition, including a vestryman who urged Bennett to resign, which he did that day, to avoid a parish split.

Bishop William Fisher Lewis in Seattle invited Bennett to 'bring the fire' north and offered him the run down church of St. Luke's, Seattle, which rapidly became a nationally known charismatic Episcopalian church, and model for hundreds of other denominational churches.

Typically, charismatic renewal disrupts established congregations, and is usually expressed in renewal home groups in the church or in a renewal service during the week or on Sunday night. However, it is often an uneasy partnership. Many people shift toward independent congregations or Pentecostal assemblies for a fuller expression of this dynamic renewal, as is examined in chapter nine: charisma and institutions.

1960 - May: Darjeeling, India (David Mangratee)

A revival broke out in Darjeeling in 1960. God used David Mangratee. Born into a Hindu family, he had a wonderful birth. His father died in the year 1933, and was to be taken for burial. People had made everything ready. He was kept inside the coffin ready for taking him the burial place. But before they could take him he woke up and lived again. David reported:

> During this time two death angels were taking him somewhere. There was a big dark hell which had a wide door. Inside were animals and skeletons of human beings and animals. But as the angels were about to take him in, the door suddenly become small and they could not take him in. Instead a voice was

heard: "Go back to earth. Your time has not come." After this my father lived for another 20 years and died again in 1953 never to rise again.

During a vision I asked the Lord whether this was true. The Lord answered, "Yes, because I wanted a man with a miracle birth." It was God's great grace that He raised me for this great work which one can see at present among the Nepalese. It is now, according to some, the fastest growing church in the world. I accepted the Lord as my personal saviour on 3rd June 1953, after the death of my father.

I underwent a Bible Training Programme at Southern Asia Bible Institute (now College) and returned to Darjeeling. Rev. David Dutt of Calcutta, Rev. Virus Shipley of Baraily, U.P., and I went Gospel Trekking to East Sikkim beginning from Rhenock, and covered Rorathang and Rongpo. Then we went to Kalimpong. We did not receive a warm welcome in Kalimpong and so we went to Darjeeling. We came to Mt. Hermon and held three days of special meetings. 35 people expressed their desire to know more about the Lord and this led to my staying back in Darjeeling looking after the 35 newly converted.

Regular church services were started and week day meetings were also started. New songs in Nepali folk tunes were composed. Songs that were already used were translated from English hymns. The new songs were in popular tunes and folk tunes which attracted many people but mainly the young people. Gospel preaching was carried on vigorously. Many souls began to take an interest in the Lord.

On Pentecost Sunday in the month of May 1960, one of our church members got filled with the Spirit of

God. She spoke in tongues and prophesied. Then in the month of June that same year the Holy Spirit came upon the believers mightily. They were filled with the Spirit of God and God blessed them with gifts of the Spirit, especially the word of wisdom and the word of knowledge. By this, lost money was found, lost souls traced, sick healed and sin uncovered.

The revival took place in a small fellowship of newly converged souls in Sikkim. The Spirit fell on all the believers, and that village become the centre of evangelism. Today much of Sikkim is evangelised. There are more than 300 churches in the small state of Sikkim with a population of less than 5,000. If the growth rate remains undiminished Sikkim will be a Christian state should Jesus tarry.

Many miracles took place in the ministry, even raising of the dead. The work faced a lot of opposition in the beginning but the changed lives of first Christians made their mouths shut. Many missionaries are working now in Nepal or Bhutan and different parts of India like Assam, Manipur and Nagaland. Not only the Nepalese among whom our major work was concentrated but also tribes like Bodos, Santhals, Nagas, Rajbansis, and many other tribal people got saved.

This revival continues. This resulted in the worlds fastest growing church. The Lord said many things about our people, the Nepalese: "I love the Nepalese very much; I will send you throughout the world to preach"; and so on. Once the Lord told me: "All my children will see Me. That is, they would see the Lord with their physical eyes." This was fulfilled to the last letter. The Lord said: I will send even greater revival than before. We are praying to Him who is a covenant keeping God.[12]

1962 - August: Santo, Vanuatu (Paul Grant)

Australian Apostolic missionary pastor-teacher, Paul Grant, saw early stirrings of revival in Vanuatu. He commented in an unpublished report:

> It is important to note the following components in the lead-up to later visitation and reviving:
>
> 1. A shared concern of missionaries for revival.
>
> 2. A significantly developed interest in the quickening power of the Spirit among west Ambai church members and leaders through teaching of the Scriptures and news of revival and the power-works of the Spirit in other parts of the world, e.g. a Series of talks on the East Africa revival, the Welsh revival, signs and wonders and healings as reported from the Apostolic Church in Papua New Guinea, and inspiring records in other magazines.
>
> 3. An emphasis on prayer meetings, both between missionaries and in local churches.
>
> 4. Regular and frequent prayers for a visitation of God's Spirit by Apostolic Churches around the world. The first Monday night of each month was observed as a prayer night for worldwide missions.
>
> 5. Concentrated, sustained Scripture teaching in the classrooms of the primary school where students later would experience the power of God.
> By 1961, I had spent nine years among the people learning many valuable lessons in cross-cultural service and feeling myself being incorporated into their

'family' stage by stage. Church services were free and open for much congregational participation. During 1961 in the construction and opening of a new school building a spirit of prayer was noticeably intense.

A week of prayer prior to the special ceremonies for the dedication of the school building was a markedly powerful time. On Santo Island in the town of Luganville a non-professional missionary of the Apostolic Church, a builder, was experiencing a surge of power in the local church fellowship consisting principally of people from Ambae working in this urban situation. Then came a series of significant episodes.

Beginning in the Santo church on August 15th 1962 and continuing there and in churches on Ambae (commencing in Tafala village in October) over a period of about 12 weeks the power of God moved upon young people. There were many instances of glossolalia, healings, prophetic utterances, excitation, loud acclamations to God in public services, incidents of deep conviction of sin, conversions, restitutions, and other manifestations of holiness of life.

From diary and report records I have the following observations:

1. Shouts and liberty and outstreached arms, fervent praying by all ... for one hour (24 August).

2. I've never seen such passionate fervency (7 September).

3. Abraham (young man) through the day had sought the Lord ... at night he was filled with the Spirit (8 October).

4. ... these baptisms (in the Spirit) have produced a reverence and spiritual quickening of depth and sincerity (October 14).

5. ... reverence is prominent.

6. ... Stanley (young man) in the classroom broke forth in other tongues during a Bible lesson on 2 Corinthians 4 ... prayer ... four students committed themselves to Christ (2 December).

7. Thomas (an older man) told me he was drawn by the Spirit to the school building to listen (3 December).

8. Williamson ... has thrown away his cigarettes ... agitated over temptation ... asked for prayer (3 December).

9. ... infusion of new life and power in the weekly meetings (2 January 1963).

This visitation resulted in a liveliness not known before. Initially it was mainly among young people. In later months and years it spread among all age groups and to my present knowledge was the first such visitation in the history of the Christian Church in Vanuatu. To me the gratification I gained centred upon the following particulars:

1. The Holy Spirit had animated and empowered a people who were well taught in the Scriptures. Records show a lift in spiritual vitality in all the village churches.
2. It brought the church as a whole into a more expressive, dynamic dimension and also a charismatic gift function. They were much more able to gain victory over spirit forces so familiar to them.

3. It began to hasten the maturation processes in developing leadership.

4. The reality matched the doctrinal stand of the church. There was now no longer a disparity.

5. It confirmed to me the very great importance of being "steadfast, unmovable, always abounding in the work of the Lord forasmuch as you know that your labour is not in vain in the Lord" (1 Corinthians 15:58 AV).

6. It led to significant outreach in evangelism, both personal and group. ...

In the following years some of the young men and women served God in evangelistic teams, school teaching, urban witness, government appointments, and as pastors and elders to their own people. One of them has with his wife been an effective missionary... in Papua New Guinea.[13]

Similar Spirit movements such as this characterise revival in the islands with their animistic involvement in spirit activity. Christians affirm the power of the Holy Spirit over traditional occult spirits. Many local revival movements have flared up in Vanuatu and the South Pacific. This typical report is from Ruth Rongo of Tongoa Island dated August 28, 1991:

I've just come back from an Evangelism ministry. It lasted for three months. God has done many miracles. Many people were shocked by the power of the Holy Spirit. The blind received their sight, the lame walked, the sick were healed. All these were done during this evangelism ministry. We see how God's promise came into action. The prophet Joel had said it. We people of Vanuatu say "The spirit of the Lord God is upon us because he has anointed us to preach the Gospel to the poor people of Vanuatu." Praise God for what he has done.

In where I live, in my poor home, I also started a home cell prayer group. Our goal is that the revival must come in the church. Please pray for me and also for the group. Our prayer group usually meets on Sunday night, after the night meeting. We started at 10:30 pm to 1 or 3:30 am. If we come closer to God he will also come close to us. We spent more time in listening and responding to God.[14]

These revival movements continue to increase in the Pacific, especially as indigenous teams minister in other areas with the Spirit's fire. The church grows stronger, even through opposition. Indigenous Christians live and minister in New Testament patterns from house to house, from village to village.

1965 - September: Soé, Timor (Nahor Leo)

Spirit movements of revival influenced many thousands of people in Indonesia during the troubled and politically uncertain times there in the sixties. Much of it happened outside the established church, with a later acceptance of it in some churches. Thousands of animistic Muslims were converted, the biggest Christian impact on Islam in history.

The Indonesian government and army's victory over the attempted Communist coup opened the way for the savage killing of 400,000 suspected Communists or sympathizers, so the numbers of nominal Muslims and Christians multiplied. This external motivation explains only part of the rapid multiplication of the church during this period, however. Many nominal animistic Muslims turned to the church not out of fear but out of revulsion toward their fellow Muslim's slaughter of suspected Communists.

The Indonesian Bible Institute, established by Worldwide Evangelisation Crusade missionaries in 1959 at Batu in East Java experienced revival in the sixties with deep repentance, confession, renunciation of occult practices, burning fetishes and amulets, and a new humility and unity among staff and students. Individual students and teams engaged in effective evangelism in many islands.

A team of Indonesian students accompanied by a German Lutheran missionary teacher visited Timor during 1965 and saw evidences of revival beginning which burst into unprecedented power in September 1965. Christians and new converts burned amulets, pastors and leaders broke with animistic practices, prayer meetings multiplied, giving increased, heavy drinking of palm wine and chewing the narcotic betel nut was curtailed, and youth, traditionally the hardest to reach became the most responsive. They formed evangelistic teams of their own to take this new- found gospel of deliverance to outlying villages.

This revival spread in the uncertain days following the attempted communist coup on the night of 30 September and 1 October, 1965, in Indonesia when six of the eight Indonesian army generals were killed and mutilated, with only Suharto and Nasution narrowly escaping execution. General Suharto became acting president, keeping the popular President Sukarno without power till his death in 1971.

At the time of the coup a powerful revival movement had begun in Timor at Soé, a mile high mountain town of about 5,000 people where Rev. Daniel pastored the Reformed Church. A young man, Nahor Leo, was convicted by a vision of Jesus, destroyed a hidden amulet, and confessed publicly in the

Reformed Church on the evening of Sunday, 26 September. The church experienced a Pentecost style Spirit movement.

The editors of Tyndale House Publishers, hearing of unusual revival reports from Timor, sent Don Crawford, a trained reporter, to investigate the revival in Indonesia, especially in Timor. He reported this way:

> Calls to enter an evangelistic ministry came to young people in unusual fashion. Nahor Leo, a high school athlete with a reputation as a rebel, was stirred by a dynamic challenge to Christian service given by the headmistress of a Soé school. Later, studying in his room in Pastor Daniel's home with two fellow students, he suddenly called out, "Who turned out the light?" Assured it was still burning, Leo stumbled to his bed. "I'm going to rest."
>
> He slept a few minutes. Then, as if wrenched from the bed, he fell to the floor and appeared to be struggling with an invisible force. Leo groped his way to his clothes box and thrust his hand to its bottom, then pulled up the root of a plant which was wound with red string. "Yes," Leo muttered, as if answering the unseen visitor, "this is my *djimat*."
>
> Leo's companions recognized the strange object as an instrument of witchcraft. "It's true," Leo spoke again. "I have used it to ask the spirits to help me win races and to attract girls." The unusual conversation continued for a moment. Then Leo collapsed on the floor. "What's the matter? Who were you talking to?" one of the boys shouted. Leo slowly turned his sightless eyes toward his companions. At length the white-faced youth replied, "I saw the Lord. He made me reveal the *djimat* I had never given up. He told me

he wanted me to serve him alone. And . . ." his voice trembled . . . "he told me I must have Pastor Daniel pray for me - or I will die. Would you get him, please?"

Pastor Daniel came swiftly at the desperate summons. After a prayer of confession, the fetish was burned. Then, reminiscent of the Apostle Paul when he was ministered to by the man of God, Leo's sight was restored. And, like Paul, Leo became a persuasive evangelist, inspiring others to follow the Christian way.

It was the zeal of young leaders like Nahor Leo who formed wide-roving evangelistic teams that fanned the religious fire in Timor, Mr. Daniel told me, and continuing "signs and wonders" have fueled the flame. For in every case of a supernatural occurrence, there has followed a significant turning to the Christian faith.[15]

On Sunday night, September 26, 1965, people heard the sound of a tornado wind and saw flames on the church building which prompted police to set off the fire alarm to summon the volunteer fire fighters. Many people were converted that night, many filled with the Spirit including speaking in tongues, some in English who did not know English. By midnight teams of lay people had been organised to begin spreading the gospel the next day. Eventually, about 90 evangelistic teams were formed which functioned powerfully with spiritual gifts.

Nahor Leo, the young man who testified that night in the Reformed Church, chose 23 young people who formed an evangelistic group, Team 1. They gave themselves full time to visiting churches and villages and saw thousands converted with multitudes healed and delivered. In one town alone they saw 9,000 people converted in two weeks.

Another young man, Mel Tari witnessed this visitation of God and later became part of Team 42. He reported on this revival in two widely read books.[16] Healings and evangelism increased dramatically. Specific directions from the Lord led the teams into powerful ministry with thousands becoming Christians. They saw many healings, miracles such as water being turned to wine for communion, some instantaneous healings, deliverance from witchcraft and demonic powers, and some people raised from death through prayer.

The teams were often guided supernaturally including provision of light at night on jungle trails, angelic guides and protection, meagre supplies of food multiplied in pastors' homes when a team ate together there during famines, and witchdoctors being converted after they saw power encounters when the teams' prayers banished demons rendering the witchdoctors powerless. Crawford, who gives the most cautions report, gives examples:

> I had already heard about some of the early Soé miracles from my missionary friend in Kupang, Marion Allen of the Christian and Missionary Alliance. In visits to Soé during dry seasons he was able to investigate the happenings there. He had told me that almost every type of New Testament miracle had been repeated in the Soé area. One evangelistic team, for example, had gotten to their destination by walking across a flooded mountain stream. At first they had dismissed the feeling that they should walk on the water even though it had come to the team leader after prayer about the problem. After three successive prayer sessions, with the same apparent answer, the leader took a tentative barefoot step into the water. When he did not sink, the others followed - to the amazement of stranded travelers who witnessed the strange event from both sides of the stream.

Another team, desiring to celebrate the Lord's Supper but having no wine, were in a similar fashion instructed to use water from a nearby spring. As at the wedding Christ attended in Cana, the water, when drunk for the communion celebration, had become wine. On a hike around the Soé area, Sardjito [the Bible School principal] showed me the spring from which the water-turned-to-wine had come.

Mr. Allen had talked to both of the major participants in another drama. An elderly woman among the mourners at the funeral of a young boy felt a strong impression to pray for the lad's life. At first she resisted the impulse. The boy had been dead several hours and in that climate it was imperative that an unembalmed body be buried soon after death. But her feeling persisted. When it came time to put the lid of the wooden coffin in place, she felt compelled to act. She asked if she could offer a prayer. The ceremony was stopped to humor the old woman. While she was praying, the boy stirred, then rose up.

To many observers the fact that the "dead" boy is alive today represents a miracle. But to the believers in Soé the miracle lies rather in how the event was useful in bringing a large number of animist worshipers to faith in Christ. Sardjito and the Soé church's two pastors, Rev. Daniel and Rev. Binjamin Manuain, all asserted that such occurrences - as well as the testimony of those who had been delivered from the grip of witchcraft - spurred a remarkable growth of Christianity on the island. From Indonesian statistical sources I learned that in the first three years of the movement the Christian population of Timor grew by 200,000.[17]

The teams learned to listen to the Spirit of the Lord and obey him. His leadings came in many biblical ways:

1. God spoke audibly as with Samuel or Saul of Tarsus,

2. many had visions as did Mary or Cornelius,

3. there were inspired dreams such as Jacob, Joseph or Paul saw,

4. prophecies as in Israel and the early church occurred,

5. the still small voice of the Spirit led many as with Elijah or Paul's missionary team,

6. the Lord often spoke through specific Bible verses,

7. circumstances proved to be Godincidences not just coincidences,

8. often when leadings were checked with the group or the church the Lord gave confirmations and unity as with Paul and Barnabas at Antioch.[18]

The American wife of Mel Tari, Nori Tari noted that revival phenomena in Timor were neither obvious nor advertised, even though continually occurring, because the people live in greater awareness of spirit powers, do not talk about miracles except to a spiritual advisor or mentor, and do not expect everyone to be healed. They acknowledge God's sovereignty, especially in what may happen, when and how it happens and to whom it may happen.[19]

The Reformed Church Presbytery on Timor recorded 80,000 conversions from the first year of the revival there, half of those being former communists. They noted that some 15,000 people had been permanently healed in that year. After three years the number of converts had grown to over 200,000. In those three years over 200 evangelistic teams were formed. On another island with very few Christians 20,000 became believers in the first three years of the revival.

These people movements can be studied from a range of perspectives beyond the scope of this thesis, such as the political, social, economic and historical dynamics involved. However, a crucial element of the Timor revival was the perceived authority and power of the Christians' God over animistic gods and the confrontation with the authority and the magical powers of the local shaman. Significant church growth, people movements and evangelism continually demonstrate such a power encounter between God's Spirit and local gods or spirits.

1968 - July: Brisbane, Australia (Clark Taylor)

Clark Taylor (1937-) founded Christian Outreach Centre (COC), and Worship Centre, based in Brisbane, Australia. Now COC is a global movement with over 16,000 churches, many schools and its Christian Heritage College which awards government accredited degrees in ministry, education, social sciences and business.

> Clark Taylor became a Christian in Brisbane in 1959 at a Billy Graham Crusade and began to train for the Methodist ministry in 1961. In 1963, he suffered from Cerebral Malaria. I was married to him in 1964, and we had three children.

His wife Ann tells his story:

He was baptized in the Holy Spirit in 1967. Another miracle happened in 1967. At times, Clark would become unconscious as a result of the Cerebral Malaria. By 1967, he was having these unconscious turns frequently. One morning, when he was in Oxley Methodist Church, he felt that God said to him, "It's time for you to be healed." He told this to the minister, who replied, "Come down on Tuesday night when the prayer meeting is on and I will pray for you." This was quite remarkable, because in 1967, such things as healings and the baptism in the Holy Spirit were rare in the Methodist Church. At the prayer meeting, Clark started to lapse in unconsciousness, but the people laid hands on him and prayed for him and he was totally healed in that instant.

We were appointed to the Holland Park Methodist circuit in 1968 to assist the senior minister. Soon after his arrival, Clark commenced Thursday night Bible studies in the manse. Although it was holiday time, fifteen attended the first night. By April, there were 100 hundred attending Bible studies.

Prayer meetings were commenced three times a week. These were a good indication as to who had been baptized in the Spirit, because those who had previously found 7am to be an early rising time suddenly found great joy in getting up at 4am in the dark to go to the 5am prayer meeting. Now something quite miraculous happened while we were at St. Paul's and this is the beginning of the story. The Lord moved mightily on July 17, 1968. One of the ladies who have been prayed for several times had not received the gifts of tongues. The Lord spoke to her that there was going to be a special meeting on Sunday and that He would bring people from the highways and the byways and not to prepare for that meeting. Now we are used to doing things quite spontaneously in meetings, but in those days for a preacher to step out into a meeting unprepared was absolutely terrifying. God named specific people who would be attending. Those people were unknown to her at the time, but she was to pray for them. Those people did attend the meeting on July 21, and were saved and healed.

The children and I were away at this time, as Clark was supposed to be studying for exams. Clark spent much time in prayer, seeking the Lord about the special Sunday night meeting. There was much joy and excitement among the newly baptised-in-the-Spirit Christians who met each night to pray and seek the Lord. The presence of the Lord was very evident, and the fear of the Lord also. There was much conviction and cleansing from sin. Those few days before the Sunday nights were really dynamic.

On the night of Sunday, July 21, the church was packed. The building was a modern, low-set structure which could hold a few hundred people, although there was normally only a handful on Sunday nights. What occurred on that night is probably the most amazing thing I have seen. I believe it is a foretaste of what God will do in revival. The building was absolutely packed. The foyer was packed and there were people outside looking in through the windows. There had been no advertising. The Spirit of God drew the crowds. Many healing miracles occurred, one after another. Later on in the night, Clark preached a very short gospel message and many people streamed forward to be saved. Over the next few days, people came to our home one by one and they were baptised in the Holy Spirit, some of them seeing visions.

The Methodist Church leaders decided to put Clark into Kings College, their theological college at the University, so he became a student there in 1969. In between his studies, he began what became known as the Corinda meetings. George Nichols, the man who had introduced Clark to the baptism in the Holy Spirit, had a large home in the Brisbane suburb of Corinda. These meetings commenced on May 10, 1969. These numbers grew to about 200 hundred during the following two years.

Following time with Trevor Chandler at Windsor Full Gospel Church and then Christian Life Centre, we began travelling. Later, we began Christian Outreach Centre.

The first step was a meeting, attended by twenty-five people, in our home at Keperra on June 16, 1974. One week later, 126 people participated in Communion. Christian Outreach Centre was under way.

Faith in God was one of our foundational beliefs. Christian Outreach Centre Bibles automatically fall open at the 11th chapter of Mark. We had to have a faith in God because we had nothing else - no financial backing, no parent body to launch us, no experience in starting churches. Some people described us as 'ecclesiastical nobodies' and they were right.

We then spread out to other parts of Queensland and Australia, and then overseas. We started planting churches in towns close to Brisbane, one reason being that we really needed each other. Training took place on the run, as the first Christian Outreach Centre Pastors were some farmers, carpenters and milkman.

Christian Outreach Centre men and women were committed to "Australia for Christ." They put their money where their mouth was. People gave sacrificially and the staff worked for very low wages. One of the secrets of success in the early days had to be that people has a will to work.

By 1976, Clark was beginning to talk television. "A New Way of Living" went to air on Channel Nine in Brisbane on July 17, 1977. The program was given that name because it was a popular song at the time and people were experiencing what the words described.

"A New Way of Living", was shown on sixteen stations in Queensland, as well as going to air in South Australia, Victoria and New South Wales. At that time, we had a congregation of 800 and TV was costing about $5,000 per week. Large numbers of people throughout Australia will be eternally grateful that God used the medium of television so mightily.[20]

Clark Taylor led Christian Outreach Centre during its first fifteen years. Then Neil Miers became its International President and Clark later travelled in healing evangelism and then founded the Worship Centre in Brisbane in 2000.

1970 - February: Wilmore, Kentucky, North America (Asbury College)

A revival broke out in Asbury College in Wilmore, Kentucky, on Tuesday, February 3, 1970. The regular morning chapel commencing at 10 o'clock saw God move on the students in such a way that many came weeping to the front to kneel in repentance, others gave testimonies including confession of sin, and all this was mixed with spontaneous singing. Lectures were cancelled for the day as the auditorium filled with over 1,000 people. Few left for meals. By midnight over 500 still remained praying and worshipping. Several hundred committed their lives to Christ that day. By 6 am next morning 75 students were still praying in the hall, and through the Wednesday it filled again as all lectures were again cancelled for the day. The time was filled with praying, singing, confessions and testimonies.

As they continued in prayer that week many students felt called to share what was happening with other colleges and churches. Invitations were coming from around the country as news of the revival spread. So teams went out from the next weekend to tell the story and give their testimonies. Almost half the student body of 1,000 was involved in the teams witnessing about the revival. In the first week after the revival began teams of students visited 16 states by invitation and saw several thousand conversions through their witnessing.

After six weeks over 1,000 teams had gone from the college to witness, some of these into Latin America with finance provided by the home churches of the students. In addition, the neighbouring Theological Seminary sent out several hundred teams of their students who had also been caught up in this revival.

Those remaining at the college prayed for the teams and gladly heard their reports on their return. The Holy Spirit did similar things wherever they went. So that revival spread. The college remained a centre of the revival with meetings continuing at night and weekends there along with spontaneous prayer groups meeting every day. Hundreds of people kept coming to the college to see this revival and participate in it. They took reports and their own testimonies of changed lives back to their churches or colleges so sharing in the spread of the revival.

Revival also spread among the hippie dropouts in the early seventies. Thousands were converted in mass rallies on the beaches and in halls. They developed their own Jesus People magazines, music and evangelism.

1970 - July: Solomon Islands (Muri Thompson)

Muri Thompson, a Maori evangelist from New Zealand, visited the Solomon Islands in July and August 1970 where the church had already experienced significant renewal and was praying for revival. Many of these Christians were former warriors and cannibals gradually won to Christ in spite of initial hostility and the martyrdom of early missionaries and indigenous evangelists.

Beginning at Honiara, the capital, Muri spent two months visiting churches and centres on the islands. Initially the national leaders and missionaries experienced deep conviction and repentance, publicly acknowledging their wrong attitudes. It was very humbling. A new unity and harmony transformed their relationships, and little things which destroyed that unity were openly confessed with forgiveness sought and given.

Then in the last two weeks of these meetings the Holy Spirit moved even more powerfully in the meetings with more deep repentance and weeping, sometimes even before the visiting team arrived. That happened on Sunday morning 23 August on the island of Malaita where the whole congregation was deeply moved with many crying even before the team arrived from their berth in the ship the *Evangel* which carried the mission team of 40 people.

Muri preached powerfully. Then he said, "If anyone wants to come forward ..." and immediately the whole congregation of 600 surged forward across the dirt floor under the thatched leaf roof. Most people including pastors cried with loud sobs of repentance, which soon gave way to outbursts of joy. Many saw visions of God, of Jesus on the cross or on his throne, of angels, or of bright light. Some spoke in tongues. Some were healed. Most came into a new experience of God with a deep awareness of the need for humility and being sensitive to the Holy Spirit.

The following Thursday, 27 August, at another village on Malaita the team found a people well prepared through many weeks of repentance, unity, and a growing longing to be filled with the Spirit. After preaching Muri asked for a time of silent prayer and the 2,000 people bowed in prayer. Then he heard a growing sound.

> "At first," he said, "I thought it was audible prayer among the congregation, but realized it was above, in the distance, like a wind, and getting louder.

> "I looked up through an opening in the leaf roof to the heavens from where the sound seemed to be coming. It grew to be roar - then it came to me: surely this is the Holy Spirit coming like a mighty rushing wind. I called the people to realize that God the Holy Spirit was about to descend upon them."[21]

Three praying leaders in a nearby prayer house heard the silence, and then the roaring sound. They came outside and heard it coming from immediately above the church. In the church people broke into wailing, praying and strong crying. Conviction of sin increased, followed by deliverance and great joy. Weeping turned to joyful singing. Everywhere people were talking about what the Lord had done to them. Many received healings and deliverance from bondage to evil spirits. Marriages were restored and young rebels transformed. Everywhere people were praying together every day. They had a new hunger for God's Word. People were sensitive to the Spirit and wanted to be transparently honest and open with God and one another.

Normal lectures in the South Seas Evangelical Church Bible School were constantly abandoned as the Spirit took over the whole school with times of confession, prayer and praise.

Teams from these areas visited other islands, and the revival caught fire there also. Eventually pastors from the Solomons were visiting other Pacific countries and seeing similar moves of God there also.

1971 - October: Saskatoon, Canada (Bill McLeod)

Wilbert (Bill) McLeod, a Baptist minister in his midfifties, had seen many people healed in answer to prayer, often praying with a group of deacons. He once anointed a woman with oil and prayed with her when she was dying of cancer. While Bill prayed the woman had a vision of Jesus coming to her and touching her. She was healed. Bill saw nothing.

Bill invited the twin evangelists Ralph and Lou Sutera to speak at his church in Saskatoon. Revival broke out with their visit which began on Wednesday 13 October 1971. By the week-end an amazing spirit gripped the people. Many confessed their sins publicly. The first to do so were the twelve counsellors chosen to pray with inquirers. Numbers grew rapidly till the meetings had to be moved to a larger church building and then to the Civic Auditorium seating 2,000.

The meetings lasted many hours. People did not want to leave. Some stayed on for a later meeting called the Afterglow. Here people received prayer and counsel from the group as they continued to worship God and pray together. Humble confession of sin and reconciliations were common. Many were converted.

Taxi drivers became amazed that people were getting cabs home from church late into the night or early into the morning. Others were calling for taxis to take them to church late into the night as they were convicted by the Lord. Young people featured prominently. Almost half those converted were young. They gave testimonies of lives that had been cleaned up by God and how relationships with their families were restored. The atmosphere in schools and colleges changed from rebellion and cheating to cooperation with many Bible study and prayer groups forming in the schools and universities.

Criminals confessed their sins and gave themselves up to the police. Restitution was common. People paid overdue bills. Some businesses opened new accounts to account for the conscience money being paid to them. Those who cheated at restaurants or hotels returned to pay their full bill. People returned stolen goods.

Christians found a new radical honesty in their lives. Pride and jealousies were confessed and transformed into humility and love. As people prayed for one another with new tenderness and compassion many experienced healings and deliverance.

Not all welcomed the revival. Some churches remained untouched by it or hostile to it. This seems common to all revivals.

Sherwood Wirt, editor of the Billy Graham Association's magazine *Decision* reported:

One day late in 1971, I read a strange report from Canada. Curious things were taking place in some congregations in the western provinces. Brothers and sisters, it was said, had been reconciled to each other; shoplifted articles had been returned; crimes were being reported by the culprits; church feuds were being resolved; pastors were confessing their pride.

But then I heard this word: "We're walking kneedeep in love up here."[22]

In November a team went to Winnepeg and told of the revival at a meeting for ministers. The Holy Spirit moved powerfully and many broke down confessing their sins. Rivalries and jealousies were confessed and forgiven. Many went home to put things right with their families. The ministers took this fire back into their churches and the revival spread there also with meetings going late into the night as numbers grew and hundreds were converted or restored.

Sherwood Wirt reported on Bill McLeod preaching at Winnepeg on 15 December 1971:

> I confess that what I saw amazed me. This man preached for only fifteen minutes, and he didn't even give an invitation! He announced the closing hymn, whereupon a hundred people came out of their seats and knelt at the front of the church. All he said was, "That's right, keep coming!"
>
> Many were young. Many were in tears. All were from the Canadian Midwest, which is not known for its euphoria. It could be said that what I was witnessing was revival. I believe it was.[23]

Bill McLeod and a team of six brought the revival to the eastern Canada when they were invited to speak at the Central Baptist Seminary in Toronto. The meeting there began at 10 am and went through till 1:15 am next morning. Dinner was cancelled as no one wanted to leave. They did stop for supper, then went on again.

When the Sutera brothers commenced meetings in Vancouver on the West Coast on Sunday, May 5, 1972, revival broke out there also in the Ebenezer Baptist Church with 2,000 attending that first Sunday. The next Sunday 3,000 people attended in two churches. After a few weeks five churches were filled.

The revival spread in many churches across Canada and into northern U. S. A. especially in Oregon. Everywhere the marks of the revival included honesty before God and others with confession of sin and an outpouring of the love of God in those who repented.

The German speaking churches were also touched by the revival and by May 1972 they chartered a flight to Germany for teams to minister there.

The Afterglow meetings were common everywhere in the revival. After a meeting had finished those who wanted to stay on for prayer did so. Usually each person desiring prayer knelt at a chair and others laid hands on them and prayed for them. Many repented and were filled with the Spirit in the Afterglow meetings which often went to midnight or later.

Sherwood Wirt reports on his experience of an Afterglow. As he sat in a chair people came to pray for him. They told him to,

Ask God to crucify you.
Crucify me? I wasn't even sure the idea was theologically sound.

"To do what?" I stammered.
"Nail you to the cross" was the reply ...

"Now ask God to fill you with his Spirit and thank him for it." ...

"You probably don't have much of a sensation of blessing now... Don't worry. The feeling will come later and how!"

She was right. It came. And it has never left ...

The Holy Spirit used a divine solvent... to dissolve the bitterness in my heart... In his own time and at his own pleasure he sent a divine solvent into this troubled heart. It was like the warmth of the sun burning off the layers of fog.

I don't know just how the love came in, but I know that all the bitterness I held against others including those near to me disappeared.
Resentment hostility hurt feelings you name it.
They all dissolved. Evaporated. Went.[24]

He commented on this laying hands on people for prayer, which was normal in Afterglows: "Call it revival, renewal, a fresh touch, an anointing, times of refreshing, or what you will. I needed it."[25]

That deep work of the Spirit continues now across the world. Its expressions vary with different cultures and denominational traditions. However, the divine Spirit deeply impacts those who continue to seek the Lord.

1973 - September: Enga District, Papua New Guinea

During September 1973 pastors from the Solomon Islands Enga Baptist churches in the highlands of New Guinea. They conducted meetings throughout the area including sessions with village pastors.

Revival broke out in many villages on Sunday 16 September when the pastors had returned to their churches. Hundreds of people, deeply convicted of sin, repented and were reconciled to God and others with great joy. Pastors in one area held a retreat from Monday to Wednesday in a forest which previously had been sacred for animistic spirit worship. Others joined the pastors there. Healings included a lame man able to walk, a deaf mute who spoke and heard, and a mentally deranged girl was restored.

Work stopped as people in their thousands hurried to special meetings. Prayer groups met daily, morning and evening. Most villages established special places for prayer such as groves near the village where people could go and pray at any time. In the following months thousands of Christians were restored and thousands were converted. The church grew in size and maturity.

This was followed in the eighties by tough times. Tribal conflict, destruction and bloodshed erupted. Revival often precedes hard times and equips God's people to endure, or even to suffer for him.

1973 - September: Phnom Penh, Cambodia (Todd Burke)

In September, 1973, Todd Burke arrived in Cambodia on a one week visitor's visa. Just 23 years old, he felt a strong call from God to minister there, the only charismatic missionary in the country. Beginning with two English classes a day, conducted through an interpreter, he taught from the Good News Bible. Those interested in knowing more about Jesus stayed after class and he saw regular conversions and people filled with the Spirit and healed. Revival broke out in the war torn capital of Phnom Penh and rapidly spread to surrounding areas.

During that September, Todd's wife DeAnn joined him and their visas were extended. A capable interpreter, Thay, joined their team and they received government permission to hold a crusade from 28 September, on the afternoons of Friday to Sunday in the athletic stadium. A singing team from the States arrived the day before the crusade began and led each meeting for half an hour with songs and testimonies.

Todd Burke described that first meeting:

> About five thousand people were in the audience, most of them middle and lower class people. Among them was a large number of refugees. Seated to my left was a whole section of soldiers dressed in battle fatigues. Many of them had been wounded or had suffered the loss of a limb and I was touched by the look of hope written on their attentive faces. Before the meeting I overheard a reporter interviewing one soldier who was leaning on crutches near the platform. He had lost his right leg in combat. "I don't understand what this is going to be about," he said, "but maybe this Jesus

can help to relieve our pain and sorrows." That was my prayer too. ...

As the time drew near for me to speak, I began praying for God to anoint me with the Holy Spirit. I needed his power to proclaim the Lordship of Jesus to these people who had never heard his message. ...

Thay was interpreting phrase by phrase and we seemed to have the people's attention. "I can't prove to you that Jesus offers more than you have in Buddha on in any other religion. Only Jesus can prove that to you as he did in the days when he walked the earth."

Then I began to relate the story of the paralytic man who had been healed by Jesus. During Thay's interpretation I prayed silently that the Holy Spirit would breathe life into those words and cause them to pierce each individual heart. ...

With a silent prayer (at the end of the message), I continued, "All of you who would like to know whether Jesus is Lord and has this power to save you and to heal you, please raise your hands." They went up all over the stadium; an air of restlessness crept over the crowd.

"Now," I shouted into the microphone, "put your other hand on the area of your body where you need a healing. Or place your hand upon your heart if you want to have your sins forgiven and to find a new life in Christ." Slowly I prayed a simple prayer so Thay could interpret every word clearly. ... I felt a surging confidence that the Holy Spirit was doing a mighty work at that moment.[26]

Todd invited those who had been healed to come forward and testify. After a brief pause hundreds streamed forward. A lady who had been blind for many years testified that right after the prayer she could see. A lame man who had been carried into the meeting found he could walk again. There were too many healings for everyone to testify.

Each afternoon the crowds increased, and so did the impact of God's presence. American TV crews, pulled in off reporting the war, filmed the final crusade. It was shown across America. Todd described the final meeting:

> Nearing the end of the message, I noticed people were already moving toward the front. Why are they coming already? I wondered. Have they been healed while I was speaking? ... Some were coming for prayer, but most of them had been healed already.

> I quickly ended my message and prayed with the entire audience, as I had done the two preceding days. When Thay invited people to come to the front and testify of what God had done for them, the response was incredible. For several hours, hundreds of people streamed across the platform as we watched in amazement.

> When the procession was finished, Thay asked the remaining audience whether they believed Jesus had proved himself to be the Lord. They roared their agreement and then applauded spontaneously. "How many of you want to receive Jesus as your Saviour and Master?" he asked. A sea of hands raised before us. Our students and workers moved into the crowd to pray and counsel with as many as they could reach, handing out tracts and gospel portions and instructing people where they could go to learn more about Jesus.[27]

161

Many of those saved and healed began home churches. A powerful church spread through a network of small house churches. Todd met with the leaders of these groups at early morning prayer meetings every day at 6 a.m. Most pastors were voluntary workers holding normal jobs. Some cycled in from the country and returned for work each morning. Healings, miracles and deliverance from demonic powers were regular events, attracting new converts who in turn were filled with the power of the Spirit and soon began witnessing and praying for others.

When the country fell to the communists in 1975 the Burkes had to leave. They left behind an amazing church anointed by the power of God before it was buried by going underground to survive.

Endnotes

[1] Allan Anderson, 2004, An Introduction to Pentecostalism, Cambridge University Press, p. 58.

[2] Richard Riss, 1988, A Survey of 20th Century Revival Movements in North America, Hendrickson, p. 106.

[3] Riss, 1988, p. 126.

[4] T L Osborn, 1986, Healing the Sick, Harrison, pp. 394-395.

[5] Osborn, p. 397.

[6] Eddie Hyatt, 1998, 2000 Years of Charismatic Christianity, Revival & Renewal Resources, p. 192.

[7] Riss 1998, pp. 112-113.

[8] Colin Whittaker, 1984, Korea Miracle, Kingsway, p. 159.

[9] David Pytches, 1989, Does God Speak Today? Hodder & Stoughton, pp. 49-51.

[10] Report given by Rev. Y Y Murry of the Latter Rain Revival Ministry.

[11] Dennis Bennett, 1960, Nine O'clock in the Morning, Logos, p. 51.

[12] Edited from unpublished notes by David Mangratee, April 2000, in Darjeeling.

[13] Paul Grant, 1986, unpublished notes, pp. 7-10.

[14] Ruth Rongo, 1991, personal letter to Geoff Waugh.

[15] Don Crawford, 1972, Miracles in Indonesia, Tyndale, pp. 22-24.

[16] Mel Tari, 1971, Like a Mighty Wind, and Mel and Nori Tari, 1974, The Gentle Breeze of Jesus. These books give autobiographi-

cal reports of the revival, especially the mission teams. Other reports were gathered by Kurt Koch in his undated book The Revival in Indonesia.

[17] Don Crawford, 1972, pp. 25-28.

[18] Tari, 1971, gives many examples of these revival phenomena.

[19] Tari, 1974, pp. 8-12.

[20] Ann Taylor, from www.worshipcentre.com.au July, 2010.

[21] Alison Griffiths, 1997, Fire in the Islands, Shaw, p. 175.

[22] Sherwood Wirt, 1975, Knee Deep in Love, Coverdale, p. 23.

[23] Wirt, p. 46.

[24] Wirt, pp. 11-15.

[25] Wirt, p. 127.

[26] Todd & DeAnn Burke, 1989, Anointed for Burial, Logos, pp. 22-25.

[27] Burke, pp. 32-33.

Chapter 5

Late Twentieth Century Revival:
Renewal and Revival

The spread of charismatic renewal continued to widen into traditions resistant to using Pentecostal or charismatic terminology but open to the impacts of the Spirit in revival. Peter Wagner labelled this development the Third Wave of renewal encompassing traditional evangelical churches, following the Pentecostal and Charismatic waves. These streams, combined with the growing networks of independent churches, characterised renewal and revival in the last third of the twentieth century. Many international evangelists promoted powerful Spirit movements in their crusades, which in turn impacted churches of all denominations. Revival in Africa produced astounding growth in independent churches in networks of renewal and revival.

International ministries from the seventies of such people as Benny Hinn, Reinhard Bonnke, Rodney Howard-Browne and John Wimber transcended denominational differences while strongly demonstrating healing evangelism.

1974 – December: North America (Benny Hinn)

Benny Hinn, born in Jaffa, Israel, lived there with his parents, five brothers and two sisters, during his youth.

Although raised as Greek Orthodox, he studied in a private Catholic school. His educational experience in the Catholic school nurtured a desire at an early age to dedicate his life to ministry. Because he lived in Israel, his studies often included an opportunity to visit the sites about which he was studying. These experiences added much to his understanding of Bible history, helping to prepare and equip him for future ministry.

A stuttering problem made speaking extremely difficult for him. Although he was a very good student, his stuttering inhibited his ability to communicate.

In July 1968, he and his family left Jaffa and emigrated to Toronto, Canada. The greatest change in his life took place occurred when some of his high school classmates shared the message of God's love with him. He surrendered his heart and life to Jesus Christ and was born again.

Following his conversion, a deep spiritual hunger to know God more drew him to prayer and Bible reading. The Holy Spirit became his teacher and companion. He spent many hours each day alone in his room studying God's Word, praying, worshipping, and fellowshipping with the Spirit.

This went on for more than a year. It was during this period in his life that he attended a Kathryn Kuhlman service in Pittsburgh. During the service, the presence and power of the Holy Spirit was evident as Kathryn Kuhlman talked about her friend, the Holy Spirit. That night back in Toronto, alone in his room, he whispered words that would transform his life: "Holy Spirit, Kathryn Kuhlman said you are her friend. I don't think I know you. Can I meet you?" That was the beginning of an incredible spiritual journey for Benny Hinn.

Once while sharing his experiences with close friends, he was invited to share his story in a church meeting that evening. As he stood before the group, he was apprehensive because of his stuttering problem. But as he opened his mouth to speak, his tongue was loosed and he spoke clearly for the first time in his life.

That was Saturday, December 7, 1974. From that moment on, miracles began to take place for Benny Hinn. His family members came to know the Lord, one by one.

The ministry of Benny Hinn touches millions each year through television, Miracle Crusades, books, and pulpit ministry. He was the Pastor/Founder of World Outreach Center in Orlando, Florida, where he served a growing congregation of 12,000 each week, and then became committed to his full time evangelism and healing ministry. As an evangelist he reaches millions each year through daily television and Miracle Crusades around the world. In addition he is a best-selling author and outstanding teacher of God's Word.

As the host of the daily half-hour television program, *This Is Your Day*, Benny Hinn shares the message of God's love and miracle-working power with an international audience of millions. Through dynamic ministry, music, and miracles viewers are invited to believe for their miracle because "nothing is impossible when you put your trust in God!"

Benny Hinn is a man with a mandate from God, who told him to take the message of God's saving and healing power to the world. He does so through the many avenues of his ministry. His anointed, Spirit-led pulpit ministry sets him apart as a man who knows and loves God. This, combined with his understanding of God's Word, enables him to effectively communicate the biblical principles in word and deed.[1]

1975 - April: Gaberone, Botswana (Reinhard Bonnke)

German missionary to Africa, Reindard Bonnke (1940) founded Christ For All Nations (CFAN) which now ministers to millions.

Converted at nine, he had a missionary zeal. As a teenager Reinhard saw Johannesburg in South Africa in a vision of a map of Africa. At 19, he headed off to the Bible College of Wales to train as a missionary, even though he couldn't speak English. Three months later he was preaching in English! There he learned practical principles of living by faith.

After a short pastorate in Germany where he married Anna, they left for missionary service in Africa. Working as traditional missionaries from 1967 to 1974 in Maseru, the capital of the small landlocked country of Lesotho, they saw meagre results.

Near the end of that time Reinhard's interpreter broke down during his message at a healing meeting one Sunday morning and sank weeping to the floor because of God's awesome presence. Waiting for the interpreter to recover Reinhard 'heard' the Lord speak 'words' which amazed him: *My words in your mouth are just as powerful as my words in my own mouth.*

The 'voice' repeated the sentence. He 'saw' it like a movie in Scripture Jesus told the disciples to speak in faith and it would happen. "I suddenly realised that the power was not in the mouth the power was in the Word," said Reinhard.

Then, when the interpreter had recovered enough to speak, as he was preaching Reinhard 'heard' the Spirit say, "Call those who are completely blind and speak the word of authority."

He did. About six blind people stood. He boldly proclaimed, "Now I am going to speak with the authority of God and you are going to see a white man standing before you. Your eyes are going to open."

He shouted, "In the name of Jesus, blind eyes open!" It shocked everyone as his voice resonated loudly against the bare brick walls.

Then a woman's voice shrieked, "I can see! I can see!" She had been totally blind for years. The other blind people also saw. The place erupted in excited cheers. A woman handed her crippled boy through the milling crowd to Reinhard who sensed the power of God on the boy and watched amazed as his crippled legs shook and straightened. That boy was healed. The meeting went for hours as people screamed, shouted, danced and sang.

At the end of 1974, Reinhard relocated to Johannesburg and established Christ For All Nations. Early in January, when he was ill, he had a vision of Jesus similar to the Joshua's vision (Joshua 5:13-15). He wrote:

> I was very sick. I didn't think I would make it. I went to doctors. Nothing helped. I was crying to God: "Lord what are you doing? What is your plan?" One afternoon I retired to my study. A thirst for prayer came over me and I was hardly on my knees when I saw a

most wonderful vision. I saw the son of God stand in front of me in full armour, like a general. The armour saw shining like the sun and burning like fire. It was tremendous and I realised that the Lord of Hosts had come. I threw myself at His feet. I laughed and I cried ... I don't know for how long, but when I got up I was perfectly healed.[2]

When Bonnke flew to Gaberone in Botswana to buy time on radio there the Lord told him to hire the 10,000 seater sports stadium for a crusade. The local Pentecostal pastor who helped prepare for the crusade felt apprehensive. He had only 40 in his congregation!

The crusade in April 1974 with Reinhard's evangelist friend Pastor Ngidi started in a hall which could seat 800. On the first night 100 attended. Healings happened every night, and people fell to the floor overwhelmed. That was new to Reinhard.

By the end of the first week 2,000 people were packed into the hall. So they moved into the stadium! Thousands attended. People were saved and healed every night and over 500 people were baptised in water within two weeks.

One night in the stadium, the Holy Spirit urged Reinhard to pray for people to be baptised in the Holy Spirit. So he asked an African coworker to give a message on the Holy Spirit.

About 1,000 people responded to the call to be baptised in the Spirit. As soon as they raised their hands they all fell, shouting and praising God in new languages on the ground. Reinhard was amazed. He had never seen anything like that before. It continued to happen in his crusades.

Eventually Reinhard used an enormous tent which could seat 30,000 people. Some of Christ For All Nations crusades in Africa have reached huge open air crowds of 600,000 to 800,000 people. Always hundreds or thousands are saved, healed and delivered as the power of God moves on the people.

1977 - March: Min District, Papua New Guinea (Diyos Wapnok)

Pastors from the Solomon Islands spoke about their revival at a pastors and leaders conference at Goroka in the highlands of Papua New Guinea. Diyos Wapnok attended from the Baptist Mission area at Telefolmin. He heard God call his name three times in the night there and realised that the Lord was drawing his attention to some special challenge.

Later, on Thursday afternoon 10 March, 1977 at Duranmin in the rugged Western Highlands, where Diyos was the principal of the Sepik Baptist Bible College, while he spoke to about 50 people they were all filled with the Holy Spirit and great joy.[3]

The students experienced a light brighter than day, filling the room where they were. Many simultaneously felt convicted of unconfessed sin and cried out for mercy and forgiveness. All became aware of the majesty, authority and glory of God.

Revival had come to Duranmin and the Sepik. This glimpse of God's greatness gave a new dimension to the students' preaching. The movement spread beyond the churches to their unreached neighbours and to most of the villages in the whole Sepik area. Many churches of new believers were established and in the next three years at least 3,000 new believers were baptised.

1979 - March: Elcho Island, Australia (Djiniyini Gondarra)

The Lord poured out the Holy Spirit on Elcho Island in northern Australia on Thursday, 14 March, 1979. Djiniyini Gondarra was then the Uniting Church minister in the town of Galiwin'ku at the south of the island. He had been away on holidays to Sydney and Brisbane, returning on the late afternoon Missionary Aviation Fellowship flight.

He was travel weary and just wanted to unpack and get to bed early. Many of the people, however, had been praying for months, and especially every day while he had been away, so they wanted to have prayer and Bible study with him in his home. This is his account of that Pentecost among Australian Aborigines in the Arnhem Land churches across the north of Australia:

> After the evening dinner, we called our friends to come and join us in the Bible Class meeting. We just sang some hymns and choruses translated into Gupapuynu and into Djambarrpuynu. There were only seven or eight people who were involved or came to the Bible Class meeting, and many of our friends didn't turn up. We didn't get worried about it.
>
> I began to talk to them that this was God's will for us to get together this evening because God had planned this meeting through them so that we will see something of his great love which will be poured out on each one of them. I said a word of thanks to those few faithful Christians who had been praying for renewal in our church, and I shared with them that I too had been praying for the revival or the renewal for this church and for the whole of Arnhem Land churches, because

to our heavenly Father everything is possible. He can do mighty things in our churches throughout our great land.

These were some of the words of challenge I gave to those of my beloved brothers and sisters. Gelung, my wife, also shared something of her experience of the power and miracles that she felt deep down in her heart when she was about to die in Darwin Hospital delivering our fourth child. It was God's power that brought the healing and the wholeness in her body.

I then asked the group to hold each other's hands and I began to pray for the people and for the church, that God would pour out his Holy Spirit to bring healing and renewal to the hearts of men and women, and to the children.

Suddenly we began to feel God's Spirit moving in our hearts and the whole form of our prayer suddenly changed and everybody began to pray in the Spirit and in harmony. And there was a great noise going on in the room and we began to ask one another what was going on.

Some of us said that God had now visited us and once again established his kingdom among his people who have been bound for so long by the power of evil. Now the Lord is setting his church free and bringing us into the freedom of happiness and into reconciliation and to restoration.

In that same evening, the word just spread like the flames of fire and reached the whole community in Galiwin'ku. Gelung and I couldn't sleep at all that night because people were just coming for the ministry, bringing the sick to be prayed for, for healing. Others came to bring their problems. Even a husband and wife came to bring their marriage problem, so the Lord touched them and healed their marriage.

Next morning the Galiwin'ku Community once again became the new community. The love of Jesus was being shared and many expressions of forgiveness were taking place in the families and in the tribes. Wherever I went, I could hear people singing and humming Christian choruses and hymns! Before then I would have expected to hear only fighting and swearing and many other troublesome things that would hurt your feelings and make you feel sad.

Many unplanned and unexpected things happened every time we went from camp to camp to meet with the people. The fellowship was held every night and more and more people gave their lives to Christ, and it went on and on until sometimes the fellowship meeting would end around about midnight. There was more singing, testimony, and ministry going on. People did not feel tired in the morning, but still went to work.

Many Christians were beginning to discover what their ministry was, and a few others had a strong sense of call to be trained to become Ministers of the Word. Now today these ministers who have done their training through Nungilinya College have been ordained. These are some of the results of the revival in Arnhem Land. Many others have been trained to take up a special ministry in the parish.

The spirit of revival has not only affected the Uniting Church communities and the parishes, but Anglican churches in Arnhem Land as well, such as in Angurugu, Umbakumba, Roper River, Numbulwar and Oen-pelli. These all have experienced the revival, and have been touched by the joy and the happiness and the love of Christ.

The outpouring of the Holy Spirit in Arnhem Land has swept further to the Centre in Pitjantjatjara and across the west into many Aboriginal settlements and com-munities. I remember when Rev. Rronang Garrawurra, Gelung and I were invited by the Warburton Ranges people and how we saw God's Spirit move in the lives of many people. Five hundred people came to the Lord and were baptised in the name of the Father, the Son, and the Holy Spirit.

There was a great revival that swept further west. I would describe these experiences like a wild bush fire burning from one side of Australia to the other side of our great land. The experience of revival in Arnhem Land is still active in many of our Aboriginal parishes and the churches.

We would like to share these experiences in many white churches where doors are closed to the pow-er of the Holy Spirit. It has always been my humble prayer that the whole of Australian Christians, both black and white, will one day be touched by this great and mighty power of the living God.[4]

The Renewal Fellowship in Brisbane invited team from Elcho Island to minister at a combined churches Pentecost week-end in 1992. Over 20 Aborigines paid their airfare to come, saying they rarely had such opportunities. When they were asked to pray for the whites responding after their messages, they said, "We don't know how to pray for whites. We haven't done that." They soon learned, and prayed with the faith and

gracious insights typical for them. Asked why white churches did not invite Aborigines to minister to them, and why the
revival did not touch white churches they replied softly, "You
are too proud."

A small Aboriginal community of about 30 adults with their
children live at the far northern end of Elcho Island, acces-
sible by four wheel drive over a 50 kilometre dirt track. That
community has been praying daily for revival in Australia and
across the world for over 20 years. They meet for prayer
each morning, during the day and again each evening.

Features of this revival have been repeated in many aboriginal communities in Australia, particularly in North Queensland
from July 1999. It includes the desperate, repentant prayers
of a remnant of Christians, a strong impact of the Spirit of
God bringing widespread confession and freedom from addiction to social vices including drunkenness, immorality and
gambling, the restoration of harmonious family life and civil
order with peace and joy.

1979 - July: Port Elizabeth, South Africa (Rodney Howard-Browne)

Rodney HowardBrowne has seen hundreds of thousands
converted through his ministry, and many more renewed in
their love for the Lord and empowered by the Holy Spirit. His
ministry remains controversial because of the manifestations
involved, especially laughter.

In July 1979, when he was eighteen Rodney HowardBrowne
of Port Elizabeth, South Africa, attended an interdenominational prayer meeting with about eighteen young people. He
had been desperately crying out to God, and at that meeting he prayed with the abandonment of youth, "God, either

you come down here tonight and touch me, or I'm going to die and come up there and touch you." He began shouting "God, I want your fire."

After crying out for twenty minutes he suddenly he felt engulfed in the fire of God, was totally overwhelmed, weeping, laughing, and praying in tongues. That continued for four days till he cried out, "God, lift it. I can't bear it any more. ... Lord, I'm too young to die, don't kill me now." For two weeks he felt that intense presence of God. Then that intensity lifted for about
ten years but later became common in his ministry.

In 1980, while he was ministering with a group of young people in a Methodist Church in South Africa, a woman in pain asked for prayer in the vestry before a service. He told what happened:

> I got up from my seat. I was going to put my hand on her head. And I lifted my hand and got it about here ... like you'd pull a sixgun out of a holster and point it at somebody. And when my hand got about here, it felt like my fingertips came off, and out of my hand flowed a full volume of the anointing and the power of God, and it flowed right out of my hand and it went right in to her forehead and she crumbled in the floor. There was nobody in the room more amazed than me. And I looked down at the woman and I looked at my hand, and I'll tell you what my hand the fire of God the anointing of God the virtue the dunamis was still coming out of my hand. It felt like my hand was a fire hose. And now you start getting nervous you think, I'd better look out where I point this thing. This thing's loaded now.

> And so the rest of the team came in, and I didn't know what to do with it other than what we'd just done, so

I said, "Lift your hands." ... Bam, they're all out in the back of the vestry. Now I'm in trouble. If the priest comes back, I'm finished. So I went around and just managed to get them just right and sober them up and say, "Get up and pull yourself together, we've got to go in to the meeting." We managed to get them all up except one girl. We had her propped between two men and got them out into the auditorium.

I get into the service, and that night I had to speak and I said to the Lord, "Lord, you know I'm not allowed to talk about Holy Ghost. You know I'm not allowed to talk about tongues. You know I'm not allowed to talk about "fall" and "power" and these words. Lord, how can we have what happened in the back room happen out here?" And the Lord said to me, "Call all those that want a blessing." Everyone raised their hands. So I said, "All right, get up, come up, and line up." And so I was going to go down and lay my hands on the first person's head. And the Lord said to me, "Just be very careful, and so don't put your hands on them because some people [will] think you'll push them over if you do." I take my finger, put it on the forehead of the first person and I said, "In the name of Jesus..." It looked like an angel stood there with a baseball bat and smacked them up the side of their head. And the person hit the floor. And I went down the line. Bam, Bam, Bam, Bam. The whole row was out under the power of God. Some of the people were pinned to the floor ... for an hour and a half. Some of them, the moment they hit the ground they were speaking with other tongues, and we had said nothing about it. And that anointing stayed again for a period of two weeks.

Let me tell you right now for an eighteen year old to experience that kind of anointing it's dangerous.

And then suddenly, it was gone. I prayed for people, they would fall down, but it was not the same. And I thought I'd lost the anointing. So now I'm starting to pray to get before God and find out: "What have I done to lose the anointing, and what formula must I use to get it back?" He said, "You can't do anything to get that anointing back. That anointing is not you. That anointing is all me. It has nothing to do with you." He said, "I just gave you a taste of what will come later on in your ministry, if you are faithful." He said, "If I gave it to you now, you'd destroy yourself. I can't give it to you now. There's no formula for it. If there was a formula for it, you'd do it and you'd get it, and you'd think it was you. From now on, whenever that anointing comes, you'll know it's not you and you'll know it's all me and you'll have to give me all the glory and all the praise and all the honour."

Rodney Howard Browne moved to the United States in 1987 for evangelistic work. Then from April 1989 in Clifton Park, near Albany in upstate New York he experienced powerful impacts of the Spirit during his meetings. He described it this way, "The power of God fell in the place without warning suddenly. People began to fall out of their seats, rolling on the floor. The very air was moving. People began to laugh uncontrollably while there wasn't anything funny. The less I preached, the more people were saved."

His influence soon reached worldwide proportions, with hundreds being saved in his meetings and thousands being overwhelmed in many ways.

1980 - May: Anaheim, North America (John Wimber)

In 1977, John Wimber began leading the fellowship of about 40 people which had been commenced by his wife, Carol. It later became the headquarters of the Vineyard Christian Fellowships. John preached from Luke's gospel and began to pray for healings with no visible results for nine months although the worship and evangelism attracted many people. Then healings began to happen and became a regular part of Vineyard ministry.

John Wimber summarized their story:

> Beginning some time in September of 1976, Bob Fulton, Carol Wimber, Carl Tuttle, along with others, began assembling at the home of Carl Tuttle's sister. The agenda was simple: praying, worshipping and seeking the Lord. By the time I came several months later, the Spirit of God was already moving powerfully. There was a great brokenness and responsiveness in the hearts of many. This evolved into what became our church on Mother's Day in 1977.

> Soon God began dealing with me about the work of the Spirit related to healing. I began teaching in this area. Over the next year and a half God began visiting in various and sundry ways. There were words of knowledge, healing, casting out of demons, and conversions.

> Later we saw an intensification of this when Lonnie Frisbee came and ministered. Lonnie had been a Calvary Chapel pastor and evangelist, being used mightily in the Jesus People Movement. After our Sunday

morning service on Mother's Day [1980[6]], I was walking out the door behind Lonnie, and the Lord told me, "Ask that young man to give his testimony tonight." I hadn't even met him, though I knew who he was and how the Lord had used him in the past. That night, after he gave his testimony, Lonnie asked the Holy Spirit to come and the repercussions were incredible. The Spirit of God literally knocked people to the floor and shook them silly. Many people spoke in tongues, prophesied or had visions.

Then over the next few months, hundreds and hundreds of people came to Christ as the result of the witness of the individuals who were touched that night, and in the aftermath. The church saw approximately 1,700 converted to Christ in a period of about three months.

This evolved into a series of opportunities, beginning in 1980, to minister around the world. Thus the Vineyard renewal ministry and the Vineyard movement were birthed.[7]

Wimber's controversial ministry through the Vineyard movement rapidly spread worldwide through conferences, books and music characteristic of the "Third Wave" of renewal. A term coined by C. Peter Wagner at Fuller Theological Seminary to describe the acceptance of charismata in evangelical churches which are not identified with the charismatic movement.

1984 - June: Brugam, Papua New Guinea (Ray Overend)

In the Sepik lowlands of northern Papua New Guinea, a new visitation of God burst on the South Seas Evangelical

Churches at Easter 1984, sparked by Solomon Island pastors. It was characterised by repentance, confession, weeping and great joy. Stolen goods were returned or replaced, and wrongs made right.

Australian missionary Ray Overend reported:

> I was preaching to an Easter convention at a place called Walahuta during the recent Sepik revival in Papua New Guinea. The words the Lord gave us were from Isaiah 6 ... After the last word of the message the whole church rose to its feet and clapped loudly something completely new to me! I knew they were not applauding me. They were acknowledging to God in praise the truth of his Word. ... Then I sat down in the only spare little space in the overcrowded church and the whole congregation began to sing one song after another. ...
>
> Many faces were lifted to heaven and many hands raised in humble adoration. The faces looked like the faces of angels. They were radiating light and joy. And then I noticed something. Right beside me was a man who had heard the Word and now he just watched those radiant faces lost in praise. Then he hung his head and began to sob like a child. He was ministered to. Demons were cast out. And he received the Lord Jesus right into his heart. Then he too began to clap in gentle joy.
>
> But who was he? A pastor came over to tell me that he had been until this moment the leader of the Tambaran cult in the Walahuta area that Satanic cult of which the whole village lived in mortal fear and traditionally the whole of the Sepik feared that cult.[8]

The man who was second-in-charge of the Tambaran cult in that area was also converted that day while he was listening to the worship from a distance as God's love and power overcame him. Revival began to move through the area, until eventually it impacted the main mission station at Brugam. Ray Overend reported:

I will never forget [Thursday] June 14th, 1984. Revival had broken out in many churches around but Brugam itself, with many station staff and many Bible College and Secondary School students, was untouched. For a whole week from 8th June a well known preacher from New Zealand (Fred Creighton) had brought studies on "Life in Christ by the power of His Spirit." There was much very thorough teaching. On Tuesday afternoon in prayer I had a real peace that the Lord would break through in Brugam. Then early on Thursday night, the 14th, Judah Akesi, the Church Superintendent, invited some of us to his office for prayer. During that prayer time God gave him a vision. In the vision he saw many people bowed down in the front of the church building in the midst of a big light falling down from above just like rain.

So after the ministry of the Word that night Judah invited those who wanted to bring their whole heart and mind and life under the authority of Christ to come forward so that hands might be laid on them for prayer.

About 200 people surged forward. Many fell flat on their faces on the ground sobbing aloud. Some were shaking as spiritual battles raged within. There was quite some noise...

The spiritual battles and cries of contrition continued for a long time. Then one after another in a space of about three minutes everybody rose to their feet, singing spontaneously as they rose. They were free. The battle was won. Satan was bound. They had made Christ their King! Their faces looked to heaven as they sang. They were like the faces of angels. The singing was like the singing of heaven. Deafening, but sweet and reverent.[9]

The whole curriculum and approach at the Bible School for the area changed. Instead of having traditional classes and courses, teachers would work with the school all day from prayer times early in the morning through Bible teaching followed by discussion and sharing times during the day to evening worship and ministry. The school became a community, seeking the Lord together.

Churches which have maintained a strong Biblical witness in he area continue to stay vital and strong in evangelism and ministry, filled with the Spirit's power. Christians learn to witness and minister in spiritual gifts, praying and responding to the leading of the Spirit.

Many received spiritual gifts they never had before. One such gift was the "gift of knowledge" whereby the Lord would show Christians exactly where fetishes of sanguma men were hidden. Now in Papua New Guinea sanguma men (who subject themselves to indescribable ritual to be in fellowship with Satan) are able to kill by black magic... In fact the power of sanguma in the East Sepik province has been broken.[10]

In 1986, a senior pastor from Manus Island came to the Sepik to attend a one year's pastors' course. He was filled with the Spirit. When he went to with a team of students on outreach they prayed for an injured child who couldn't walk. Later in the morning he saw her walking around the town. The revival had restored New Testament ministries to the church, which amazed that pastor because he had never seen that before the revival.

A significant feather of these pacific revivals have been the ministries of indigenous people to other indigenous groups, usually without western missionary involvement initially. Later, indigenous leaders have often turned to missionary teachers to explain the revival phenomena biblically, which has usually meant a fresh approach to teaching on the Holy Spirit.

1987 – November: Bougainville (Ezekiel Opet)

Royree Jensen[11] tells the story of powerful revival in Bougainville, east of Papua New Guinea, during the decade of war from 1988, sparked by the Bougainville Revolutionary Army (BRA) to defend their land and culture from devastation caused by mining. Spiritual leaders also worried about the western evils that arrived with the mining: pornography, alchohol abuse, drugs, smoking and immorality.

> Friday, November 6, 1987 marked the first supernatural revival event. It was at this time that the crisis was about to boil over. The stories of that day and the period of time that followed have been told to me by Papa Luke, a genteel man - white haired, 73 years of age, a school teacher, world-travelled. He lives on Saposa Island, 30 minutes by banana boat from Buka Island. He was a small boy during World War II and can remember the time when the Japanese invaded his island. Having lived through so much turbulence, Papa Luke now spends most of his days sitting with God. When we finally found him, he was sitting by the ocean reading his Bible.

Both teacher and story-weaver, he began to talk, vividly recalling the day the revival began, in the circular story-telling style of the Melanesian people.

"Before revival came up, I wrote a drama about God that mixed the culture with the Word of God. We had a drama group of young people who travelled around Buka area. Around this time, nine people got sick from black magic. Out of the nine, five died and four were left."

"My cousin Salome was one of the four people who didn't die. She was brought to the hospital in Buka but she didn't recover, so she was referred to Arawa General Hospital. She didn't recover there. The Indian doctor told her and her husband that he had seen witchcraft in India and knew that this poison came from the witchcraft. The doctor discharged her and she came home."

"They had a ritual ceremony where they asked for the sorcerers to release her by making a sacrifice to free her. She was meant to get better but didn't improve. After black magic failed, her brother, the chief, requested for the drama group to come back to our village and pray."

"By Sunday morning, my cousin was still sick. My family brought her to the Lotu (church service). They prayed for deliverance and healing. She got healed immediately along with the other three who were still sick. Five dead. Four healed. On that Sunday, many spiritual gifts fell. Everyone received a spiritual gift - all different kinds of gifts."

"Now the group went to the island where Salome and the others got sick. They were going to heal the island of the witchcraft that had killed the people. They put their hands into the ground without having to dig and they pulled out the poison. Their hands went through the ground to the exact spot of the bones or whatever artifacts had been used for the witchcraft. Their eyes were closed but the Holy Spirit led them to these places." (As he told me this, he shaped his hand as they had shaped theirs - like a rigid blade extending straight from the arm.)

Walking on water

"Now things became wild, exciting and interesting. Supernatural things began to happen. By the power of the Holy Spirit, my cousin Salome discerned that there was some witchcraft poison on another nearby island (a burial site) that was put there by a sorcerer. We began to pray. While we prayed, fifteen people stood with their eyes shut. Still with their eyes shut, they began walking on the water from our island to the nearby island. The Holy Spirit led them while they walked. When they reached the other island, they put their hands into the ground and pulled out small parcels of scraped human bone. This powder was being used by sorcerers in their witchcraft rituals. They brought these parcels of scraped bones back to our island, still walking on top of the water with their eyes still shut. They did not swim."

"We prayed over the parcels and threw them away into salt water. This broke the power of witchcraft. We don't know how they did the walking on the water except by the power of God. Plenty of people saw them walking on the water. There were plenty of eye witnesses. The distance between the two islands is one kilometre."

"The effect that this had on the island was that we became very excited about God. Many became Christians and worshipped God. It didn't stop there. Some of our school boys and girls, including my son, visited another island. All the mothers prepared food for them to share out. My son climbed a tree leaving his plate of food for a friend. The friend ate the food and died, along with eight other children and their teacher. My pikinini only got sick."

"This was not the only group to visit that island and die so we were waking up to the fact that the island had something no good on it. We notified all the ministries around us. For one week, we fasted, prayed and read the Bible."

"First we went back to the island where our 15 people had walked. We found more black magic - enough to fill a 10kg bag of rice. We prayed over it and threw it in the water. A big flying fox with legs like a man settled on top of the house where I was staying with another pastor. We could feel the wind from his wings. We rebuked this evil, black magic. It was powerful and even those who were praying fell down. This battle went on for quite a while but the people in our church were skilled in deliverance and intercession and eventually we started to win over this black magic."

"Two days later, we visited the island where the school children had died. We circled the island in a small boat worshipping God. We were all a little bit afraid. First people who could discern black magic went ashore. Then those who could fight black magic went ashore. Then we all went ashore."

"We stood together and worshipped God. Then we split into two groups, heading around the island in opposite directions. Just before we joined up, one team stood under a tree and looked up. They saw a live bird that they knew was part of black magic. They said, 'In the name of Jesus come down.' The bird died and began to fall. By the time it hit the ground, only the skeleton of the bird was left."

"One month before, some plantation workers had been on the island. A man had sat under that tree to rest. He took sick, went to hospital and died. However, after we fought the black magic, it was okay. Even today, 20 years later, people live there and no one gets sick. There is good food, good fish and everything grows. It is no longer a witchcraft island."

"These things marked the beginning of the revival. Demonic spirits were being chased out of our land."

More miracles

Albert was a young Christian during the crisis. He adds: "I now see, feel and walk on the power of God. I didn't know these things when I was a young Christian but I saw it in others. There were those who were operating on the high voltage power of God. These were people who would walk through a hail of bullets and not get hit. I would say that the host of heaven caught some of the bullets for me."

"There was one instance in 1993 when I was leading a group of chiefs from up in the mountains to sign a peace agreement. I was not doing this job of my own accord but because it was my job to do. I prayed to my God, "The fighting is all around us and I am a Christian. If You are going to go with me, talk with me tonight, Papa God. I don't want to lead them through the bullets."

"At 2 a.m., my elder son who was three spoke in English. He did not know English. He said, 'Daddy, Daddy, Daddy, you can go.' He was fast asleep. Fifteen years later, the memory still brings tears to my eyes and a reverent awe of God. This was not the time of meetings, conferences, mobile phones or encouragement. This was a hard time and we only had God."

"I woke up in the morning with peace. That day, 15 of the chiefs started to run back to the mountains. I told them that God was with us and that not one single man must run away even if there is gunfire. I told them that, if one runs, then the guns will get us but that if no one runs, we will all be safe."

"There was a place called Ambush Corner always maintained by BRA. They knew where I was taking these chiefs and why. They didn't want anyone to sign peace papers. I was in the front of the line. The Holy Spirit stopped me and I heard a voice tell me to take the chiefs to one side. I stopped them and said, 'We are about to enter Ambush Corner and I am afraid that there are people ready to kill us. However, last night, I felt the peace of God. Don't run but stand strong beside me.' We walked ahead and the BRA descended upon us. I said to them, 'In Jesus' name, I am a servant of God."

"They pointed their weapons to the sky and fired them off, then they pointed their guns at us but the guns wouldn't fire. The chiefs kept following me saying that the peace must come from God. The peace we enjoy today in Bougainville is because of that document."

"One time, I was holding my son on my shoulders going for a tramp. We came to a flooded river which was odd because there had been no rain so we took another route. Later I found out that there was an ambush waiting to kill us. The unnatural flood changed our direction."

During the late 1980s when war erupted, life was going on in its exotic daily routines in the jungle. Yet there was one clan leader who decided to stay in his village, 2 kms from the coastline and about 80 kms from Panguna Mine. Such villages were caught between flying bullets. Pastor Ezekiel made a home there he made called Aero Centre. Here are just a few stories that have been told directly to me some ten years since the guns were laid down.

A boy's story: "During the crisis, PNGDF men entered the little house I lived in with my mother. I was 12 years old. They demanded kerosene and food at gunpoint. My mother was a Christian and so she began to pray. They held a gun to her head but she said, 'No'. Kerosene was more valuable than gold for us. Without it, we couldn't run our home. The soldier pulled the trigger. The gun didn't go off. All this time, I watched my mother. They pulled the trigger a second time. The gun didn't go off. The soldier went outside our hut, pulled the trigger and it went off. The gun was loaded and it exploded. These soldiers realised that God was with my mother. They quickly ran away. We kept our kerosene."

By the time that 12 year old boy told me this story, he was a young man, yet the awe of God was still on him. He had witnessed his mother's faith in God and he is still walking in the fear of God.

Ruth, a vivacious school teacher recalls her experiences of being a woman during the crisis and the revival: "In the time of the crisis, God helped my family in a big way. We had no money to buy clothes, food and soap. God showed us how to use coconut and lemon to wash our clothes to make them white as snow. He showed us how to use coconut oil from our own coconut trees for our lamps. Before the crisis, we used to buy kerosene for our lamps. Now there was no money and no kerosene. Salt was also not available so He showed us how to cook our food in salt water from the ocean, adding grated coconut for our flavours. Sometimes we would boil the ocean water until all we had left was the powdery salt. In these ways, God showed me that He loved women in their domestic situation; that even in a crisis He could provide all we needed by looking after our clothes and our bodies."

"God also blessed the ground during the crisis. Food that we hadn't planted appeared – sweet potato, yam, taro, casava, chinese taro, banana and other fruit. This didn't just happen in one place. It happened all over the island. In fact, there is now a category of sweet potato called *crisis kaukau*!"

Jane: "When the crisis came, people ran away to the mountains leaving their chickens behind. It seemed that those chickens found their way to our village so we had plenty of meat for a long time during the crisis."

10 years after the surrender of guns, young men and women - some married with children - are going to great lengths to complete primary and secondary education. Schools are being built or re-built but teachers are few and often minimally qualified. Because of the crisis, those who should now be teaching are themselves still in formal education. Those educated be-

fore the crisis are helping those who are now study-ing. Those who are uneducated are making their living from working the cocoa plantations.

With no help from the neighbouring giant, Australia, and with the confusion and betrayal of brother fighting brother, they turned to God, sometimes praying from 6 in the morning to 6 at night. As the saying goes, "When God is all you have you find that He is enough."

Pastor Ezekiel Opet and his Wife, Jane

The head of the clan living in Aero Centre was, and still is, a remarkable man known everywhere as simply 'Pastor' and rightly so. He is generally regarded as a leader in the revival of the church in Bougainville. Eze-kiel is softly spoken and powerful in word. His wife is beautiful, equal to him in every way.

I asked Ezekiel, "Why did you stay in the village during the crisis instead of fleeing to the mountain jungles?"

He replied, "It was my pastoral responsibility. The presence of God came so close to us during those times. We had never experienced God before like this. It became a very big encouragement. It filled in the space where perhaps our neighbours - village by village and nation by nation - could have and should have been."

Pastor Ezekiel had been a United Church pastor since his training for the ministry. He had received the spiri-tual experience known as the Baptism in the Holy Spirit at the time of his salvation. This experience turns knowledge into spiritual energy and liturgy into dynamic power. Knowing *about* God is exchanged for knowing Him personally. Icy religion is melted by joy and hope. It was not surprising, therefore, that he became a key player in the revival in Bougainville.

Pastor Ezekiel was told to close down his Bible School. Because of the crisis, all of the schools on the island had been closed down and he was to comply. He refused. He said that it was not his place to close it down. God had opened it and God would have to shut it. He was viciously beaten as a result of this decision, and on a number of other occasions. Over 500 people, including many women, have graduated from his Bible School. Many are now missionaries in other countries.

Another extraordinary side effect of the crisis was the subsistence diet. Many times I have heard it said that they came out of the crisis 10 years younger than they used to be because all the refined food was taken out of their diet. They ate from the soil. "Our bodies got healthy and strong."

Prayer Mountain

A Prayer Mountain emerged deep into the crisis years. Its origins were mysterious and its role in the crisis and in the revival was equally other-world.

A contributing factor to the glory of God over Bougainville and to the revival has to have been this Prayer Mountain. In Bougainville and in other parts of the world, it is not uncommon for a geographical site to be set aside as a prayer mountain. However, when I began to hear stories of this one particular Prayer Mountain, I knew that God had met with this people in a rare manner, not unique, but certainly rare.

Pastor Ezekiel's strength and focus on God encouraged others to become giants in faith also. David Gagaso is one such giant. This strong and good looking young man with a soft, melodic voice was the one who received the word from God about this mountain.

David made a choice as a young man to live an uncompromising life of faith in Jesus Christ. He was diligent in his pursuit of spiritual things leading him to a series of miraculous experiences. Phenomena in the night sky, visions, and voices helped him locate a certain mountain on which he, his brother and friends built a bush house for prayer. This became known as Prayer Mountain. In the context of the chronology of the crisis, the Prayer Mountain phenomenon was most intense just prior to the final attempts by the Bougainville Revolutionary Army and Papua New Guinea to bring peace to the island.

He said, "In that bush house, the presence of God came down. The place was totally covered and filled with thick fog and smoke. We could hardly see other people in this little house. Pastor began using Prayer Mountain, hosting prayer seminars and prayer programs."

"We began to see manifestations of God. People began to receive songs and others saw angels. We were lost in prayer and fasting."

"If Pastor was going out to speak at a crusade, we would first go up the mountain to pray. Then, while he was speaking, people would stay on the mountain praying. My older brother saw an angel dressed in white."

"When people were disobedient, lightning would appear and wrap itself around the people. For instance, God had showed us how to build the house on Prayer Mountain. It was hard work. We cut the trees down the mountain and then carried the wood up the mountain to the place where we were building. One day, three men decided to go hunting instead of doing this hard work. The lightning appeared and wrapped itself around them. They nearly died. They smelt bad and could hardly speak. They were out of their senses. After an hour, they began to talk to each other, asking how they felt about the lightning. My brother told them the reason for the lightning - that they didn't follow instructions."

"In 1999, we replaced the bush house with one that had a tin roof. At the opening service for that house, I felt the presence of Jesus Christ as we were worshipping. Everyone was flat on the ground, face down. Even the musicians were on the ground with their instruments. It was an awesome incredible experience for me that I will never forget. We had to stop the whole service because we enjoyed God's presence so much. It took us a very long time to come back to the rest of the service. We could not pray or dance or sing but could only be flat on the ground before the presence of God."

"Normally before people set foot on Prayer Mountain, the sky would be clear. When people entered the prayer house, cloud would cover up the whole place even though there were no other clouds in the sky."

"We never slept at Prayer Mountain, but would always come back to the foot of the mountain to sleep."

"By 2004, we were not using Prayer Mountain any more. Until this present day, pig hunters who go up there still see footprints in the dusty floor of men walking inside the house of prayer. This is at least six years after the time of serious prayer. These are the footprints of angels who still enjoy the presence of God in that house."

David paused and then continued. "Our experience in the crisis produced people who can be involved in missions. We are not scared about any situation. We learn language easily; we eat anything or nothing; we sleep anywhere; we need nothing; we carry fire."

"I personally believe that God is going to raise up very aggressive missionaries from our island. One of the things I believe is that the Church should be involved in mission. Our Church in Bougainville is now reaping what we were planting up there in Prayer Mountain. We prayed for Africa and now we have missionaries there. Same with Indonesia. We are becoming the answer to our own prayers. I myself am about to go to a place that is not safe for Christians."

Jane took up the story. "Prayer Mountain was where the Spirit of God fell. Things happened that are foreign to the western mind."

"It started when we took Bible School students up to Prayer Mountain for a retreat. We planned to be there for two weeks, praying and fasting, before sending them out on a ministry trip."

"At the time of this two week stay on Prayer Mountain with the students, we were not thinking in terms of a revival. We were just being obedient to why we believed God had established Prayer Mountain."

"Soon, people were lifted up off the ground during worship and prayer. One girl was lifted up, flew past me and landed outside the building. Other students went through the wall, breaking it on their flight, landing outside."

"We tried to stop them; to quiet them down; to bring them back inside the building. But there was a fear of God and a fear of the unknown. We were afraid that if we stopped it, we would be touching something that was God."

"One time Ezekiel was up Prayer Mountain. On his way back to Aero Centre, he met two 'white men' who were glowing. They asked him where he was going. He said, 'Home' and then passed them. He turned around. They were gone."

"Another time a group were cleaning the building at the top of Prayer Mountain. They arrived to find footprints all around the house. You must understand that this is not a place where anyone lived and those on cleaning duty would have seen anyone leave the house on their way up the mountain. They knew straight away that these were the footprints of angels."

"I have to say that, even though we do not now go up the Prayer Mountain, the impact still remains. When we meet for worship, we don't need to be gee-ed up. Rather, we begin to worship God from the start. We are aware of the danger of following a routine or a program."

There is no doubt that this mountain played a crucial part in both the revival and in the beginning of the end of the crisis. Ezekiel's adds:

"Before Prayer Mountain, and into the second year of the crisis, people were singing worship songs to God. The sound of the singing was heard around the mountains."

"When it was time to be in church, people would run to the front of the church, casting themselves down on the smooth rocks that were alongside the front of the church. There were times when the dirt floor of the church was indented by the banging of heads in repentance and worship."

"Then came Prayer Mountain. We stopped at the bottom of the mountain to confess our sins and if we didn't do this well enough on the first stop, such conviction would come on us that we would stop again. Finally we would reach the prayer house at the top of the mountain and the presence of God would come down. We wouldn't talk but could only whisper because of the awareness of the Holy Spirit. The day came, after the building was completed, for its dedication. I put a big ceremony on the doors and then we went inside. When we were about to sing the first song we found that we couldn't stand. We were prostrate on the floor before God. Prophecy after prophecy came."

"We had not expected this. The prophecies spoke against the war. In fact, when the Peace-Keeping Forces arrived in Bougainville, God reminded us of the prophecies from that meeting. What is more, we were praying on Prayer Mountain when they arrived in Bougainville."

"Another time, the Holy Spirit showed Himself by thunder and lightning. I became aware that we needed to keep ourselves holy while on Prayer Mountain. Twice, lightning came and hit the ground. People tried to run away but a lightning bolt picked them up and rolled them all over Prayer Mountain. Seeing these things increased the fear of God."

"It was during this time, around 1995, that I returned from Fiji where I had completed a divinity degree at the theological college. A big hit of revival was happening at the mountain. One of the ladies, an unschooled woman who could not read or write, stood and told me to put knowledge aside and to learn from the Holy Spirit. Straight away, my ears were opened to hear the voice of the Holy Spirit. This was now 1996. When thunder came, she would write. When the thunder was over, she would stop writing. People would have to stand beside her to keep paper up to her, so fast was she writing. I was asked to read what she was writing to the people. I remember saying that these were words of encouragement to us during the time of crisis and that it was biblical."

"During the revival, people were writing songs prolifically. One of the great songs of the revival was:"

Lord I give my heart in worship as I stand in Your presence
I bow down and I say there is none like You
And my worship captures Your heart
And Your presence lifts me up
And takes me to Your holy place where I can commune with You.

Pastor Ezekiel told me of its final days. "By 1999, a prophetic message came that we had to leave the mountain. God began to speak from John 4:21-24. The message of those verses came to me as, *"I am no longer just in that mountain. Meet Me here as you met Me on the mountain."*

"This process of obedience gave us further under-standing of the holiness and presence of God. "We began to question God. "Why are we not experiencing what we experienced before?"

"Then God began to give us the understanding that Prayer Mountain was not just for ourselves but was for taking the Gospel to other people. He spoke to us about mission. Now we were to plant churches and experience things that used to only happen on Prayer Mountain. We have done this. For instance, we now even have missionaries in Africa."

"We had to learn about the omnipresence of God. Some young people went back to Prayer Mountain to try to get back what we had experienced but nothing happened. It was a time and a season and a place for a specific purpose."

"In 2000, we launched Christian Missionary Fellowship in Bougainville. We are now sending missionaries into PNG and to the rest of world."

1988 - March-April: Solomon Islands District, PNG (Jobson Misang)

Jobson Misang, an indigenous youth worker in the United Church reported in a letter on a revival movement in the Solomon Islands District of Papua New Guinea in 1988:

Over the last eight weekends I have been fully booked to conduct weekend camps. So far about 3,500 have taken part in the studies of the *Living in the Spirit* book.[12] Over 2,000 have given their lives to Jesus Christ and are committed to live by the directions of the Spirit. This is living the Pentecost experience to-day!

These are some of the experiences taking place:

1. During small group encounters, under the directions of Spiritfilled leadership, people are for the first time identifying their spiritual gifts, and are changing the traditional ministry to body ministry.
2. Under constant prayers, visions and dreams are becoming a day to day experience which are being shared during meetings and prayed about.
3. Local congregations are meeting at 4 am and 6 am three days a week to pray, and studying the Scriptures is becoming a day to day routine. This makes Christians strong and alert.
4. Miracles and healings are taking place when believers lay hands on the sick and pray over them.
5. The financial giving of the Christians is being doubled. All pastors' wages are supported by the tithe.
6. Rascal activities (crimes) are becoming past time events and some drinking clubs are being overgrown by bushes.
7. The worship life is being renewed tremendously.

The traditional order of service is being replaced by a much more lively and participatory one. During praise and worship we celebrate by clapping, dancing, raising our hands to the King of kings, and we meditate and pray. When a word of knowledge is received we pray about the message from the Lord and encourage one another to act on it with sensitivity and love.[13]

Problems encountered included division taking place within the church because of believers' baptism, fault finding, tongues, objections to new ways of worship, resistance to testimonies, loss of local customs such as smoking or chewing beetlenut or no longer killing animals for sacrifices, believers criticized for spending too many hours in prayer and fasting and Bible studies, marriages where only one partner is involved and the other blames the church for causing divisions, pride creeping in when gifts are not used sensitively or wisely, and some worship being too unbalanced.

This is a further example of a strong indigenous Spirit movement needing biblical teaching and guidance to avoid becoming a cult or sliding into error.

1988 - August: Kambaidam, Papua New Guinea (Johan van Bruggen)

Johan van Bruggen, a missionary at the Lutheran Evangelist Training Centre at Kambaidam near Kainantu in the Eastern Highlands of Papua New Guinea, wrote in his circulars:

> Tuesday afternoon, August 2, 1988: I was by myself watching a video of Bill Subritzky, an Anglican Evangelist in New Zealand, who has been mightily blessed by the Lord with ministries of healing and of deliverance from demons. A large group of Anglican Christians had been baptised in the Holy Spirit and were on the point of receiving gifts of the Spirit. I watched quite unemotionally when Bill said: "I will mention the gifts slowly and then just let the Holy Spirit impress on your mind which gift(s) he will give you."

> He had just started with the first one: Words of Wisdom when suddenly I was surrounded by Divine Presence. When it started I wanted to run away, scared stiff! But back came the words: Don't hold back, do not fear! So I stayed and said, "Come Holy Spirit, fill

me completely." *Now* I know what it is to be drunk in the Spirit. I couldn't stand on my feet. I slumped on the bed, hands raised, trembling all over, tingling all over. I felt something moving up my gullet and I just said, "Out, out," and I literally threw up. Don't worry, I didn't make a mess. I just got rid of the spirit of fear and doubt! And oh, I felt absolutely fantastic. I cried and laughed and I must have been quite a sight! It rained hard and that rain was a solid muffler! Nobody knew. I came around again because there was the noise of the video set with a blank screen. The programme was finished and I did not know how. I have had earlier fillings of the Holy Spirit but nothing like this time with that sense of being overwhelmed.

Then came Thursday, August 4, a miserable day weather wise, although we had great joy during our studies. Evening devotions not all students came, actually a rather small group. I too needed some inner encouragement to go as it was more comfortable near the fire. We sang a few quiet worship songs. Samson, a fellow who by accident became one of our students last year, well, this Samson was leading the devotions. We had sung the last song and were waiting for him to start. Starting he did, but in an unusual way. He cried, trembled all over! ... Then it spread. When I looked up again I saw the head prefect flat on the floor under his desk. I was praying in tongues off and on. It became quite noisy. Students were shouting! Should I stop it? Don't hold back! It went on and on, with students praying and laughing and crying not quite following our planned programme! We finally stood around the table, about twelve of us, holding hands. Some were absolutely like drunk, staggering and laughing! I heard a few students starting off in tongues and I praised the Lord. The rain had stopped, not so the noise. So more and more people came in and watched!

Not much sleeping that night! They talked and talked! And that was not the end. Of course the school
has changed completely. Lessons were always great,
I thought, but have become greater still. Full of joy
most of the time, but also with a tremendous burden.
A burden to witness. ...

What were the highlights of 1988? No doubt the actual outpouring of the Holy Spirit must come first. It
happened on August 4 when the Spirit fell on a group
of students and staff, with individuals receiving the
baptism of the Holy Spirit on several occasions later
on in the year. The school has never been the same
again. As direct results we noticed a desire for holiness, a hunger for God's Word which was insatiable
right up till the end of the school year, and also a tremendous urge to go out and witness. Whenever they
had a chance many of our students were in the villages
with studies and to lead Sunday services. Prayer life
deepened, and during worship services we really felt
ourselves to be on holy ground. ...

We have been almost left speechless by what God is
doing now through our students. We realize that we
have been led on and are now on the threshold of a
revival.[14]

A young student, David, in his early twenties from the
Markham Valley had a growing burden for his area of Ragizaria and Waritzian which was known and feared as the centre
of pagan occult practices. He prayed earnestly. As part of
an outreach team he visited nearby villages and then went to
his own people. He was concerned about the low spiritual
life of the church. He spent a couple of days alone praying
for them.

He was invited to lead the village devotions on the Saturday night at Ragizaria. Johan van Bruggen told the story in his circulars:

Since most of the Ragizaria people are deeply involved in witchcraft practices, David made an urgent appeal for repentance. Two men responded and came forward. David put his hands on them and wanted to pray, when suddenly these two men fell to the ground. They were both praising the Lord. Everybody was surprised and did not know what to think of this. David himself had been slain in the Spirit at Kambaidam in August 1988, but this was the first time that this had happened to others through him. The next morning during the Sunday service scores of people were slain in the Spirit. Said David, People entered the church building and immediately they were seized by God's power. They were drunk in the Spirit and many could not keep standing. The floor was covered with bodies. It did not only happen to Lutherans, but also to members of a Seventh Day Adventist congregation (former Lutherans) that were attracted by the noise and commotion.

David reported that there was a sense of tremendous joy in the church and people were praising the Lord. Well, the service lasted for hours and hours. Finally David said, "And now the people are hungry for God's Word and not only in my village, but also in Waritzian, a nearby village. And they want the students to come with Bible studies. Can we go next weekend?"

We all felt that some students together with Pastor Bubo should go. ...

Pastor Bubo told me, "Acts 2 happened all over again!" For three days all the people were drunk in the Spirit.

God used the students and Bubo in a mighty way. On Saturday night the Holy Spirit was poured down on the hundreds of people that had assembled there. From then on until the moment the school car arrived on Monday noon, the people were being filled again and again by the Spirit. There was much rejoicing. There were words of prophecy. There was healing and deliverance. And on Monday morning all things of magic and witchcraft were burned. Everybody was in it, the leaders, the young, yes even little children were reported to be drunk in the Spirit. ... The people did not want to go and sleep, saying, "So often we have had drunken allnight parties. Now we will have a divine party until daybreak."

This area had been a stronghold of evil practices. Many people received various spiritual gifts including unusual abilities such as speaking English in tongues and being able to read the Bible. People met for prayer, worship and study every day and at night. These daily meetings continued to be held for over two years.[15]

That revival kept spreading through the witness and ministries of the Bible School graduates. In November 1990, Johan van Bruggen wrote:

This is what happened about two months ago. A new church building was going to be officially opened in a village in the Kainantu area. Two of our last year=s graduates took part in the celebrations by acting the story in Acts 3: Peter and John going to the temple and healing the cripple.

Their cripple was a real one a young man, Mark, who had his leg smashed in a car accident. The doctors had wanted to amputate it, but he did not want to lose his useless leg. He used two crutches to move around the village. He could not stand at all on that one leg. He was lying at the door of the new church when our Peter and John (real names: Steven and Pao) wanted to enter. The Bible story was exactly followed: "I have got no money, but what I have I give you. In the name of Jesus Christ of Nazareth, rise up and walk!" Well, they acted this out before hundreds of people, among them the president of the Goroka Church District and many pastors and elders. Peter (Steven) grabbed the cripple (Mark) by the hand and pulled him up. And he walked! He threw his crutches away and loudly praised the Lord! Isn't that something? What a faith!

Their testimony was given at a meeting of elders when Kambaidam was discussed. Mark was a most happy fellow who stood and walked firmly on his two legs. He also had been involved in criminal activities, but in this meeting he unashamedly confessed his faith in the Lord Jesus.

Later I talked with them. Steven (Peter) told me that the Lord had put this on his heart during a weeklong period of praying. "I had no doubt that the Lord was going to heal Mark, and I was so excited when we finally got to playact!" And Mark? He told me that when Steven told him to get up he just felt the power of God descend upon him and at the same time he had a tingling sensation in his crippled leg: "I just felt the blood rushing through my leg, bringing new life!" Mark is now involved in evangelistic outreach and his testimony has a great impact.[16]

1988 - Madruga, Cuba

In 1988, revival broke out in a small church in Madruga, Cuba. "People would begin to weep when they entered the church," said their pastor. More than 60 churches experienced a similar move of the Spirit. And today the Holy Spirit's presence is still being felt. Despite gestures of tolerance towards Christians, believers in Cuba still experience much hardship and oppression. Nevertheless, God is moving amongst the 10 million people of Cuba, just as in the early church.

The revival produced more than 2,400 house churches more than all the official churches put together. Though open evangelism is still outlawed, teenagers were joining the children and adults to witness boldly in parks, beaches, and other public places, regardless of the risk.

There is a "holy and glorious restlessness" amongst the believers, said one pastor. "The once defensive mood and attitude of the church has turned into an offensive one, and Christians are committed to the vision of "Cuba Para Cristo!" Cuba for Christ![17]

1988 saw astounding revival. The Pentecostals, Baptists, independent evangelical churches and some Methodist and Nazarene churches experienced it. One Assemblies of God church had around 100,000 visit it in six months, often in bus loads. One weekend they had 8000 visitors, and on one day the four pastors (including two youth pastors) prayed with over 300 people.

In many Pentecostal churches the lame walked, the blind saw, the deaf heard, and many people's teeth were filled. Often 2,000 to 3,000 attended meetings. In one evangelical church over 15,000 people accepted Christ in three months. A Baptist pastor reported signs and wonders occurring continuously with many former atheists and communists testifying to God's power. So many have been converted that churches cannot hold them so they must met in many house churches.

In 1990, an Assemblies of God pastor in Cuba with a small congregation of less than 100 people meeting once a week suddenly found he was conducting 12 services a day for 7,000 people. They started queuing at 2 am and even broke down doors just to get into the meetings.[18]

1989 - Henan and Anhul, China

Dennis Balcombe, pastor of the Revival Christian Church in Hong Kong, regularly visits China.   He has reported on revival there.

In 1989, Henan preachers visited North Anhul province and found several thousand believers in the care of an older pastor from Shanghai. At their first night meeting with 1,000 present 30 were baptised in the icy winter. The first baptised was a lady who had convulsions if she went into water. She was healed of that and other ills, and found the water warm. A 12 year old boy deaf and dumb was baptized and spoke, "Mother, Father, the water is not cold, the water is not cold." An aged lady nearly 90, disabled after an accident in her 20s, was completely healed in the water. By the third and fourth nights over 1,000 were baptised.

A young evangelist, Enchuan, 20 years old in 1990, had been leading evangelistic teams since he was 17. He said, "When the church first sent us out to preach the Gospel, after two to three months of ministering we usually saw 2,030 converts. But now it is not 20. It is 200, 300, and often 600 or more will be converted."

Sister Wei, 22 years old in 1991, spent 48 days in prison for leading open air worship. She saw many healings in prison and many conversions.

On March 12,1991, *The South China Morning Post*, acknowledged there were a million Christians in central Henan province, many having made previously unheard of decision to voluntarily withdraw from the party. "While political activities are coldshouldered, religious ones are drawing large crowds."[19]

Dennis Balcombe reported in a newsletter on August 27, 1994: "This year has seen the greatest revival in Chinese history. Some provinces have seen over 100,000 conversions during the first half of this year. Because of this, the need for Bibles is greater than ever. This year we have distributed to the house churches over 650,000 New Testaments, about 60,000 whole Bibles, one million Gospel booklets and thousands of other books."

Revival continues in China with signs and wonders amid severe persecution, just as in the early church.

Tony Lambert[20] describes current revival in China:

> A genuine spiritual revival may be defined as occurring when:
>
> • The people of God are stirred to pray fervently for the low state of the church, and for the unconverted world.
>
> • Powerful preachers of the gospel are raised up by God to proclaim the gospel with unusual force.
>
> • The church is convicted of a deep sense of sin before a holy God.

- Individuals and churches repent of specific sins.

- A new sense of joy permeates the church, making the gospel and the things of God become real.

- The Christian church has a marked impact upon the surrounding community.

- God works visibly in supernatural ways.

Explosive revival continues in China. Estimates of the growth of the Chinese church now exceed 100 million. Only the United States has more Christians than China, but China would have the largest number of Spirit-filled, on-fire Christians in the world today.

Endnotes

[1] Adapted from "Benny Hinn" by Maureen Saaman, http://wwspn. com.

[2] Ron Steele, 1984, *Plundering Hell,* Sceptre, p. 55.

[3] This account is gathered from written and verbal reports by missionaries who attended that meeting, particularly Keith Bennet.

[4] Djiniyini Gondarra, 1991, *Let My People Go,* UCA, pp. 14-19; also 1993, *Renewal Journal,* No. 1.

[5] Richard Riss, 1995, internet research.

[6] John Wimber, 1994, "A Season of New Beginnings" in *Vineyard Reflections*, May/June. Publications (including earlier editions of *Flashpoints of* Revival!) have varied dates for this pivotal impact of the Spirit, but careful researchers identify it as 1980, the date of the cassettes of the service, not 1979 which Wimber had stated in his article originally, and which therefore was often reproduced incorrectly.

[7] Wimber, 1994.

[8] Ray Overend, 1986, *The Truth will Set you Free,* South Seas Evangelical Mission, pp. 9-10.

[9] Overend, pp. 36-37.

[10] Overend, pp. 23-24.

[11] Royree Jensen, 2009, *Sons of Thunder,* Royree Jensen Ministries.

[12] Geoff Waugh, 1987, 2009, *Living in the Spirit.*

[13] Jobson Misang, 1988, from a personal letter to Geoff Waugh.

[14] Johan van Bruggen, 1988-1990, from personal circulars.

[15] van Bruggen, 1989.

[16] van Bruggen, 1990.

[17] *Open Doors*, September, 1993.

[18] Stuart Robinson, 1992, *Praying the Price,* Sovereign World, p. 14.

[19] Newsletters from Dennis Balcombe, Hong Kong, 1991.

[20] Ron Davies 1992, *I will Pour out my Spirit,* Monarch, 24, citing Tony Lambert, 1991, *The Resurrection of the Chinese Church.*

Chapter 6

Final Decade, Twentieth Century
River of God Revival

Revival movements of the last decade continue to demonstrate specific impacts of the Spirit on Christian communities, often described as the River of God. These Spirit movements have been largely localised revivals affecting churches and local communities, particularly where churches co-operate in an area. Some local revivals have become influential worldwide, such as the ones in Toronto in Canada, Brompton and Sunderland in England, and Pensacola in North America.

1992 - Buenos Aires, Argentina (Claudio Freidzon)

Beginning from 1982, especially following the trauma of defeat in the Malvinas (Falklands Islands), revival stirred in Argentina. Large crowds attended meetings with Carlos Annacondia, a businessman turned evangelist. His healing evangelism included thousands reporting healings, deliverance from demons, and miracles including teeth being filled. Thousands of people accepted Christ as Saviour and virtually every church grew. Pastors meet every week to pray with Annacondia for revival in the nation and the world.

In 1992, another movement of revival began with Claudio Freidzon, founder of a Buenos Aires church that in four years has grew to 3,000 people. Freidzon experienced a deep encounter with the Holy Spirit, after which his ministry became famous for the manifested presence of God, long services of worship and adoration, and a dramatic increase of healings and deliverance in the worship and ministry.

A significant feature of Freidzon's ministry has been that people have received an unusual anointing when Freidzon laid hands on them and prayed for them. Their own ministries in turn became more effective in evangelism, healings and imparting anointings of the Spirit to others around the world.

Freidzon's ministry began small with much discouragement, but became global. He reports:

> For seven years my congregation stayed at seven people. During some worship services I was completely alone; not even my wife could be present. Sometimes other pastors who were friends of mine came to visit and would find me alone in the meeting. I felt like dying: I wished I could disappear. ...

> One day I thought, *This isn't for me. I'm going to give up this pastoral work. I'm going to resume my engineering studies and get myself a job*. But deep down I knew that was not God's plan.

> I visited the superintendent of my organization with the purpose of handing in my credentials. ... That day the superintendent spoke to me before I could tell him what I had come to see him about. "Claudio, I have something to say to you. God has something wonderful for you. You don't see it, but God is going to use you greatly." This man was not one to go round say-

ing such things. He continued, "Look - I started in a very precarious house and had no help from anybody. Sometimes I had nothing to eat and I suffered greatly. But we prayed and God provided for each day. We felt grateful. I knew we were doing God's will. And when I think of you, Claudio, I know you are going to be useful to God and that you are within His will. I don't know what your problems are, but keep on. By the way, what brings you here today?"

I put my credentials back into my pocket and said, "Well, nothing in particular. I thought I would just come by and share a moment with you." I couldn't say anything else. When I got home Betty was weeping. I said, "Betty, we're going to continue," and I embraced her tightly. We started all over again. ...

In 1985, I had a vision of God in my room. It must have been two or three o'clock in the morning. I was asleep. Suddenly God woke me up and showed me a vision on the wall, right before my eyes. I saw the picture of a public square in the district of Belgrano in Buenos Aires. The square was filled with people who were celebrating an evangelistic campaign similar to the ones that Carlos Annacondia undertook. And the Lord said to me, "This is your new field of work."[1]

Freidzon began holding meetings in Belgrano from February 1985. Immediately from the first meeting large umbers were converted and healed, including the crime boss in the area, to the astonishment of the police. Soon crime diminished as hundreds, then thousands, were converted in Freidzon's meetings. His church grew to over 4,000 in a decade.

The Argentinian revival ministries of Claudio Friedzon, Hector Giminez, Carlos Annacondia and Omar Cabrera have won

hundreds of thousands to the Lord. All of them have powerful ministries in evangelism with many signs and wonders,
healings and miracles. Not only do these and other evangelists make an astounding impact on the nation, but ordinary
people in hundreds and thousands are praying for revival in
Argentina and around the world.

Before the 'Toronto Blessing' erupted their church in Toronto,
Canada, John and Carol Arnott visited Argentina seeking a
fresh touch from the Lord. Various leaders prayed for them,
but so did converted prisoners, a significant example of the
current revival impact on crime and society. John Arnott reported:

> In La Plata, near Buenos Aires, there is a maximum
> security prison for 4,000 inmates. This prison was out
> of control, and basically run by gangs within the pris-
> on. But permission was given to hold meetings there.
> They had pastors who were given responsibility over
> the converts. This was under the auspices of Carlos
> Annacondia.
>
> Over a period of five years, a Christian floor developed
> in the prison, of eight hundred people. This floor had
> round the clock prayer meetings, and 180 people were
> always praying at any given time, waiting before the
> Lord, and asking God to have mercy. Over the course
> of five years, 600 men completed their sentences, and
> only one was later rearrested. Other prisoners always
> want to go to the Christian floor of the prison because
> it is safe and clean. They have corking on the bars to
> make things more comfortable. So others get saved
> as a result of going to the Christian floor. When they
> think they are ready, the prisoners apply to be trans-
> ferred to another prison, and then start some of the
> same things in other prisons.[2]

Describing Argentina as a flashpoint of revival, C. Peter Wagner, wrote:

Like a burning, dry tinder, the Spirit of God has ignited an extraordinary spiritual bonfire in Argentina over the last ten years. From the southern tip of Tierra del Fuego (Land of Fire) to breathtaking Iguazu Falls in the northeast, the flames of revival have blazed through Argentina and beyond, making the country one of the flashpoints of church growth in the world today....

Argentine evangelist Carlos Annacondia began his crusade ministry in 1982, the year of Argentina's defeat in the Malvinas, just as the Spirit of God began to spark spiritual renewal. Since then, over a million and a half people have made public commitments to Christ during the course of Annacondia's ministry.

Hector Giminez was a drug addicted criminal when God called him into the Kingdom. He began ministering to troubled youth; and within a year, was leading a congregation of 1,000. Since 1986, his church in downtown Buenos Aires has exploded in size to over 120,000 members, making it the third largest church in the world.

The world's fourth largest church is also in Argentina. Omar Cabrera and his wife Marfa began their ministry during the tough years of the 1970s. Long before most Argentine pastors, they began experiencing God's blessing as they learned the power of prayer to liberate people from sin, sickness, and the forces of evil. Now their church, centred in Santa Fe, ministers to 90,000 members in 120 cities.

The revival that began in the early 1980s has touched virtually every evangelical denomination. ... The stirrings of revival have drawn Argentine Christians into unprecedented forms of unity. ACIERA, the national association of evangelical Christian churches, and the monthly evangelical tabloid *El Puente* (The Bridge) has helped believers focus on common goals.[3]

Unprecedented unity, fervent prayer, and New Testament ministries of signs and wonders give Argentina's revival worldwide impact now. Leaders from around the world visit such flashpoints of revival, receive inspiration and impartation, and ignite others as they preach and pray in the power of the Holy Spirit, just as Jesus taught the disciples to do.

1993 - May: Brisbane, Australia (Neil Miers)

Jill Austin from Kansas City in America spoke at the pastors' conference for Christian Outreach Centre in New Zealand in April 1993 where Neil Miers, the President of Christian Outreach Centre, also spoke.

Jill Austin is a part of the prophetic ministry team at Metro Christian Fellowship, an independent church strongly influenced by the revival in Argentina. Their leaders have visited Argentina regularly and they have had Argentinian speakers in Kansas.

Neil Miers and Christian Outreach Centre leaders from the Pacific region were strongly impacted by the Spirit in New Zealand, causing drunkenness in the Spirit, visions, prophecies, laughter, tears, and people overwhelmed on the floor.

Neil and Nance Miers returned to Brisbane, Australia, their headquarters, to lead the national conference for their regional pastors. Neil preached at their headquarters church in Brisbane on Sunday night 2 May.

Darren Trinder, editor of their magazine *A New Way of Living* (now *Outreach*) reported,

> Some staggered drunkenly, others had fits of laughter, others lay prostrate on the floor, still more were on their knees while others joined hands in an impromptu dance. Others, although showing no physical signs, praised the Lord anyway, at the same time trying to take it all in. People who had never prayed publicly for others moved among the crowd and laid hands on those present.

> "When we first saw it in New Zealand early in April we were sceptical," said Nance Miers, wife of Christian Outreach Centre International President, Pastor Neil Miers. "I've seen the Holy Spirit move like this here and there over the years. But this was different. In the past it seemed to have affected a few individuals, but this time it was a corporate thing."

> Neil Miers himself was physically affected, along with several other senior pastors, early in this Holy Ghost phenomenon. Later he viewed the series of events objectively. "It started in New Zealand and then broke out in New Guinea, and now it's here. If I know the Holy Ghost, it will break out across the world wherever people are truly seeking revival. For the moment this is what God is saying to do, and we're doing it. It's that simple."

> But despite the informal nature of the events, Pastor Miers, adopting his shepherd role, was careful to monitor the situation. "There are some who are going overboard with it; just like when someone gets drunk on earthly wine for the first time. The next time it happens they'll understand it a little better."

God is doing many things. He's loosening up the church. He's working deep repentance in certain individuals, and healing deep hurts in others. Just like the outpouring in Acts, it was the public ministry that followed which really changed the world. First God has to shake up the church and then He uses these people to shake up the world.

Splashes of this revival have touched people's lives throughout the Christian Outreach Centre movement around the nation and the world.[4]

This unusual Spirit movement at Christian Outreach Centre in Brisbane affected people deeply for weeks. Office staff when prayed for were overwhelmed, resting on the floor, so sometimes the phones rang unanswered. The Bible College cancelled lectures as staff and students were powerfully affected, often "drunk in the Spirit". They had vivid visions, and prayed for others constantly. Children in the primary and high schools were similarly overwhelmed, saw visions, and worshipped and prayed as never before. Many people now in full time ministry were powerfully impacted then.

This fresh impact of the Spirit spread through the pastors to Christian Outreach Centres in every state of Australia within two weeks, and the Christian Outreach Centre movement continues to grow rapidly internationally, with over 200 churches in Australia and over 600 overseas. They have developed an international education facility from pre-school to tertiary offering accredited degrees in Education, Arts, Social Science, Business and Ministry to post-graduate level.

1993 - November: Boston, North America (Mona Johnian)

Another early version of the current revival, typical of hundreds, then thousands, around the world since, touched the Christian Teaching and Worship Centre (CTWC) in Woburn, Boston from November 1993. Mona Johnian and her husband Paul lead the 450 member church.

Revival broke out in their church after they attended revival meetings led by Rodney HowardBrowne in Jekyll Island Georgia, in November of 1993. At first, Mona was not impressed by the various phenomena she observed there, but she was surprised that her own pastor, Bill Ligon of Brunswick, Georgia, fell to the floor when Rodney Howard Browne laid his hands upon him. "Bill is the epitome of dignity, a man totally under control," she said. The first chapter of her book describes a meeting at her church in which revival broke out while Bill Ligon was there as a guest minister. From the Johnians' church, the revival spread to other churches, including Bath Baptist Church of Bath, Maine, pastored by Greg Foster.

In a video entitled Revival, produced in his church in August of 1994, Paul Johnian said, "We cannot refute the testimony of the Church. ... What is taking place here is not an accident. It's not birthed by man. It's by the Spirit of God. ... The last week in October of 1993, Mona and I went down to Georgia. We belong to a Fellowship of Charismatic and Christian Ministries International, and we went down there for the annual conference. And hands were laid on us. And we were anointed. And I'm just going to be completely honest with you. What I witnessed there in the beginning I did not even understand. I concluded that what was taking place was not of God ... because there was too much confusion. ... I saw something that I could not comprehend with my finite understanding. And it was only when I searched the Scriptures and asked God to show me and to reveal truth to me that I saw that what was taking place in the Body of Christ was a sovereign move of the Almighty. And I, for one, wanted to humble myself and be a part of the sovereign move of the Almighty. And I came back. I really didn't sense any change within me. But I came back just believing God that He was going to be doing something different in our congregation."[5]

That story has now been multiplied in various forms in thousands of churches touched by this current impact of the Spirit. This was one of the early reports of recent revival phenomena that then became well known from 1994.

1994 - January: Toronto, Canada (John Arnott)

One of the most widely publicised Spirit movements in the nineties began in a congregation of 120 in January, 1994. John Arnott, senior pastor at the Toronto Airport Christian Fellowship (then called the Toronto Airport Vineyard Christian Fellowship) tells about the beginnings of what they call the Father's blessing:[6]

In October 1992, Carol and I started giving our entire mornings to the Lord, spending time worshipping, reading, praying and being with him. For a year and a half we did this, and we fell in love with Jesus all over again. ...

We heard about the revival in Argentina, so we travelled there in November 1993 hoping God's anointing would rub off on us somehow. We were powerfully touched in meetings led by Claudio Freidzon, a leader in the Assemblies of God in Argentina. ...

We came back from Argentina with a great expectation that God would do something new in our church.

We had a taste of what the Lord had planned for us during our New Year's Eve service as we brought in 1994. People were prayed for and powerfully touched by God. They were lying all over the floor by the time the meeting ended. We thought, "This is wonderful, Lord. Every now and then you move in power." But we did not think in terms of sustaining this blessing.

We invited Randy Clark, a casual friend and pastor of the Vineyard Christian Fellowship in St. Louis, Missouri, to speak because we heard that people were being touched powerfully by God when he ministered. We hoped that this anointing would follow him to our church.

Yet, Randy and I were in fear and trembling, hoping God would show up in power, but uncertain about what would happen. We were not exactly full of faith but God was faithful anyway.

On January 20, 1994, the Father's blessing fell on the 120 people attending that Thursday night meeting in our church. Randy gave his testimony, and ministry time began. People fell all over the floor under the power of the Holy Spirit, laughing and crying. We had to stack up all the chairs to make room for everyone. Some people even had to be carried out.

We had been praying for God to move, and our assumption was that we would see more people saved and healed, along with the excitement that these would generate. It never occurred to us that God would throw a massive party where people would laugh, roll, cry and become so empowered that emotional hurts from childhood were just lifted off them. The phenomena may be strange, but the fruit this is producing is extremely good.[7]

People were saved and healed, more in the next two years than ever before. Other visitors experienced this renewal, discovering a new deep love for the Lord which they then passed on to others.

Word spread. Thousands flew or drove to visit the little church at the end of the runway at Toronto Pearson International Airport. The church had to relocate into larger premises. The blessing still continues. British journalists called this renewal the "Toronto Blessing" which soon became the term used worldwide.

Salvation. Healing. Release from oppression. Weeping. Laughter. New zeal for the Lord. Leaders impacted by the Spirit of God finding their own churches similarly impacted. These results have been reported by hundreds of thousands of visitors to Toronto.

It is controversial. As with all strong moves of God's Spirit, people react in many ways. The media highlight anything unusual or strange. However, the vast majority of people prayed for at Toronto report profound blessing, and in turn bless others with their zeal for God.[8]

Thousands of people continue to travel to Toronto and related centres of this renewal, its speakers are invited to many countries, and books and audio and video cassettes proliferate.

The Vineyard conferences of the eighties with John Wimber and his teams opened much of the conservative church to the importance of the supernatural in renewal and revival in what Peter Wagner described as the Third Wave. During the nineties the phenomena associated with Rodney Howard-Browne and Toronto spread widely in western churches involved in renewal.

Now, after more than five years of the spread of this renewal and its pockets of revival this Spirit movement has demonstrated enduring renewal of hundreds of thousands of Christians and the beginnings of revival influences in the community with conversion and social transformation. Toronto in Canada, Sunderland in England, and Pensacola in North America have become the most visible centres where renewal in the church has begun impacting the community with conversions and affecting crime rates and social order.[9]

It is likely to be recorded, like Azusa Street, as a pivotal event in transmitting revival phenomena around the world, raising the expectation and experience of millions of people concerning authentic Spirit movements in revival leading into a fresh awakening.[10]

On every continent, except Antarctica, revival has been occurring with thousands coming to Christ and thousands of new churches started. By 2010, some of the fruit by associated with Toronto, not including what happened in Pensacola, Florida or in Rodney Howard Browne's meetings, include about 3,500,000 salvations and scores of thousands of new churches started in Mozambique, Brazil, Asia, and the Middle East. About 1,000,000 were through the ministry of Rolland and Heidi Baker in Mozambique. By the end of 2010, another

800,000 people in a Muslim country were saved through the ministry of Leif Hetland. Both Heidi and Leif were powerfully touched by the Holy Spirit when Randy Clark laid hands upon them. In addition, an estimated 1,500,000 more salvations came through many others who either were touched powerfully in Toronto or by someone who came from Toronto. For example, Henry Madava of Kiev, Ukraine received a powerful impartation when Randy Clark laid hands upon him and prayed for Henry and his church. Henry saw over 60,000 people saved the first year after this impartation. His meetings have since increased and conservatively about 900,000 people have been saved in his healing evangelistic crusades. Like Leif and Heidi there is an important dimension of healing to their evangelistic harvest. The other 600,000 would consist of people saved through the ministries of the many itinerates who have gone out from key leaders who were touched in Toronto.

The night before Randy Clark went to Toronto, he received a personal prophecy from Richard Holcomb, a Texas land developer whom God used in Randy's life during the preceding 10 years. The prophecy follows: "Randy, the Lord says, 'Test me now, test me now, test me now. Do not be afraid, I will back you up. I want your eyes to be opened to see my resources for you in the heavenlies, even as Elisha prayed for Gehazi's eyes to be opened. And, do not become anxious because when you become anxious you can't hear me.'" The prophecy created such a strong expectation of a visitation from God in Toronto that it still brings encouragement to Randy today.

Randy served as the Evangelist used to birth the Toronto Blessing. For the next 60 days he would minister 42 days for John Arnott, either in Toronto or in one of the other seven churches in Ontario. Wherever he went, extended meetings broke out. This was the strategy of John Arnott to make more room in the store-front church where the awakening broke out.

John Arnott asked Randy Clark several times become the full-time evangelist in Toronto as Steve Hill was in Pensacola, FL. However, Randy never felt this was the will of God for him. Instead, he felt called to take what God was doing in Toronto all over the world.

These extended, 6 nights a week meetings would continue for twelve and one half (12 ½) years in Toronto, becoming the longest protracted meeting in the history of the Western Hemisphere.[11]

1994 - May: London, England (Eleanor Mumford)

The Anglican Church, Holy Trinity Brompton (HTB) near Kensington in London has been powerfully affected by the current awakening and widely reported in the media.

Eleanor Mumford, assistant pastor of the SouthWest London Vineyard and wife of John Mumford (the pastor and the overseer of the Vineyard Churches in Britain), told a group of friends about her recent visit to the Toronto Airport Vineyard in Canada. When she prayed for them the Holy Spirit profoundly affected them.

Nicky Gumbel, Curate of Holy Trinity Brompton, was there. He rushed back from this meeting with his wife, Pippa, to the HTB church office in South Kensington where he was late for a staff meeting. The meeting was ready to adjourn. He apologised, told what had happened, and was then asked to pray the concluding prayer. He prayed for the Holy Spirit to fill everyone in the room.

The church newspaper, "HTB in Focus," 12 June 1994, reported the result:

> The effect was instantaneous. People fell to the ground again and again. There were remarkable scenes as the Holy Spirit touched all those present in ways few had ever experienced or seen. Staff members walking past the room were also affected. Two hours later some of those present went to tell others in different offices and prayed with them where they found them. They too were powerfully affected by the Holy Spirit many falling to the ground. Prayer was still continuing after 5 p.m.[12]

The church leaders invited Eleanor Mumford to preach at Holy Trinity Brompton the next Sunday, 29 May, at both services. After both talks, she prayed for the Holy Spirit to come upon the people. Some wept. Some laughed. Many came forward for prayer and soon lay overwhelmed on the floor.

Multiplied hundreds of cassette tapes of those services circulated in many hundreds of churches in England. A fresh awakening began to spread through the churches involving over 7,000 churches in England alone, and spreading through Europe and internationally through visitors to centres of renewal and revival. These are some of Eleanor Mumford's comments:

> A Baptist pastor [Guy Chevreau], was involved in this remarkable move of the Spirit of God which seems to be taking place in eastern Canada. He's written this: "At meetings hosted by the Airport Vineyard, Toronto, there has come a notable renewal and revival of hope and faith and of expectation. Over the past eighteen weeks, now about 130 days consecutively, the Spirit of God has been pouring out freedom, joy,

and power in the most remarkable ways. Six nights a week," because they take a day off for Monday, six nights a week "between 350 and 800 people at a time gather for worship, testimony and ministry. Rededications are numerous. Conversions are recently being witnessed and ministry to over 2,000 pastors, clergy, and their spouses has been welcomed by a diverse cross-section of denominational leaders." ...

And with all of this there has come a renewing of commitment, and enlarging and clarification of spiritual vision, and a rekindled passion for Jesus and for the work of His kingdom. Some of the physical manifestations accompanying the renewal are unsettling for many people, leaving them feeling that they have no grid for evaluation and no map to guide them, which is a sort of safe way of saying there are very bizarre things going on. ...

And so when I went forward on the first night, because they said on the first night, "Anyone who's not been here before we'd like you to come first for us to pray for you." And I went up unapologetically and the lovely pastor said to me, "What would you like? What are you here for?" And I said, "I want everything that you've got. I've only got two days, and I've come from London," sort of defiantly. And behind this I was saying, "I've paid the fare and I'm determined to get my money's worth. So what will you do?" ...

The whole climate of this thing is surrounded with generosity. God has poured His Spirit out on a people in an improbable little church, and they are now spending their time from morning to night giving away as fast as they can what God is giving to them. And as new people hit town, and as pastors hover across the horizon, they sort of savour as if it were fresh meat and they just long to come to you and lay their hands on you and give you all that God has given them, which I take to be a mark of the Lord. I just take it to be the generously of Jesus to His people. ...

These are ordinary people ministering in the name of an extraordinary God. And their pastor, John Arnott has said, "God is just using nameless and faceless people to minister His power in these days." And that's what I love. There is no personality attached. There's no big name involved. There's no one church that's got a corner in the market. This is something that Jesus is doing. And the people and the church are simply preoccupied with the person and the power of the Lord Jesus. No personalities. Just Him. And I love that, because I'm tired of all that stuff. I'm tired of the heroes and the personalities. I just want Jesus. I just want Him and His Church straight. And that's what I think I received. I saw the power of God poured out, just as it was in the books of Acts, and as I said this morning, I didn't see tongues of flame, but I suspect it was because I wasn't looking. And I have heard recently in this country of a meeting which took place where the Spirit of God was poured out and the building shook. The building shook, and three separate witnesses quite independently, came home and said the building actually shook. So we're in the days of the New Testament. This is kingdom stuff, and it's glorious. But it's not new.

And so I scurried back to Scripture and I scurried back to Church history and I have discovered glorious things in the writings of Jonathan Edwards, who was the initiator of the Great Awakening in America during the mideighteenth century, and he wrote this, which is remarkably similar to what I saw in Toronto just last week, two weeks ago. "The apostolic times seem to have returned upon us. Such a display has there been of the power and the grace of the Spirit." Jonathan Edwards speaks of extraordinary affections of fear, sorrow, desire, love, joy, of tears, of trembling, of groans, loud cries, and agonies of the body, and the failing of bodily strength. He also says we are all ready to own that no man can see God and live. If we, then, see even a small part of the love and the glory of Christ, a very foretaste of heaven, is it any wonder that our bodily strength is diminished? ...

I have discovered a new heroine in the last few days, who is the wife, or was the wife, of Jonathan Edwards. And she was a very godly and wonderful woman. And she fell under the power of the Spirit of God to such a degree in the 1740s, that for seventeen days, she was insensible. She was drunk for seventeen days. She could do nothing. (Now the Baptist pastor in Toronto had had to do all the school runs and all the school picnics for two days, because his wife was out for the count for fortyeight hours. And he was driving, and he was packing the lunches, and he was doing their homework he was doing everything and he said, "God, when are you going to lift off my wife, so that this home can get back into order?") But poor Jonathan Edwards had seventeen days in which his wife was insensible. And on one occasion she decided it was time to arise from the bed and to try and minister to the household, and they had a guest. So she got dressed in her best . . . and she went downstairs and lurching a little while, and as she passed the study where the door was open and Jonathan Edwards was talking to his friend about the Lord, as she heard the name of Jesus, her bodily strength left her, and she hit the floor. So they carried her back to bed, and there she stayed. And as it's said in the history books, no one recorded who made the lunch. So this thing is taking people over in the most remarkable way. And at the end of this time, Jonathan Edwards' wife said, "I was aware of a delightful sense of the immediate presence of the Lord, and I became conscious of His nearness to me, and of my dearness to Him." And I think it's this one phrase that has impressed itself upon my Spirit in the last week, and what I think is the key to this whole thing, is that the Lord in His mercy is pouring out His Spirit in order to persuade us, His people, of "His nearness to me, and of my dearness to Him." ...

I heard a story just this afternoon of a woman who had left a meeting rather as I had done, but she was reeling, and unwisely, she decided to drive home. This was all over the place, and she was stopped by the police. Honest to God, this is true. She was stopped by the police, and she got out of the car, and the policeman said, "Madam, I have reason to believe that you're completely drunk." And she said, "Yes, you're right." So he said, "Well, I need to breathalyse you," so he got his little bag, and as she started to blow into it, she just fell to the ground laughing. At which point, the policeman fell, too, and the power of God fell on him, and he and she were rolling on the freeway laughing under the power of God. And he said, "Lady, I don't know what you've got, but I need it," and he came to church the next week and he found Jesus. He got saved.

And this is happening. People are going out and telling each other about Jesus with a recklessness that they've never known before. I don't know about you, but when people say 'evangelism' the hairs in the back of my neck go up and I get guilt and I feel awful and I feel destroyed and defeated. Evangelism is a breeze, people. It's such fun like this. So there was a woman who had left one of the meetings and she had been laughing on the floor for two hours, and she got really hungry. So she went to the Taco Bell ... and she sat down ... and she looked across, and she saw a whole family eating burritos. And she said to them, ... "Do you want to be saved?" And they all said, "Yes!" All of them! And they were all saved and led to Christ on the spot.

And another man left a meeting and he went into a restaurant, and a man was watching him, and for about ten minutes, he watched him. And he had this ... young man who came up to him and said, "Excuse me, but are you a Christian?" And this chap had just left the meeting he said, "You bet." And he said, "Well, my wife has just left me. I've just lost my home. I've just lost my job, and I'm about to take my life. ... What can help me?" And he led him to Christ. And ... this is good news, people. This is news for the people out there. People are getting saved right and left. And they are now discovering even in the Toronto area that there are several hundreds of people that are getting saved. People right and left are coming to know Jesus, because Jesus is the joy of our lives. It's a wonderful, wonderful thing. ...

People are being restored by the mercy and the sweetness of God. And, quite honestly, whether one stands or falls, whether one laughs or cries, whether one shakes or stands still, whether you go down could matter not, it just doesn't matter a bit. It doesn't matter how you go down. What matters is how you come up.

It doesn't matter what goes on in the outside. What counts is what Jesus is doing in our bodies and in our souls, in our hearts and in our spirits.

We have a woman in my prayer group who is a hair dresser. And she's married to a Muslim, and her life is not easy. And she said that in the course of the last week, she's been reading her Bible like never before. But she said, "I'm not reading it." She said, "I hear the voice of Jesus reading it to me. As if I were a child, Jesus reads me His book." Wonderful things. ...

I think if we come receptive and childlike, there is infinite blessing for the people of God at this time. I've discovered in myself a love for Jesus more than ever. I've discovered in myself an excitement about the kingdom I wouldn't have believed possible. I've discovered that I'm living in glorious days. There's no other time; there's no other place where I would have chosen to be born and to live than here and now.[13]

The church newsletter describing that Sunday's services circulated widely and triggered publicity in the media. Crowds flocked to the church in the following weeks including large numbers of church leaders involved in charismatic renewal, especially Anglican and other denominational ministers. A HTB staff member referred to the 'Toronto Blessing' a term the media quickly adopted to describe this enthusiasm and fervour for God. This renewal, refreshing or touch of revival has been reported often as spreading to over 7,000 churches in England within two years.

Another significant initiative emerging from HTB is the charismatically based Alpha course prepared by Nicky Gumbel in 1993, revised in 1995. This 10-14 week introduction to Christianity includes sessions on being filled with the Spirit and gifts of the Spirit such as healing. HTB's leadership in Anglican charismatic renewal has helped spread the Alpha course to over 14,000 locations in 105 countries by 1999 including 640 Alpha courses in New Zealand and 1,000 in Australia.

Along with other expressions of the deep impact of God's Spirit, this blessing helps to bring fresh vitality to Christian life and witnessing around the world. The huge influence of 'HTB' stems from its leadership in charismatic Anglican churches and its prestige asan historic church in Kensington in the heart of London. Its leadership has shown statesmanship in nurturing this renewal in the churches, and its influence through the Alpha course continues to proliferate.

1994 - August: Sunderland, England (Ken Gott)

Ken and Lois Gott founders of Sunderland Christian Centre (SCC) in 1987 in the northeast of England, felt dry and worn out in 1994. Ken Gott and four other Pentecostals visited Holy Trinity Brompton in London. The presence of God among Anglicans humbled and amazed those Pentecostals. Bishop David Pytches prayed for them and they caught new fire. Their Sunderland church then sent Ken, Lois and their youth leader to Toronto for a week of soaking in God's anointing.

> On August 14th, the first Sunday morning back from Toronto, the effect on the church was staggering. Virtually the whole congregation responded to Ken's appeal to receive the same touch from God that he and Lois had received. They decided to met again in the evening, although normal meetings had been postponed for the summer recess. The same experience occurred. They gathered again the next evening and the next ... in fact for two weeks without a night off. Quickly, numbers grew from around a hundred

and fifty to six hundred. Word reached the region and, without advertising, people began the pilgrimage to Sunderland from a radius of around 70 miles.

By September a pattern of nightly meetings (bar Mondays) was established and each night the same overwhelming sense of God was present. That pattern has continued ever since, with monthly leaders' meeting on a Wednesday or Thursday afternoon (with usually around 300 in attendance) and a daily 'place' of prayer being added.

The effect on many churches and on thousands of individuals has been profound.[15]

The church began two meetings a day with a daily afternoon prayer meetings from January 1995. Many former criminals were saved, and crime dropped in the community. Within two years a youth group of 60 former criminals had been established in the church, led by 'Jim and Marie' a converted criminal and his wife.

Philip Le Dune, an associate pastor at Sunderland, sent this email message in August, 1996:

Sunderland Christian Centre is located in a high density low cost housing area with all the problems associated with inner city deprivation. Prior to the start of Renewal we had had very little contact with the local population, and gave very little indication that we really wanted anything to do with them! The church was heavily protected against burglary with shutters and polycarbonate windows, and a high security fence and video cameras helped the security guards protect the cars not a very welcoming sight to any would-be church attenders from the area. Our neighbours saw us turning up in our nice cars, wearing our smart clothes and carrying big black bibles. Many of the on lookers had no car, no nice clothes and some had no food.

Renewal has changed us forever. When God pinned a local gangster to the floor of the church one evening, only God knew that he was soon to be employed by the church, together with his wife, as youth workers. Jim & Marie now hold daily "meetings" with the people from the local community who are increasingly coming to see SCC as "theirs".

Recently the atmosphere in the youth club, held up-stairs in the church hall while the Renewal meetings are held in the sanctuary downstairs, changed significantly. The youths, many of whom are already well experienced in criminal activities, had begun to take less interest in the usual youth club activities like pool and became much more interested in the ministry time that Jim & Marie had introduced. Last week all of the kids decided to stay behind for prayer and the Holy Spirit turned up! One young lad, aged about 12, called Billy received prayer, and the Holy Spirit laid him out on the carpet.

Billy is notorious in the area and is considered by many, including his social workers to be beyond control. He has tried to break in to the church on numerous occasions and has been involved in petty theft as well as assaulting members of the church staff! Despite this he has been welcome to join with his peers in the youth meeting and has been enjoying himself! Jim asked him, "Why do you come out for prayer Billy?" and he replied, "It's the only time in the week I feel clean."

A few days ago three teenagers turned up one evening to the youth meeting. They were well known as "hard cases" in the community and they stood at the bottom of the stairs mocking Jim and his team and calling them "Bible bashers" and other less savoury names! Jim invited them up, but when it came to ministry time they stayed put in their seats, laughing at the others who were receiving prayer. Jim called them out. "I'm going to pray for you three now," he said. "What are you going to do?" they asked. "I'm going to do nothing. I'm not even going to touch you. I'm just going to pray and the Holy Spirit is going to do the rest."

Jim began to pray and the three of them froze. After 16 minutes, with everyone else having left the room Jim came back and the three of them were still standing stock still, eyes closed in total silence. When they came round one of them said, "Well, what can you say? Now I know that God exists, but what do I do about it?" Jim was able to explain what he should do and he went away with a lot to think about, but came back the next night saying, "I want Jim to pray for me again!"

One of his two companions described how he had felt hands pressing on his chest and face but when he'd opened his eyes there was noone there. The other said he felt like he'd been "pulled in all different directions inside".

Keep praying, as this is surely the start of the Youth Church that we want to establish here in Sunderland.[16]

The awakening or refreshing or renewal which impacted Sunderland Christian Centre also spread to churches across Europe and as visitors from around the globe visited them and as they took teams to many countries, that same fire ignited people and churches worldwide. Then 1995 saw a further explosion of revival fire.

1994 - November: Mt Annan, Sydney, Australia (Adrian Gray)

Pastor Brian Shick, a member of the staff at Christian Life Centre Mount Annan, Sydney, reported on the beginning of this renewal in their church in November, 1994, where Adrian and Kathy Gray are the senior pastors.

> Having desired for some time to find a permanent home for the church which Adrian and Kathy Gray have pastored since February 1975, the current property was purchased in 1984 … An outstanding prophetic sign occurred a short while before this outpouring took place when a helicopter flying over the church called the fire department reporting our building on fire. Thirteen fire trucks screamed up the church driveway looking for the fire to extinguish, but there was no fire. When the realisation came that it was a spiritual fire that had been witnessed great awe came upon the church. This happened at the conclusion of ten days of prayer and fasting for revival.

> At the arrival of the move of the Holy Spirit on the first weekend of November 1994, like the church in Toronto, Canada could only be described as sovereign. Randwick Baptist Church, which is in more central Sydney, experiencing the same outpouring at exactly the same time testifies to the reality of it being a sovereign event. In fact there were numbers of churches around the nation that experience a similar occurrence about the same time.

For many months the church had been praying for a visitation of God without perhaps really realising what that meant. An evangelistic crusade with an "end-times emphasis" had been planned for that weekend. The evangelist, recently returned from Toronto, Canada, preached his evangelistic message and called people forward who wanted a fresh touch from God. Immediately over 300 people responded and as the evangelist and pastors prayed the presence of God came. The Father's heart of love was revealed to the people and as hands were gently laid on them they fell to the floor under the anointing of the Holy Spirit. They lay there for a long time and when they got up there were dozens of amazing testimonies of healing and restoration and life changing transformations. The next day, Sunday, the Holy Spirit came again, and then again on Monday and Tuesday and in every meeting held since that time. The anointing was so strong that many people in those first months would fall to the floor as soon as they came through the door.

Renewal did not just become an appendage to the existing program, it became the entire program. The Holy Spirit is free to move however he wants in any of the services. While most pastors would say that this is the case in their churches, many have actually limited the style of meeting that is characteristic of this current move, to one or two services a week and the other meetings are "normal".

Mid week services were started almost immediately and have continued. These are held Wednesday 10:30 a.m. and 7:30 p.m. and Friday 7:30 p.m. On Saturday nights there is a youth service at 7:30 p.m. There is also the Waves of Power International Ministry School at 7:30 p.m. on Tuesday nights. These services and the ministry school attract many people from other denominations much like the renewal/revival meetings around the world. Every occasion that the church gathers is a revival time.

Approximately 200,000 people have attended in the first four years since the outpouring began. The official membership has grown from 300 prior to renewal to 700 at present. With all the services added together, 1,200 people are ministered to per week with many more during conferences.[17]

The church emphasises team and 'body ministry' - the whole body of Christ using all the spiritual gifts. In four years the staff expanded from three to nineteen full and part-time members. The youth group expanded from 25 to 90. Their predominantly lay pastoral care team involves 60 people and the worship team involves 90 people.

The church has a prayer ministry team of approximately 120 members who are trained to pray for people at the five services each week and at the various conferences. They hosted around 20 conferences over in the first four years, bringing international revival speakers within the reach average believers here in Australia.

Whereas the similar Spirit movement in the Christian Outreach Centres of May 1993 touched mainly that movement and was regarded by other churches as rather excessive, this Spirit movement in an established Pentecostal church found greater acceptance within pentecostal groups, attracting visitors from around the nation.

1994 - November: Randwick, Sydney, Australia (Greg Beech)

Another outpouring of the Spirit transformed the mildly charismatic Randwick Baptist Church in Sydney the same weekend. The minister, Greg Beech, discussed this in their church magazine a year later, reporting on these events:

> Many Christians are talking about a significant work of God that is sweeping the church today which has become known as the *Toronto Blessing*. At Randwick Baptist Church (hereafter RBC), some of these phenomena have been present in lesser degrees for about nine years. They occurred spontaneously and without prompting or discussion.
>
> Late 1993 and the first seven or eight months of 1994 had been a considerable time of change for RBC involving difficult decisions, change of staff, relational tensions, loss of some members, and a rethink of the church's vision. The 'ship' of the church had slowed and was making a careful, yet sure change, in direction.

Factors leading up to the outpouring at RBC include :

- A gradual renewal of the church's prayer life with new prayer meetings and a number of people joining the 'prayer watch'.

- A four month teaching series on the Holy Spirit was undertaken on Sunday evenings.

- A stronger sense of 'grace' in the church.

- A sense of expectation. We had been feeling spiritually dry for sometime. We believed in the work of the Spirit but were not seeing much power. A sense of a new day dawning.

- A couple in the church visited Toronto and were dramatically touched by the Holy Spirit. Upon arriving home on 1st November they prayed for some of us. We were powerfully ministered to. They also brought back from Toronto some resources, in particular three videos. Watching one of these I was touched with joy by the Holy Spirit.

- Sunday, 6th November, was a remarkable day for a number of reasons. In the early morning prayer meeting there was a sense of expectation. At the worship service an American Pastor, Roy Kendall and his family, (who pastor a church in Jerusalem) led a wonderful time of praise. Roy spoke on the subject of praise including a word about spiritual dryness, and thirst for God. A number of people received ministry after that service but it wasn't until the evening service that we saw power being poured out. Chris Acland preached on Isaiah 55, Steve and Cathy testified on their experience in Toronto, and afterwards we saw some of the signs that have since increased in intensity and breadth.

We recognise and wish to emphasise that the outpouring was not so much a result of anything we did but was a sovereign movement of God. The outpouring seems to have transferred from the Toronto Airport Vineyard, and is being transferred to churches around the world. We have been thrilled to learn of other churches in Sydney also being touched.

While we had prayed for the outpouring of the Spirit, it still caught us by surprise! The sheer intensity and broad sweep of the Spirit's work has been staggering.

The current refreshing is not some kind of new 'latest and greatest' programme which has been introduced to revitalize church services. The 'refreshing' is not something that pastors introduce to see if new life can be breathed into their church. We believe what we are witnessing is a sovereign work of the Holy Spirit. It was with considerable amazement that we stood back and watched God pour out His Spirit in November 1994 at R.B.C. We found it difficult to come to terms with the sheer power and intensity of God's work.

For over a year we have pastored this movement, prayed for discernment, discussed, theologized, debated with our critics, searched the Scriptures, and carefully watched and examined the fruit. We are convinced this is a true work of God. However, we acknowledge that any work of God which involves a human element, will encounter sinful tendencies, perhaps demonic attack, and therefore must be carefully dealt with.

There are a number of 'streams' of refreshment and renewal that God is using around the world. For example, God is using the Toronto Airport Vineyard to refresh his church. We have been greatly blessed by them although we ask that people assess RBC based on what we teach and practice, not on what another church does. Each stream of the movement needs to be assessed on its own merits. The conclusions and positions we have reached, both in theology and practice, may well be rejected by other churches. We do not believe that ours is the only orthodox position.[18]This

Spirit movement gained significance as one of the first of the current revival phenomena reported in an Australian denominational church. As such it stirred considerable press interest. A broadening stream of personal and church witnesses testify to the significance of this Spirit movement for personal and church growth and life.

1995 - January: Melbourne, Florida, North America (Randy Clark)

Five local churches in Melbourne, Florida, invited Randy Clark as guest speaker at the Tabernacle Church on Sunday, 1 January, 1995. Unusual revival broke out including large numbers falling down, laughter, weeping, and many dramatic physical healings. Thousands flocked to meetings held six days a week. Pastors and musicians from fifteen different congregations hosted the meetings in a new expression of cooperation and unity. Randy Clark reported:

In 1994 I spent about 150 [days] in renewal meetings. During that time I never was in a meeting which I felt had the potential to become another Toronto type experience. That was until I went to Melbourne, Florida [on] January 1, 1995. Another revival has broken out. Many sovereign things have occurred which indicate this place too will be [the site of] unusual renewal meetings. I shall share some of these.

First, what made me expect something special at these meetings? I never schedule over four days for meetings, but I scheduled fifteen days for this meeting. Why? I believed there were things going on which indicated a major move of the Spirit was imminent. The Black and White ministerial associations merged a few months prior to my going. The charis-matic pastors had been meeting together for prayer for six years, and pastors from evangelical and char-ismatic and pentecostal churches had been meeting and praying together for over two years. There was a unity built which would be able to withstand the pres-sures of diverse traditions working together in one re-newal/revival meeting.

The meetings are held at the Tabernacle, the largest church in the area. It holds 950 comfortably. This was Jamie Buckingham's church, now pastored by Michael Thompson. The church sanctuary is filled by 6:15 with meetings beginning at 7:00. About 1,200 are crowded into the sanctuary, another 150 fill a small overflow room, and another 200-300 sit outside watching on a large screen.[19]

Staff of the Christian radio station WSCF, FM 92 at Vero Beach, Florida, an hour's drive south of Melbourne, inter-viewed Randy Clark on Friday, 6 January, 1995. The General Manager of the radio station, Jon Hamilton, reported on that visit. The report is significant concerning the specific impact of the Spirit on the staff and the subsequent impact on listen-ers and on the community including impacting unchurched people. Hamilton reports as an experienced, mature, scepti-cal, cautious participant-observer:

January, 1995
Dear Friend of Christian FM 92:

I had already put the finishing touches on my first let-ter of 1995. I really liked it. It was full of optimism and inspirational resolutions for the New Year.

It will never make it to the printer.
Instead, I am compelled to offer to you a testimony

and witness as to a most remarkable day. I pray that it may serve to encourage those who seek God, and terrify those who oppose Him.

January 6, 1995 began in a rather ordinary way. It was Friday, it had been a busy week, but I was looking forward to a slow day. As I was leaving the house, I actually told my wife, "There's not much on my calendar, I may try to take the afternoon hours off and come home early."

I had agreed to interview a pastor from St. Louis, Randy Clark that morning. Randy was the guest speaker at The Tabernacle Church's renewal services nightly, and since "The Tab" is a good friend of FM 92 (and many other area churches were participating in the meetings), we had decided to clear a slot on the morning show for a brief interview.

My guest was one of the leaders of the socalled "Toronto Revival". I had read about the Toronto meetings, but frankly, I've heard a lot of "revival rumours" over the years and have learned not to pay much attention. Normally, I don't do the interviews myself, but I was feeling cautious and let the "morning guys" know I'd be there during the show.

The interview was innocent enough at first. The subject turned to a discussion of the Holy Spirit's manifest presence in a meeting (as opposed to His presence that dwells within our hearts always). Rather suddenly, something began to happen in the control room.

It began with Gregg. He was seated behind me listening, and for no apparent reason, he began to weep. His weeping turned to shuddering sobs that he attempted to muffle in his hands. It was hard to ignore, and Randy paused midsentence to comment "You can't see him, but God is really dealing with the fellow behind you right now." I looked over my shoulder just in time to see Gregg losing control. He stood up, only to crash to the floor directly in front of the console, where he lay shaking for several minutes.

I don't know if you have ever tried to conduct a radio interview in such circumstances, but let me assure you I never have. I was mortified. We have always attempted to avoid any extremes at FM 92, so it was difficult to explain to our listeners what was happening. I had always known Gregg to act like a professional, so I knew something was seriously going on. I did my best to recover the interview under the embarrassing circumstances. I thanked the guest and wrapped it up. (And thought of ways to kill Gregg later!)

After when we have a guest minister in the station, we ask him to pray for the staff. Before Randy Clark left, we asked him to say a word of prayer.

We formed a circle and began to pray for the staff one by one. My eyes were shut, but I heard a thud and opened them to see Bart Mazzarella prostrate on the floor. He had fallen forward on his face. What amazed me most was that Bart was known to be openly sceptical. He simply did not accept such things. Within seconds, another and another staff person went down. Even those that remained standing were clearly shaken.

When they prayed for me, I did not "fall down". What did happen was an electric sensation shot down my right arm, and my right hand began to tremble uncontrollably. My heart pounded as I became aware of a powerful sense of what can only be called God's manifest presence.

Remember, our staff is not primarily Charismatic. We are Episcopalian, Nazarene, Evangelical, Pentecostal .... and a couple of "not quite sure". While I personally am associated with an Assembly of God church, I'm quite the skeptic when it comes to "weird stuff". I don't watch many evangelists on TV, because too often I am turned off by what I see. This was completely new to us.

Randy was scheduled elsewhere, so after just a few minutes of prayer, he thanked me graciously and left quickly. Our staff remained in the control room, staring at each other wide eyed, and hovering over Bart, who still appeared unconscious on the floor. (He was completely immobile for over half an hour).

There was a sweet atmosphere of worship in the room, so I told someone to put one of the Integrity Worship CD's on air while we continued to pray together.

I thought the atmosphere would abate after a few minutes and return to normal... but instead, our prayers grew more and more intense. The room became charged in a way that I simply cannot describe. After an hour of this, we realized that it was 10:30, the time we normally share our listener's needs in prayer.

I switched on the mike, and found myself praying that God would touch every listener in a personal way. After prayer, with great hesitation I added this morning God has really been touching our staff, so we've been spending the morning praying together. If you're in a

Geoff Waugh

situation right now where you are facing a desperate need, just drop by our studios this morning and we'll take a minute to pray with you." This was the first time we had ever made such an invitation.

This is where everything went haywire.

Within a few minutes, a few listeners began to arrive. The first person I prayed with was a tall man who shared with me some tremendous needs he was facing. I told him I would agree with him in prayer. As I prayed for his need, a voice in my head was saying "It's a shame that you don't operate in any real spiritual gift or power. Here's a man who really needs to hear from God and you've got nothing worth giving him!" I continued to pray, but I was struggling. I reached up with my right hand to touch his shoulder, when suddenly he shook, and slumped to the floor. (He lay there without moving for over 2 hours.) I was shocked and shaken.

Two others had arrived at this point, and staff members were praying with them. Suddenly, they began weeping uncontrollably, and slumped to the floor. This scene was repeated a dozen times in the next few minutes. It didn't matter who did the praying, whenever we asked the Lord, he immediately responded with a visible power, and the same manifestations occurred.

I didn't know whether to be terrified or thrilled, but clearly, something completely unusual was going on. A young man cautiously entered the room, and began to tell us that he was "just happening" to be scanning the radio dial when he heard "something about prayer". He reported that he was immediately overcome with conviction. Years before, he had contem-

252

plated going into the ministry, and had even attended a couple of years at a Christian College, but he had since strayed from God. As a chill of conviction swept him, he felt God suddenly tell him it was now or never. He drove to the station. We prayed with him to receive Christ as Lord, and afterward, he too slumped to the floor.

One by one they came. We continued to play praiseoriented music, and every hour (sometimes on the halfhour) we'd invite people to come.

Fairly early in all this, we ran out of room. The radio station floor was wall to wall bodies... some weeping, some shaking, some completely still. People reported that it was like heavy lead apron had been placed over them. They were unable to get up. All they could do was worship God.

Fortunately, our offices are inside of the complex at Central Assembly, so when the crowd began to grow, we moved across into the Church, leaving the radio station literally wall to wall with seekers.

Some teachers at Indian Christian School had heard what was happening, and asked us to pray for certain children they were bringing in the room. As we prayed for the kids, many began to shake and fall to the floor. Some would begin to utter praises to God. Others lay completely immobile for periods of over an hour. (If you've ever tried to make a seven year old lay still, you know it's a miracle!) A few simply experienced nothing at all.

By now I was convinced that we were experiencing a bona fide move of God. I had read about such manifestation experiences being common in the revival meetings of great men like Jonathan Edwards and John Wesley. I had also read of the great camp meeting revivals in the early 1800's, where thousands upon thousands experienced being 'slain', but I never imagined I would really live to see it.

The crowd continued to grow, and lines began to form. The power of God continued to fall on those coming. It was almost like being in a dream. I would look up and see our staff members ... eyes red, faces puffy, and hands trembling, but with a fire in their eyes and the power of God upon them. I couldn't believe it was the same people I knew and worked with. In a matter of hours, something we never even dreamed of (much less aspired to) was happening.

The floor in front of the sanctuary was soon covered with men and women, boys and girls. The aisles began to fill and we were pushing aside chairs for more floor space. Usually, one of our staff would 'catch' the person as they fell, but on quite a few occasions we were caught by surprise and people fell hard on the floor. Frankly, we had no idea what we were doing. (I'm not sure I want to learn!)

At some point I looked up and saw a local Baptist Pastor walk in the door. I must confess that my first thought was, "Oh Boy...I'm in trouble!" While I knew this brother to be a genuine man of God, nevertheless I was concerned about how a fundamental, nononsense Baptist might take all these goingson. (Besides, I didn't have an explanation to offer!) I walked up to greet him. He just silently surveyed the room, and with a tone of voice just above a whisper said, "This... is... God. For years I've prayed for revival... This is God."

Within minutes more local pastors began to arrive. Lutheran, Independent, Assembly of God... The word of what was happening spread like wildfire. As the pastors arrived, they were cautious at first, but within just minutes, they would often begin to flow in the same ministry. The crowd was growing and pastors began to lay hands on the seekers, where once again the power of God would manifest and the seeker would often collapse to the ground.

It did not seem to matter who did the praying. This was a nameless, faceless, spontaneous move of God. There were no stars, no leaders, and frankly, there was no organization. (It's hard to plan for something you have no idea might happen!)

Eventually, word of what was occurring reached Fred Grewe, the Melbourne pastor who had brought Randy Clark to the station earlier that morning. He and Randy, along with several other Melbourne pastors, jumped into the car and headed down to Vero Beach. At this point, we started broadcasting live from the Church. As the group from Melbourne arrived, more and more people also began to show up asking for prayer. It seemed like there were always more than we could get to.

Amazingly, unchurched, unsaved people were showing up. I got a fresh glimpse of the power of radio as person after person told us "I'm not really a part of any church..." A few were sceptical at first, and later found themselves kneeling in profound belief.

Sometimes people would rise up, only to frantically announce to us that they had been healed of some physical problem. One woman's arthritic hands found relief. Neck pains, jaw problems, stomach disorders and more were all reported to us as healed.

We have received at least a dozen verified, credible, reliable comments from people who told us that when they switched on the radio, they were suddenly, unexpectedly overwhelmed by the presence of God (even when they didn't hear us say anything). Several told us that the manifest presence of God was so strong in their cars that they were unable to drive, and were forced to pull off the road.

The "falling" aspect of this visitation was the most visible manifestation, but it was not falling that was important. What was important was the fact that people were rising up with more love for God in their hearts than ever before. They were being changed, and their hearts set ablaze. I have lost count of the numbers of people who told me of the change God worked in their life.

It's hard to imagine the impact this has had on our staff. It seems like God has almost given me a new staff, composed entirely of men and women to tremendous zeal for God. What is occurring in our local churches is even more amazing. My phone is ringing with the calls of excited pastors. At least a dozen area churches from completely different ends of the theological spectrum are already experiencing this powerful move in their church. The leaders of many, many other local fellowships have been visiting these churches to "check it out", and they too are being touched to "take it back" with them. It's almost like a tidal wave has hit this area of Florida.

If you are sceptical, I understand and forgive you. (I might have thrown a letter like this one away just days ago.) I share this only to try and offer a faithful rendition of what has really happened.

I only ask that you remain open to whatever God wants to accomplish through you.

Christian history is full of accounts of those times when God elected to "visit" His people. When He has, entire nations have sometimes been affected. I believe you'll agree, our nation is ripe for such a revival. For such a time as this, let us look to God with expectancy.

With warm regards, I am,
Sincerely Yours,
Jon Hamilton
General Manager[20]

The revival in Melbourne continued with an astounding mixture of white, black, Asiatic, Hispanic, and American Indian people being touched by God, filled with the Spirit and witnessing to others. It became another clear example of the ecumenical and inter-racial effects of these impacts of the Spirit.

Renewal meetings five days a week continued for nine months in 1995, then eased back to weekly or monthly gatherings. Combined renewal ministries have included racial reconciliation initiatives, united campaigns and chaplaincies in the schools, a Space Coast Prayer Network of Christians united in prayer for revival and combined church gatherings for renewal and special events.[21]

It was this outbreak of the Holy Spirit that caused a significant shift in emphasis for Randy Clark, the Evangelist used of God to begin the outpouring. During the month of January

1995, Randy would see more healings than he had in the preceding 24 years of ministry. After Melobourne, healing would take a more significant place in the "renewal" for Randy after Melbourne. This change in emphasis from "renewal" to "revival" built on healing and evangelism would continue until today (2010) for Randy Clark.[22]

1995 - January: Modesto, California, North America (Glen Berteau)

Glenn and Debbie Berteau, pastors of Calvary Temple Worship Centre in Modesto, California, from January 1994, strongly sensed the Lord would give them revival there. Early in 1994, they challenged their congregation with that vision. After the 'Vision Sunday', individuals committed themselves to fast on specific days as the congregation became involved in a forty day period of prayer and fasting. In early January 1995, they had a three day fast. The church building remained open for prayer, and people prayed over names on cards left on the altar. Those able to do so met together daily for prayer at noon. Many pastors in the area began meeting each week to pray for the city.

On Sunday 15 January 1995, the church began holding performances of the play, *Heaven's Gates and Hell's Flames*. It was scheduled for three days originally but continued for seven weeks with 28 performances. Jann Mathies, pastoral secretary of Calvary Temple reported in April:

> As of this writing, approximately 81,000 have attended the performance with 90% each night seeing it for the first time. At time of printing, 33,000 decision packets have been handed out, and of that, (confirmed) 20,000 returned with signed decision cards. Over 250 churches have been represented with hundreds of people

added to the churches in our city and surrounding communities in less than one month. People come as early as 3:30 pm for a 7 pm performance. There are over 1,000 people waiting to get in at 5 pm, and by 5:30 pm the building is full. Thousands of people have been turned away; some from over 100 miles away. ... Husbands and wives are reconciling through salvation; teenagers are bringing their unsaved parents; over 6,000 young people have been saved, including gang members who are laying down gang affiliation and turning in gang paraphernalia. . . . The revival is crossing every age, religion and socioeconomic status. . . . We have many volunteers coming in every day, and through the evening hours to contact 500 to 600 new believers by phone; special classes have also been established so that new believers may be established in the faith.[23]

The play became a focus for revival in the area. Some churches closed their evening service so their people could take their unsaved friends there. One result is that many churches in the area began receiving new coverts and finding their people catching the fire of revival in their praying and evangelising.

One church added a third Sunday morning service to accommodate the people. Another church asked their members to give up their seats to visitors. Bible book stores sold more Bibles than usual. A local psychologist reported on deep healings in the lives of many people who attended the drama.

That play continues to be used effectively around the world. For example, churches in Australia have performed the play with hundreds converted in a local church. Hardened unbelievers with no place for church in their lives have been converted and now live for God.

1995 - January: Pasadena, California, North America (Che Ahn)

From January, 1995, John Arnott of the Toronto Airport Vineyard and Wes Campbell of New Life Vineyard Fellowship in Kelowna, British Columbia began speaking for two or three days each at Mott Auditorium on the campus of the U. S. Centre for World Mission. By 24 March, people gathered for meetings five nights a week, usually going very late.

John Arnott conducted powerful meetings there on Friday-Sunday 24-26 March, hosted by Harvest Rock Church, a Vineyard Fellowship. Then the combined churches in the area continued with nightly meetings from Monday, 27 March. Later that settled to meetings from Wednesday to Sunday each week. Then Wednesdays were reserved for cell groups and meetings continued from Thursday to Sunday nights.

Che Ahn, senior pastor of Harvest Rock Church wrote in their monthly magazine *Wine Press* in August 1995:

> I am absolutely amazed at what God has done during the past five months. After John Arnott exploded onto the scene with three glorious and unforgettable renewal meetings, he encouraged the pastors of our church to begin nightly protracted meetings. My mind immediately rejected the idea. I thought to myself, "The meetings were great because you were here, but how can we sustain nightly meetings without someone like John Arnott to draw the crowd?" The answer to my question was an obvious one. Someone greater than John Arnott would show up each night at the meetings Jesus. And each night since we began March 27, 1995, God has shown up to heal, to save, and to touch thousands of lives. There is no accurate way to measure the impact that the renewal meetings are having

in our city. I do believe that we are making church history, and we are in the midst of another move of the Holy Spirit that is sweeping the world. From March 27 to July 27, we have had 99 nightly renewal meetings. We have averaged about 300 people per night, some nights with more that 1,200 people and others with a small crowd of 120.

More than 25,000 people have walked through the doors of Mott Auditorium, many of them happy, repeat customers. We have seen more that 300 people come forward to rededicate their lives or give their hearts to Jesus Christ. These statistics don't come close to representing other evangelistic fruit of those who have attended the meetings. For example, two church members, Justine Bateman and Jeff Eastridge, had an outreach at Arroyo High School and more than 60 young people gave their hearts to the Lord!

We have seen marvellous healings from the hand of the Lord, many of them spontaneous without anyone specifically praying for the healing. I wish I had the time and space to share all the wonderful fruit I have seen at the renewal meetings. Seeing the need to share what God is doing, I felt that we are producing this church newsletter to share these testimonies of lives that have been impacted by God during this current outpouring of the Holy Spirit (Internet: Harvest Rock Church).

1995 - January: Brownwood, Texas (College Revivals)

Richard Riss gathered accounts of revival sweeping colleges across America beginning with Howard Payne University in Brownwood, Texas.

On January 22, 1995, at Coggin Avenue Baptist Church in Brownwood, Texas, two students from Howard Payne University, a Christian institution, stood up and confessed their sins. As a result of this incident, many others started to confess their own sins before the congregation. On January 26, a similar event took place on the campus of Howard Payne. Word quickly spread to other colleges, and Howard Payne students were soon being invited to other college campuses, which experienced similar revivals. From these schools, more students were invited to still other schools, where there were further revivals. ...

One of the first two students from Howard Payne to confess his sins was Chris Robeson. As he testified about his own life and the spiritual condition of his classmates, "People just started streaming down the aisles" in order to pray, confess their sins, and restore seemingly doomed relationships, according to John Avant, pastor of Coggin Avenue Baptist Church. From this time forward, the church began holding threeandahalfhour services. Avant said, "This is not something we're trying to manufacture. It's the most wonderful thing we've ever experienced." ...

At Howard Payne, revival broke out during a January 26 'celebration' service, as students praised God in song and shared their testimonies. Students then started to schedule allnight prayer meetings in dormitories. ...

Then, on February 13-15, during five meetings at Howard Payne, Henry Blackaby, a Southern Baptist revival leader ministered at a series of five worship services, attended by guests from up to 200 miles away. On Tuesday, February 14, more than six hundred attended, and student leaders went up to the platform to confess publicly their secret sins. About two hundred stayed afterward to continue praying. One of the students, Andrea Cullins, said, "Once we saw the Spirit move, we didn't want to leave." ...

After Howard Payne, some of the first schools to be affected were Southwestern Baptist Theological Seminary in Forth Worth, Texas, Beeson School of Divinity in Birmingham, Alabama, Olivet Nazarene University in Kankakee, Ill., The Criswell College in Dallas, Moorehead State University in Moorehead, Ky., Murray State University in Murray, Ky., Wheaton College in Wheaton, Ill., Louisiana Tech University in Ruston, La., Gordon College in Wenham, Mass., and Trinity Evangelical Divinity School in Deerfield, Illinois. In each case, students went forward during long services to repent of pride, lust, bondage to materialism, bitterness, and racism.

These revivals continued throughout and beyond 1995. They were marked by large numbers repenting publicly of sin and students witnessing enthusiastically. This Spirit movement among students has similarities to former revival in college campuses, especially those of the early nineteenth century in America. Both produced commitment to witnessing and mission. Modern technology has enabled hundreds of young people, including students, to communicate rapidly and travel widely, including short term mission visits.

Youth With A Mission (YWAM) has provided one avenue for this kind of mission and currently has a staff of over 6,000 leaders involved in conducting short term mission training programs. Significantly, YWAM began with Loren Cunningham, the international director, taking teams on outreach from the pentecostal church where he was the youth pastor. This remains a growing characteristic of pentecostal and charismatic groups, including youth groups and student groups.

1995 - June: Pensacola, North America (Steve Hill)

Over 26,000 conversions were registered in the first year of the 'Pensacola Revival'. Over 100,000 conversions were registered in the first two years.

On Father's Day, Sunday 18 June 1995, evangelist Steve Hill spoke at Brownsville Assembly of God, near Pensacola, Florida. At the altar call a thousand people streamed forward as the Holy Spirit moved on them. Their pastor, John Kilpatrick, fell down under the power of God and was overwhelmingly impacted for four days.

That morning service, normally finishing at noon, lasted till 4 pm. The evening service continued for another five and a half hours. So the church asked Steve Hill to stay. He cancelled appointments, continued with nightly meetings, and relocated to live there, where he continues to minister in revival.

John Kilpatrick, pastor of the Brownsville Assembly of God Church, reported:

> Corporate businessmen in expensive suits kneel and weep uncontrollably as they repent of secret sins. Drug addicts and prostitutes fall to the floor on their faces beside them, to lie prostrate before God as they confess Jesus as Lord for the first time in their lives. Reserved elderly women and weary young mothers dance unashamedly before the Lord with joy. They have been forgiven. Young children see incredible visions of Jesus, their faces a picture of divine delight framed by slender arms raised heavenward.
>
> I see these scenes replayed week after week, and service after service. Each time, I realize that in a very

real way, they are the fruit of a sevenyear journey in prayer, and of two and a half years of fervent corporate intercession by the church family I pastor at Brownsville Assembly of God in Pensacola, Florida.

The souls who come to Christ, repenting and confessing their sin, the marriages that are restored, the many people who are freed from bondage that has long held them captive these are the marks of revival and the trophies of God's glory. No, I am not speaking of a revival that lasted one glorious weekend, one week, one month, or even one year! At this writing, the 'Brownsville Revival' has continued unbroken, except for brief holiday breaks, since Father's Day, June 18, 1995! How? Only God knows. Why? First, because it is God's good pleasure, and second, perhaps because the soil of our hearts was prepared in prayer long before revival descended on us so suddenly.

On that very normal and ordinary Sunday morning in June of 1995, I was scheduled to minister to my congregation, but I felt weary. I was still trying to adjust to the recent loss of my mother, and my yearslong desire for revival in the church seemed that morning to be so far off. So I asked my friend, Evangelist Steve Hill, to fill the pulpit in my place. Although he was scheduled to speak only in the evening service, Steve agreed to preach the Father's Day message. We didn't know it then, but God was at work in every detail of the meeting.

The worship was ordinary (our worship leader, Lindell Cooley, was still ministering on a missions trip to the Ukraine in Russia), and even Brother Hill's message didn't seem to ignite any sparks that morning until the noon hour struck. Then he gave an altar call and suddenly God visited our congregation in a way we had never experienced before. A thousand people came forward for prayer after his message. That was almost half of our congregation! We didn't know it then, but our lives were about to change in a way we could never have imagined.

We knew better than to hinder such a mighty move of God, so services just continued day after day. We had to adjust with incredible speed. During the first month of the revival, hundreds of people walked the isles to repent of their sins. By the sixth month, thousands had responded to nightly altar calls. By the time we reached the twelfth month, 30,000 had come to the altar to repent of their sins and make Jesus Lord of their lives.

At this writing, 21 months and over 470 revival services later, more than 100,000 people have committed their lives to God in these meetings only a portion of the 1.6 million visitors who have come from every corner of the earth ...

If the prophecy delivered by Dr David Yonggi Cho [given in 1991] years before it came to pass is correct, this revival, which he correctly placed as beginning at Pensacola, Florida, will sweep up the East Coast and across the United States to the West Coast, and America will see an outpouring of God that exceeds any we have previously seen. I am convinced that you, and every believer who longs for more of God, has a part to play in this great awakening from God.[24]

Pastors, leaders and Christians have been returning to their churches ignited with a new passion for the Lord and for the lost. The awesome presence of God experienced at

Pensacola continues to impact thousands from around the world. Although the methods used are typical pentecostal approaches to church life, a significant difference is the intensity of the Spirit's impact on people's lives, the depth of repentance, and the dynamic enthusiasm of new converts and established Christians witnessing to friends and praying with them.

1995 - October: Mexico (David Hogan)

David Hogan, founder of Freedom Ministries, a mission to remote hill tribes in Mexico told in a sermon about the outpouring of the Spirit there. Particularly significant in this account is the determination of Hogan to shield the tribes from imported renewal or revival experiences. He allowed no visitors to report on revival in Toronto, Pensacola or other Spirit movements in the current awakening. He regards the Spirit movement in the Mexico hills as fully indigenous.

This account is particularly important as it provides a typical and powerful example of thousands of current indigenous Spirit movements throughout the world, most of which are still unreported, but evident through the enormous expansion of pentecostal-charismatic Christianity globally, especially since the eighties.

> I visited an outlying village. It took four hours in a 4 wheel drive and then two hours on foot, uphill very remote. There's no radio, no T.V., no outside influences. I'm sitting up there in this little hut on a piece of wood against the bamboo wall on the dirt floor. Chickens are walking around in there. And this pastor walks up to me. He's a little guy, and he's trembling. He says, "Brother David, I'm really afraid I've made a mistake." I hadn't heard of any mistakes. I was wondering what had happened in the last few days. He's got four little

churches in his area. He said, "Man, it's not my fault. I apologize. I've done everything right, like you taught me. I pray everyday. I read the Bible. I'm doing it right. What happened is not my fault."

I said, "What happened? Come on, tell me what happened." He was trembling. Tears were running out of his eyes. He said, "Brother David, I got up in our little church. I opened my Bible and I started preaching and the people started falling down. The people started crying. The people started laughing. And it scared me. I ran out of the church."

That's what I was looking for. That's what I was waiting for, when God came in our work; not because somebody came and preached it; not because I said it was okay or not okay, because I was neutral about it. I knew it was all right, but I wanted to see it in our work not because I ushered it in, but because the Holy Spirit ushered it in. And he did.

I got together with my pastors and we made a covenant to do a month's fast in September 1995. This was as well as the three days on and three days off fast that we had been doing that year anyway, so we were ready for whatever God wanted to do. God hit me on the third day of that month of fasting, but I continued the fast and on the seventh day he hit me again greater than I've ever been hit in my life up to that point. But we continued fasting for the whole month.

We were in an awesome time. I didn't know how deep we were in the river of God. I'd been fasting for a month, and I didn't know what was happening. So I decided to get my pastors together in each section. We had groups of about 3075 pastors in each section.

I went into the most conservative area of our mission first, because I wanted to see what would happen. At the first meeting, with about 75 of my pastors I got up, opened my Bible, and I shared one or two verses. Suddenly I felt: that's enough. They're used to me preaching two hours sometimes, but it hadn't been ten minutes.

I said, "Stand up." And they stood up. I said, "Receive the River of Life." You should have seen it! It looked like someone was hitting them with bats in the stomach and the head. But nobody was touching them. People were lying over benches, forward, backward, all over the place. I was trying to help, but I couldn't help. People were just flying everywhere. And these were ministers.

So I went through all the sections like that. I got into one section, and they were glad to see me. They hadn't seen me in a few months. I stood up. I opened my Bible. I read one verse about the fire of God, and the people started shaking. I thought, "Oh God, this is way out."

So I said, "Stand up." They tried to stand up. Some of them couldn't stand up. I just said the word "Fire." And the whole place fell. It was getting more and more scary to me. But people were getting healed without anybody touching them. A man in that meeting had been deaf for 27 years. I didn't know the man. He fell over and hit his head on a bench, and fell underneath the bench. He got up from there after a few minutes and he took off running out of the room. His ears had unstopped and he was running from the noise!

After I had been through all the sections, introducing this softly, it finally came time to call all the pastors together from the whole work. A couple hundred of our pastors came. I wish you had been there to see what we saw! It was amazing.

On the first day, Wednesday 25 October 1995, there were about 200 pastors there, and the whole church that was hosting us. That made about 450 people. The first day was awesome. God hit us powerfully. There were healings. I was happy. The people were encouraged.

The second day, Thursday, was even better. It was stronger. I thought we were peaking out on the second day. I got there at eight o'clock in the morning and left a ten o'clock at night, and there was ministry all day. We were fixing problems, and God was working through the ministry. It was wonderful. But I tell you, I was not ready for the third day.

I don't have words to describe what happened to us when the Holy Spirit fell on us on Friday, 27 October 1995. If you had been there, you wouldn't have words to describe it either. It's an awesome thing I've been able to witness. The river of God is here, and it's full. There's plenty for all.

We were coming in from different areas. The Indians were all there. I didn't know they had been in an all night prayer meeting. I didn't know that the Holy Spirit had fallen on them and they couldn't get up. I didn't know that they had been pinned down by the Holy Spirit all night long, all over the place, stuck to the ground. Some of them had fallen on ant beds, but not one ant bit them.

I was staying about 45 minutes away. I got in my 4 wheel drive and as I drove there I began listening on the two-way radio. Some of our missionaries were already there, and were talking on the two way radio saying, "What's happening here. I can't walk."

As I listened to them on the radio I felt power come on me. And the closer I came, the more heat I felt settling on me. I could feel heat, and I had my air conditioner going! When I got to the little church, I opened the door of the truck and instantly became hot. Sweat poured off me. I was about 300 yards from the church. The closer I got, the more intense was the heat. I could hardly walk through it, it was so thick. I'm talking about the presence of God. That was 7:30 in the morning!

I walked around the corner of the building. People were all over the place. Some were knocked out. Some were on the ground. Some were moaning and wailing. It was very unusual. By the time I got to the front of the church where the elders were I could hardly walk. I was holding on to things to get there. I could hardly breathe. The heat of the presence of God was amazing.

The people had been singing for two hours before I got there. At 8:15 on the morning of October 27th, 1995, I walked up there and lay my Bible down on that little wobbly Indian table. Hundreds were looking at me. Some were knocked out, lying on the ground. I could hardly talk.

I called the nine elders to the front and told them the Holy Ghost was there and we needed to make a covenant together, even to martyrdom. We made a covenant there that the entire country of Mexico would be saved. They asked me to join them in that pact. When we lifted our hands in agreement all nine fell at once. I was hurled backward and fell under the table. When I got up the people in front fell over. In less than a minute every pastor there was knocked out.

We were ringed with unbelievers, coming to see what was going on. The anointing presence of God came and knocked them all out, dozens of them. Every unbeliever outside, and everyone on the fence was knocked out and fell to the ground. There were dozens of them. From the church at the top of the hill we could see people in the village below running out screaming from their huts and falling out under the Holy Ghost. It was amazing.

We always have a section for the sick and afflicted. They bring them in from miles around, some on stretchers. There were 25-30 of them there. Every sick person at the meeting was healed: the blind, the cancerous, lupus, tumours, epilepsy, demon possession. Nobody touched them but Jesus. There was instant reconciliation between people who had been against each other. They were lying on top of each other, sobbing and repenting.

I was afraid when I saw all of that going on. I looked up to heaven and said, "God what are you ?" and that was the end of it. He didn't want to hear any questions. Bang! I was about three or four metres from the table. When I woke up some hours later, I was under the table. When I finally woke up my legs wouldn't work. I scooted myself around looking at what was going on. It was pandemonium! When some people tried to get up, they would go flying. It was awesome.

"And he showed me a pure river of water of life, clear as crystal, proceeding from the throne of God and of the Lamb" (Revelation 22:1). I saw that river. I actually saw the river, it's pure water of life from God's throne. If I could see it again I would know it, I saw it, I experienced it, I tasted it.

We had five open eyed visions. One small pastor was hanging onto a pole to hold himself up. He was there, but he wasn't there. He said to me, "Brother David, look at him. Look at him, Brother David! Who is it? Look how big he is! Oh, he's got his white robe on. He's got a golden girdle." It was Jesus. He said, "Brother David, how did we get into this big palace?"

I looked around. I was still on the dirt floor. I still had a grass roof over me, but he was in a marble palace, pure white. I crawled over to look at him. He was seeing things we could not see. Another of the elders, a prophet from America, who had been working with me for thirteen years, crawled over and we were watching this pastor who was in a trance. It was amazing.

The three of us were inside something like a force field of energy. Anybody who tried to come into it was knocked out. It was scary. The pastor said, "He's got a list, Brother David." And the pastor started reading out aloud from the list. I was looking around, and as he was reading from the list people went flying through the air, getting healed and delivered. It was phenomenal, what God was doing. And he's done it in every service in our work that I've been in since then. It's been over a year. It's amazing. Wonderful.

Between 150 and 500 people per month are being saved because of it, just through what the North American missionaries are doing.[25]

David Hogan reported these events in Brisbane just over a year after that powerful visitation of God in their work. The transforming presence of God continues among them with an increase of conversions and miracles, particularly healings, but also some villagers raised from the dead. Although the language of his discourse is early style pentecostal, the accounts are both modern and biblical exemplifying God's overwhelming intervention often seen in revival movements.

1996 - March: Smithton, Missouri, North America (Steve Gray)

The small rural town of Smithton, with a population of around 500, thirty miles from Kansas City in the wheat fields of Missouri, became a 'mecca' for over 100,000 visitors in the first two years of a revival Spirit movement there. The Smithton Community Church hall has been crowded six nights a week with 500-800 people since 1996. The continued influence and growth of the little church led them to relocate to Kansas City in 1999.

After twelve years in the church, 34 year old Steve Gray the pastor was feeling discouraged, so he visited the Brownsville revival in Pensacola for ten days in March 1996 hoping for renewal. He was particularly impressed with how John Kilpatrick pastored the revival at Brownsville. He found himself revitalised and phoned his wife Kathy on Sunday, 17 March saying, "I have just been in the best Sunday morning service I have ever been in. Tell our church." David Cordes, one of the elders, was deeply convicted, saying, "Why should our pastor have to travel a thousand miles to be in the best service he has ever been in?" He and others fell on the floor in repentance for their lack of support and encouragement. That spirit of repentance and brokenness continued in the Smithton church meetings that week.

Gray left Brownsville after the morning service on Sunday, 24 March to drive back, and walked into the Smithton Church at 6:12 p.m. while the congregation was worshipping at the beginning of their 6 p.m. service. They reported that at that moment Holy Spirit fell on the whole church. Everyone crowded to the front in repentance, tears, joy and deep commitment to God. Immediately they added revival services to their church schedule. The outpouring continued for with five services every week. Visitors came from all fifty states of America and many foreign countries, often exceeding the population of the town.

Thousands testify to significant change, renewal, conversion and healing. Visiting pastors have taken the fire back to their congregation. The church sends teams to many places asking for a visit. Gray says, "The longer we are in this (revival), the more I realize how badly it is needed. I didn't realize how sick the church in America is." The biggest challenge he faces, according to Gray, is to keep unity and purity in revival and protect people from 'wolves' who cause division and dissention.[26]

The mounting demands of national and international exposure, increasing numbers, and access to city facilities led the Smithton church to relocate to Kansas City in 1999, and it continues with further influence in the city, attracting visitors, and interacting with others in renewal.

1996 - April: Hampton, Virginia, North America (Ron Johnson)

The 2,200 member Bethel Temple Assembly of God experienced a revival movement from April 1996. Revival meetings were held Wednesday, Thursday & Friday. In April of 1996 a Sunday 7:30 a.m. service started and did not end till 3:24 p.m. which by-passed the 10:30 a.m. service. Church members were repenting, numerous people converted to Christ, and many were delivered of evil spirits.

Bethel Temple Church is racially diverse with 40% African-American, 50% white, and 10% Hispanic and Asian, located in Hampton, Virginia, the oldest English speaking settlement in America.

In 1996, the Senior Associate Pastor, Don Rogers, had an open vision of the Holy Spirit coming to Hampton. He saw the Spirit of the Lord coming like a storm and it blew into their church. In his vision when this happened it blew out a glass window in the church.

Fourteen months later, in June of 1997, as the Sunday service at Bethel Temple was starting. Senior Pastor Ron Johnson prayed, asking God to come "like a pent-up flood". Suddenly Johnson looked at his hands and oil was dripping from his hands. The head usher told the pastor the front window of the church has just blown out. Johnson began telling the congregation what had happened. People ran to the altar, many publicly repenting of sins. God's manifest presence filled the building. The church reports restored relationships especially the healing of marriages and sexually broken people, large numbers converted, and many being filled with the Holy Spirit.

Unity of churches in the Hampton area is growing. By 1998, twenty churches gathered together for Easter Services in the town's coliseum attended by 11,000 people.[27]

A growing phenomena of this current revival is repentance and unity. Centres of the revival report significant co-operation between churches touched by this Spirit movement. At times, as in Hampton, this is initiated through a strong and unusual impact of the Spirit in a church which has been praying for revival and growing in its response to the convicting moves of the Spirit among the people.

1996 - September: Mobile, Alabama, North America (Cecil Turner)

Calvary Assembly of God in Mobile, Alabama, is another example of one church experiencing a strong Spirit movement which then involves other co-operating churches and begins to influence the community through conversions, healings, and the related publicity.

Cecil Turner, the pastor, was a shy man with a stutter, a pipe-fitter with no Bible college education, when God he sensed the call of God to lead the small congregation from 1963. Now the church has become a centre for revival since a strong Spirit movement erupted in their annual "camp meeting" convention in the church on Sunday, 29 September, 1996. From then, meetings were held every night except Mondays, drawing 250-300 people, with 400 attending the Sunday services church, the maximum number they can pack into the sanctuary.

> Some services are exuberant and intense; others so heavy all they can do is "lay on the ground." Sometimes the Spirit is so strong during praise and worship that they throw open the altars.

> "We come in each night and never know what's going to happen," Cecil says, pausing for a moment. "I like it."

> The church started praying for revival in 1992, says Cecil's son Kevin, who has been on staff for 11 years.

"At times we wondered if revival would happen," Kevin says. "But we saw the intensity and the hunger growing."

After five years of prayer and some dry stretches, God came mightily when a travelling evangelist, Wayne Headrick, came to preach. God spoke to Headrick that if they got out of the way, God would make something happen.

That "something" keeps on happening.

"It seems like it's accelerating," Headrick told the *Mobile Register* in May 1997. "Each service there's more . . . anointing and more of the power of God."[28]

The band music is geared to reached the 'unchurched' people who are "coming in droves" to this church that sits at a 3-way stop on the western city limit of Mobile. "They may not understand it," says music pastor Kevin Turner, Cecil's son, "but they want more of it."[29]

Many attend from other denominations. Conversions have been recorded continually, 150 in the two months prior to the May 1997 report. Some say afterwards that they felt a need to come, and several testify that they were drawn in as if to a beacon. One man pulled into the parking lot, not fully understanding why he was there. The congregation prays regularly that people will be drawn by the Lord's presence. Testimonies of transformed lives, set free from addictions to alcohol, drugs and immorality, have a strong effect in the community.

Glenn McCall, pastor of Crawford United Methodist church, frequently takes members of his congregation to Calvary for revival services. "[People] are looking for something, and only God can meet that need in their spirit," he says. "I feel like it's a nationwide thing. I've heard a lot of testimonies from around the country and the world. There are some phenomenal things happening in the church world."[30]

Spirit movements transcend denominational differences. This phenomena continues to foster a fresh ecumenism, not of doctrine, but of the Spirit.

1996 - October: Houston, Texas, North America (Richard Heard)

Richard Heard led the Christian Tabernacle in Houston in growth from 250 to 3,000 members. On Sunday October 20, 1996, a move of God exploded in the church which dramatically affected it. This event is particularly significant as an example of the 'fear of the Lord' and reverent awe generated in God's manifest presence.

During the previous year the church had a strong emphasis on knowing Christ intimately. Then in August of 1996, Hector Giminez from Argentina ministered there with great power and many significant healings. Awareness of the presence and glory of the Lord increased during October, especially with the ministry of an evangelist friend of Heard, Tommy Tenny. He had spoken on the previous two Sundays, and was to speak that morning. Heard was preparing to welcome him and had just read about God's promise of revival from 2 Chronicles 7:14 when God's power hit the place even splitting the plexiglas pulpit.

Tenny told how these unique events filled the church with awe:

This body of believers in Houston had two scheduled services on Sundays. The first morning service started at 8:30, and the second one followed and began at 11.

When I returned for the third weekend, while in the hotel, I sensed a heavy anointing of some kind, a brooding of the Spirit, and I literally wept and trembled.
The following morning, we walked into the building for the 8:30 Sunday service expecting to see the usual early morning first service "sleepy" crowd with their low-key worship. As I walked in to sit down in the front row that morning, the presence of God was already in that place so heavily that the air was "thick." You could barely breathe.

The musicians were clearly struggling to continue their ministry; their tears got in the way. Music became more difficult to play. Finally, the presence of God hovered so strongly that they couldn't sing or play any longer. The worship leader crumpled in sobs behind the keyboard. …

God was there; of that there was no doubt. But more of Him kept coming in the place until, as in Isaiah, it literally filled the building. At times the air was so rarefied that it became almost unbreathable. Oxygen came in short gasps, seemingly. Muffled sobs broke through the room. In the midst of this, the pastor turned to me and asked me a question.

"Tommy, are you ready to take the service?"
"Pastor, I'm just about half-afraid to step up there, because *I sense that God is about to do something*."

Tears were streaming down my face when I said that. I wasn't afraid that God was going to strike me down, or that something bad was going to happen. I just didn't want to interfere and grieve the precious presence that was filling up that room! …

"I feel like I should read Second Chronicles 7:14, and I have a word from the Lord," my pastor friend said. With profuse tears I nodded assent and said, "Go, go."

My friend is not a man given to any kind of outward demonstration; he is essentially a man of "even" emotions. But when he got up to walk to the platform, he appeared visibly shaky. At this point I so sensed something was about to happen, that I walked all the way from the front row to the back of the room to stand by the sound booth. I knew God was going to do something; I just didn't know where. …

My pastor friend stepped up to the clear pulpit in the center of the platform, opened the Bible, and quietly read the gripping passage from Second Chronicles 7:14 …

Then he closed his Bible, gripped the edges of the pulpit with trembling hands, and said, "The word of the Lord to us is to stop seeking His benefits and seek Him. We are not to seek His hands any longer, but seek His face."

In that instant, I heard what sounded like a thunderclap echo through the building, and the pastor was literally picked up and thrown backward about ten feet, effectively separating him from the pulpit. When he went backward, the pulpit fell forward. The beautiful flower arrangement positioned in front of it fell to the ground, but *by the time the pulpit hit the ground*, it was already in two pieces. It had split into two pieces almost as if lightning had hit it! At that instant the tangible terror of the presence of God filled that room.

While all of this happened, the ushers quickly ran to the front to check on the pastor and to pick up the two pieces of the split pulpit. No one really paid much attention to the split pulpit; we were too occupied with the torn heavenlies. The presence of God had hit that place like some kind of bomb. People began to weep and to wail. I said, "If you're not where you need to be, this is a good time to get right with God." I've never seen such an altar call. It was pure pandemonium. People shoved one another out of the way. They wouldn't wait for the aisles to clear; they climbed over pews, businessmen tore their ties off, and they were literally stacked on top of one another, in the most horribly harmonious sound of repentance you ever heard. Just the thought of it still sends chills down my back. When I gave the altar call then for the 8:30 a.m. service, I had no idea that it would be but the first of seven altar calls that day.

When it was time for the 11:00 service to begin, nobody had left the building. The people were still on their faces and, even though there was hardly any music being played at this point, worship was rampant and uninhibited. Grown men were ballet dancing; little children were weeping in repentance. People were on their faces, on their feet, on their knees, but mostly in His presence. There was so much of the presence and the power of God there that people began to feel an urgent need to be baptized. I watched people walk through the doors of repentance, and one after another experienced the glory and the presence of God as He came near. Then they wanted baptized, and I was in a quandary about what to do. The pastor was still unavailable on the floor. Prominent people walked up to me and stated, "I've got to be baptized. Somebody tell me what to do." They joined with the parade of the unsaved, who were now saved, provoked purely by encountering the presence of God. There was no sermon and no real song - just His Spirit that day.[31]

The service continued to 1 a.m. Monday, and people met in the church every night for two months, repenting and seeking God. Richard Heard, the pastor, spoke about it by telephone in November, 1996, with Norman Pope of New Wine Ministries in Pagosa Springs, Colorado.

I felt the presence of the Lord come on me so powerfully I grabbed the podium, the pulpit, to keep from falling, and that was a mistake. Instantly I was hurled a number of feet in a different direction, and the people said it was like someone just threw me across the platform. The pulpit fell over that I had been holding for support, and I was out for an hour and a half. ... I could not move. And I saw a manifestation of the glory of God. ... There were thick clouds, dark clouds, edged in golden white and in the clouds there would be bursts of light that would come through, that would just go through me absolutely like electricity. ... There was literally a pulsating feeling of as though I was being fanned by the presence of the glory of God. ... There were angelic manifestations that surrounded the glory and I didn't know how long I was out. They said later that I was there for an hour and a half.

In the meanwhile, all across the building people, they tell me, were falling under the presence of God. That's not something that has happened much in our church, but people were stretched out everywhere. And the altar. We have three services on Sunday and people would enter the hallways that lead to the foyer and then into the auditorium and they would enter the hallways and begin to weep. There was such a glory of God and they would come into the foyer and not stop they would just go straight to the altar people stretched out everywhere. ... There were all kinds of angelic visitations that people had experienced. And we've got professional people in our church doctors, professors, their bodies were strewn everywhere.

When I felt the glory of God lift, I tried to get up and couldn't. It was as though every electrical mechanism in my body had shortcircuited. I couldn't make my hands or my feet respond to what I was trying to tell them to do. It was as though I was paralyzed. ... And we had one service that day, and the service literally never ended it went all the way through the day until 2:00 that morning. It had started at 8:30, and we decided to have church the next night, and I didn't want to be presumptuous, but we went on a nightly basis on that order, just announcing one night at a time, and as we got deeper into the week I could begin to see that God was doing something that was probably going to be more extended. ...

There have been numerous healings. The evangelist didn't speak at all that Sunday. In fact, the entire week he spoke maybe twenty minutes. There's been a really deep call of God to repentance. People come in and they just fall on their faces. ...

We had a great choir. We're a multiethnic congregation. A Brooklyn Tabernacle kind of sound, if you're familiar with that. Great worship and praise. Sunday morning there wasn't a choir member standing on the platform. They were all scattered like logs all over the platform. And we go in [musicians] begin to play, to lead us into the presence of the Lord, and they play very softly. Because of our background, usually our worship is very strong, very dynamic, a lot of energy. Not any more. It's like you're afraid to even lift your voice.

Like they even the notes on the piano they want to play very gently and then the Lord sweeps in. Five nights last week I wasn't even able to receive an offering. So I mean, when He begins to move there's not one thing you can do. You just get out of the way and let Him work. ...

We've cancelled everything that we had planned. We have a lot of outside activities. We have 122 ministries within the church that have helped our church to grow, and these ministries were primarily either for getting people here or holding people once they've converted. ... I was telling our staff they were asking, "Are we going to have Christmas musicals and children's pageants ever?" And we do a big passion play every year that brings in thousands and thousands of people. And I asked them, "Why do we do all of this?" and they said, "Well, we want people to come here so they can encounter God." I said, "Look at what's happening. We've got people storming in here that we've never seen, never heard of, never talked to. And God's doing it in a way that is so far superior to what we could do that whatever we've got going on, we're cancelling everything." And that's literally what we've done. ... And there hasn't been a single objection. That's what amazes me.

I think that this is probably going to end up whatever this season is that the Holy Spirit is bringing us through in terms of our commitment to Him and the deep searching of our own hearts, it has the feeling at this point like it's going to like it's building toward even a greater evangelistic outpouring.[32]

A year later people were still being converted, often 30-40 a week. Richard Heard commented that everywhere in the church the carpet is stained with the tears of people touched by God and repenting. These kind of reports are beginning to multiply across America and around the world as the power of God moves upon his repentant people who seek him above all else.

1997 - January: Baltimore, Maryland, North America (Bart Pierce)

As with the centripetal influence of Azusa Street from 1906, centres of revival in the current developments influence ever widening areas receptive to it.

A significant, on-going example is the influence of revival in places such as Houston on other areas. Bart Pierce, pastor of Rock Church in Baltimore, Maryland, with a 3,000 seat auditorium, invited Tommy Tenney to speak at his church. *Charisma* magazine reported:

Bart Pierce will never forget the day the Holy Spirit fell at his church in the rolling suburbs of Baltimore, Maryland. It wasn't gradual, nor was it subtle. God showed up during the Sunday morning service on January 19, 1997.

Pierce, pastor of Rock Church in Baltimore, and his wife, Coralee, had just returned from a pastors' retreat in St. Augustine, Florida. Pierce says he went to the retreat with "a desperate, deep hunger for more of God."

While there, he heard Tommy Tenney recount an event that occurred in a Houston church a few months earlier. ...

Tenney, a third-generation travelling evangelist, told the gathered pastors that the drama of the split pulpit was totally eclipsed by the awesome presence of God that filled the sanctuary immediately after the supernatural event. "The revival," Tenney told them, "was characterized by a deep sense of humility, brokenness and repentance."

While Tenney spoke, many of the pastors, including Pierce, fell on their faces weeping. Pierce spent much of his time at the retreat prostrated and weeping before the Lord. When it ended, he asked Tenney to come back to Baltimore with him for the weekend.
On the 18-hour drive home, Pierce, his wife and Tenney had "an encounter of God as we talked about what God was doing and what we believed," Pierce says.
"We would sit in the car and weep," recalls Tenney. They reached Baltimore on Saturday night, filled with a hunger for more of the Lord.

The next morning Pierce knew something was up as soon as he got to the church building. "Two of my elders were standing inside the door weeping," he says. "We started worshiping, then people began standing up all over the building crying out loud." Some came forward to the altar; others would "start for the altar and crumple in the aisle."

Even those outside the sanctuary were affected. "Back in the hallways, people were going down under the power of God. We never really got to preach," Pierce says. Tenney and Pierce were supposed to be leading the service, but both were too overcome by the intense presence of God to do anything but cry.

"There was a deep sense of repentance that grew increasingly more intense," Pierce recounts. At 4 p.m. there were still bodies lying all over the church floor. Pierce and Tenney tried several times to speak, but each time they were overwhelmed by tears.

"Finally," says Pierce, "we told our leadership team, 'We're going home to change clothes.' We were a mess from lying on the floor and weeping."

The two men went home and changed. When they got back to the church at 6 p.m., people were still there, and more were coming. That first "service" continued until 2 in the morning.

Monday night, people returned, and the same thing happened. It happened again Tuesday night.

"Many people simply crawled under the pews to hide and weep and cry," remembers Pierce. "At times the crying was so loud, it was eerie."

Pierce noticed new faces in the congregation. "We didn't have a clue as to how they knew about the service, because we don't advertise at all," he says. When he asked, some of the visitors told amazing stories.

One man said he was driving down the road when God told him, "Go to Rock Church." Another woman said she was sitting at her kitchen table when she got the same message. She didn't know what a "Rock

Church" was, but she found a listing in the phone book. After the service she tearfully confided that she had been planning to leave her husband the next morning.

"God had totally turned her heart," says Pierce. "She and her husband have been totally restored."

For the first few weeks, Pierce says, "every ministry at the church was turned upside down." The church has always been known for its mercy ministries — its homeless shelter for men, its home for women in crisis, its food distribution program, which moves 7 million pounds of food a year, and its ministry to revive Baltimore's inner city.

But when the revival started, everything took a back seat to what God was doing. Pierce would find his staff lying on the floor in the hallways or hear a thump against the wall and find someone lying on the floor in the next room, crying uncontrollably.

People reported supernatural events in their homes, too. One woman's unsaved husband had a dream in which everyone spoke Chinese. He came downstairs and found his wife lying on the floor speaking Chinese. His son, who was supposed to be getting ready for school, was lying on the floor in the living room, weeping and crying. That day, the man got saved.

One night a boy from a local gang came forward weeping while Tenney was still preaching. "He came to the front, looked up at me and said, 'You've got to help me, because I just can't take it anymore,'" Tenney recalls.

The church doesn't keep figures on the numbers of people who have come to faith in Jesus since the revival started because they encourage people to go back to their home churches. Many pastors bring their people to the services in Baltimore because they know that Rock Church won't steal their flock. ... "On any given night we have 12 to 20 pastors from the Baltimore area," Pierce says.

Still, some do come long distances. One night they looked out and saw 47 Koreans who had chartered a plane to come. Another time a group from Iceland was there. They have had visitors from Britain, Germany, the Ukraine and all across America. ...

Today, services in Baltimore are quieter and gentler than they were during the first few months of revival. But the worship music is powerful, and the singing draws the congregation to Jesus. Most of the songs were written by people in the church after the revival began.[33]

The convicting presence of God draws people to this church which also invests heavily in social caring ministries. Like other centres of revival, it has seen thousands make commitments to Christ, lives transformed, and it continues to minister to people in need.

Many countries worldwide have been experiencing similar Spirit movements in which a specific impact, anointing or 'baptism' of the Spirit on a group of people ignites a revival movement. This includes Australia.

1997 - November: Pilbara, Western Australia (Craig Siggins)

Craig Siggins, an Aboriginal Baptist pastor, reported on Spirit movements in Western Australia which caught the attention of the secular media, especially through the closure of a hotel at Newman, Western Australia, in the wake of the revival movement there.

My wife, Lyn, and I came to the Pilbara in 1993, settling in the town of Newman. Our vision was to see a strong, indigenous Aboriginal church raised up amongst the Martu Aboriginal people of this area. But we had not expected to see it so soon. We had expected a long, slow struggle before anything of significance developed.

Some communities were strongly anti-Christian. At one community we were told by some white Christians not to be too overt in our Christian witness. Two years later Aboriginal leaders from our Parnpajinya Church at Newman baptised many from that community. At another community a clause against teaching Christianity was written into the school constitution. Two years later we were having Christian meetings on the school verandah. Aboriginal people told me how some of the old men had threatened Christians with spears. Some of these same old men have now accepted Christ.

Against all expectations we found the Martu people to be really open to the Gospel. The seeds were sown by the 1981 revival, by the witness of the Apostolic Church and by the work of the late Jim Marsh, a gifted linguist with a pastoral heart, much respected by the people.

Teams of Aboriginal Christian men from the Plibara Aboriginal Church of Roebourne (Apostolic) came over from time to time and helped. Leaders developed. More were baptised. I became committed to taking teams from Parnpajinya (Newman) to various communities. Gifts were developed. More and more became Christians and were baptised, but the revival hadn't really come as yet. It was like the winter rains refreshing us before the main summer rains came. Communities - too many to cope with - were crying out for visits.

One of our leaders - Kerry Kelly (KK) - had gone to War-ralong and teamed up with a couple of other strong Christians. Warralong has a community that had been opposed to Christianity. But the Spirit moved there and many were baptised. We had Christian meetings (the first ever). At one meeting nearly the whole community came forward to dedicate or re-dedicate their lives to Christ. KK, less than two years old as a Christian, became one of the main leaders at Warralong and for the revival. In 1996, I had taken KK over to a Men's Training Camp in the Northern Territory. This interaction helped solidify KK in his Christian walk. KK often leads at the Lord's Supper, and when many communities come together this has been a unifying factor.

At Parnpajinya (Newman), just before and after Christmas 1997, many people were coming to the Lord and we were having multiple baptisms at the Ophthalmia Dam. This was about the time the revival really took off. People from Jigalong and other communities were also coming to be baptised, including some of the old men. Many nights we were having meetings that went to early in the morning. Some communities were having meetings every night and prayer meetings every day! Some still are.

A spiritual awakening took place in many communities in 1997. Things started at Warralong, where many became Christians and were baptised after being influenced by three Christian Aboriginal leaders. Then just before Christmas, Kurutakurru joined two other leaders at Nullagine, and many from Nullagine and other communities became Christians and came across to the dam at Newman to be baptised.

Many communities started having meetings almost every night and prayer meetings every day. Leaders travelled to different communities for the meetings and to encourage people, sometimes holding meetings at night after a funeral service when hundreds of people were gathered. Some meetings went on for eight hours or more as people shared in song, testimony, prayer, Bible reading and preaching.

When Franklin Graham visited Perth in early February, 1998, over 200 Martu people travelled the 1,150 km for his meetings. It was like one long church service all the way there and back. Everyone was bursting to sing and witness to the people in Perth.

When we got back there were more meetings and baptisms, even from communities that had previously rejected Christianity. Old people, Aboriginal elders, were turning to Christ and being baptised. Four hundred people gathered at the Coongan River near Marble Bar for three days of meetings, with many more being baptised.

Police, hospitals and others have noticed a decrease in alcohol related incidents. The media has begun to take notice. Nullagine, which had the record of being the arrest capital of Australia, became news when the pubs went broke, apparently because so many had given up the grog. 'A Current Affair' came up and did a television spot at Nullagine.

Amazingly, a simultaneous and apparently quite separate revival began at about the same time among the Pintubi people and others across the border in the Northern Territory. A team from Kiwirrkura, just on the WA side of the border, travelled across the desert and joined up with the Pilbara meetings, arriving early for our Easter Convention held in a wide dry river bed near Newman. More than 1000 people from different communities and Christian traditions came together to celebrate.

Why the revival? It is nothing more or less more than a work of the Holy Spirit. It has similarities to the revival that spread to many Aboriginal communities in the early '80s, which reached the Pilbara but never really took hold. Like that revival, people have had dreams and visions. Recently Mitchell, a leader from Punmu, got up and read from Acts 2 about Joel's prophecy and said it was being fulfilled. Not long ago, people told me they had seen a cross in the sky one morning. And like the '80s revival, it is the Aboriginal people taking the Wangka Kunyjunyu (Good News) to their own people in their own way and their own language.

Aboriginal leaders empowered by the Holy Spirit are leading the revival. These leaders would like to see the revival reaching the wider Kartiya (nonAboriginal) society. But for these shy desert people to reach out to Kartiya in these days of Mabo, Wik and the struggle for reconciliation will only be by the hand of God.[34]

Similar to the Aboriginal led revival of the eighties in Arnhem Land of Northern Australia, this Western Australian revival movement spread through other aboriginal communities.

1998 - August: Kimberleys, Western Australia (Max Wiltshire)

Max Wiltshire, the Assemblies of God Australian Aboriginal Outreach (AAO) coordinator, reported on revival in the Kimberley region of north-west Australia at the Assemblies of God state conference in August 1998.

A number of Aboriginal leaders had accompanied him to the conference, including Kenny Boomer who received his ministry credential. Their national magazine, *The Australian Evangel*, carried Max Wiltshire's story.

> The Kimberleys are ablaze. The fire of God in the hearts of his people burns brighter than ever, new churches have been started, others have doubled in size - one leaping from 10 percent of the community to 90 percent in just a few weeks. Further afield in the Pilbara area the move of God has been so intense that the local hotel went into receivership.
>
> This move has seen the number of Christians doubled in the area over the last twelve months, which means our conventions are climbing toward a thousand people in the evening meetings. Are the manifestations still occurring as at first in this move of God? Yes, in fact the increase that we are seeing is in direct relationship to the outstanding manifestations of the Spirit.
>
> But - what manifestations are we talking about? The usual? Yes, laughing, shaking, rolling, crying, running and so on continue. However, if these are the normal, what are the outstanding ones? In truth, some would make you cry in awe and wonder. Such as seeing people falling under the power of the Spirit as they give their offering to the Lord. As they have come to

the front and put their offering in the containers, they 'fall out' there and then as the blessing of giving overcomes them.

"After a recent crusade, one Aboriginal lady handed a ministry offering to the speaker on behalf of the church, and fell at his feet, again under the power and blessing of giving.

We have also seen folks falling out in the opening prayer as the very name of Jesus is mentioned. They just fall from the seats to the floor, not knowing they are meant to wait until the altar call before they let the Lord touch them. Back up singers are unable to stand, also people bringing items are unable to finish them because the anointing is so great.[35]

These reports of spirit movements among Aboriginal communities reflect different emphases in theology and ecclesiology, one conservative Baptist and one Pentecostal, but both indicate the profound impact of revival on personal and communal life.

1999 - July: Mornington Island, Queensland (Jesse Padayache)

Brian Pickering, Australian prayer co-ordinator gathered reports of revival in aboriginal communities in North Queensland. Jesse Padayache, an Indian from South Africa, now living in Australia, has led meetings in these communities and reported on revival at Mornington Island, Arakun and Weipa in the Gulf of Carpentaria, North Queensland, as well as on Psalm Island north east of Townsville.[36]

Mornington Island was noted for its drunkenness and violence. Iranale Tadulala, a Fijian Pastor was posted there as the Uniting Church minister in 1994. During 1997, he had a vision of an angel appearing to him who told him that there was to be a revival on Mornington Island and he was to facilitate it. However it would not be easy.

He began a 40 day fast from 1st June until 11th July, 1999. A colleague visited Mornington Island when Iranale Tadulala was 28 days into his fast and was deeply challenged just being with him because he was so committed, close to tears all the time.

A Christian man had been martyred in the early days of the Mission on Mornington Island. At the end of his 40 day fast Iranale Tadulala believed he had to go out to the site of the killing and fast there a further seven days. This was a rather harrowing experience which he described as doing battle with cosmic forces throughout that prayer and fasting.

At the conclusion of the fast, only days after a national prayer gathering at Uluru (Ayres Rock) in July a team began meetings at Mornington Island which began on 27th July. At the end of the first meeting 100 stayed behind for prayer and counselling. By the end of the crusade there had been 300 conversions (25% of the population) and they were still going on with 500 reported converted by September.

Five pastors in the team included three Fijians (from Palm Island, Weipa, and Mornington Island), an Australian from Townsville and the Indian South African from Brisbane. They are working on discipleship, want Bibles, and are already getting phone calls from surrounding areas asking them to go there, but are saying: "When God says it is right!"

Jesse Padayache, the South African Indian, has ministered in Australia for many years. His wife Cookie was healed miraculously from a tumour on the brain through prayer. They have medical x-rays showing the tumour and the total healing.

In February and May, Jesse had spoken at revival meetings in Palm Island north east of Townsville, among the tribes there, where there has been much drunkeness. Many were converted, delivered and set free from addiction to alcohol, tobacco and fornication. A man, angry with Jesse because his de-facto wife was converted in February and wanted to get married, was later converted. He asked Jesse to marry them during the meetings in May. Now money formerly spent on addictions is spend on food, clothes and shelter and many people are prospering for the first time.

News of the revival meetings on Palm Island then reached Mornington Island. In Mornington Island, alcohol abuse has been extreme. Drunkenness was everywhere. The place was littered with piles of beer cans. The Fijian pastor Iranale Tadulala, had been discouraged, facing continual opposition. About 10 people attended the services.

On the first night, Tuesday, 27 July, 1999, the team was casting out demons till midnight. People were healed including the deaf, cripples, and people with back pain, diabetes, blood pressure, and heart diseases. Many committed their lives to the Lord Jesus Christ and were prayed with to be set free from generational curses. A report from the pastors says: "Spirits of suicide, alcoholism were driven out and old curses of sorcery and witchcraft were broken."

On the second night, Wednesday, an angry lady with a beer can came in abusing Jesse Padayache and the team for casting out spirits. She yelled, "Me and my beer, we live together. Don't listen to this man." But the people wanted to be delivered because of the changes they saw in their friends. Many were healed and delivered. Two healed people threw away their crutches. A lady with a stroke was healed and freed from her wheelchair. The drunken lady saw the healings and eventually wanted prayer. She committed her life to Christ and became instantly sober. She said, "Pastor, I don't want this stupid habit" and gave her six pack of beer to the pastor.

A young man, lying in bed at home heard the loud speakers, and so came to the meetings to give his life to God. On Sunday the church was packed with people standing outside to listen. Many were healed in the morning, and many more on Sunday night.

Large numbers, formerly in de-facto relationships, have now married. The pastor has been busy performing marriages. Within weeks, beer consumption dropped by over 9,000 cans a week.

On the Monday they started classes for believers. More were converted then also. A drunken man came from the 'pub' to the believers class, seeking God. The believers also follow up each other, because they all know who is involved.

When Jesse Padayache passed through Weipa on his way to Arakun in the gulf country of north west Queensland in August, he met an aboriginal lady from a community of 400 people in Marpoon, north of Weipa. Her 34 year old son, looking wild, saliva dripping, and shaking, had been in a psychotic state receiving treatment for six years. He'd been separated from his de-facto wife and children for that time. The pastor saw them at the shopping centre so invited them to his place for healing prayer. The son was frightened of the pastors, staring with wild eyes. They bound spirits and cast them out. When he went back to the hospital he was pronounced totally healed. He now lives with his family and got married.

The mother asked for prayer also. She had asthma, a heart monitor, sugar diabetes, and a huge lump like a rock melon on her stomach. The lump disappeared, and the arthritis, asthma, diabetes and blood pressure were all healed immediately, medically verified. Later she came back to Weipa for meetings with a bus load of people, all seeking God because of those healings. Most of that bus load were saved, and now a church as been started in Marpoon. The previous church had been destroyed in the 1960s, and the people there had hated the gospel, till now.

The pastors caught the small plane from Weipa to Arakun. Many were drunk there. People ignored or hated the church, regarding Christianity as a religion for whites. Only about six members attended the church.

One the first night of meetings at Arakun, about 50 came into the hall with another 40 people sitting around outside listening. Noisy dogs came in. An old man, deaf in his left ear and partially deaf in his right ear was totally healed. Three weeks earlier, in a dream he had seen the dark skinned Jesse pray for his healing, and he knew he would be healed at that meeting. Then, nearly all in the hall and some from outside gave their lives to Christ that first night. Many were healed, including a man lame in his right leg.

Word spread fast. Everyone knows what is happening in the community. The next night the church was packed. Crowds stood around outside. By the end of the meetings, 170 aboriginals had given their lives to Christ for the first time. Many were healed including people blind or partially blind and deaf. Great joy filled the community. Many were delivered from alcohol addiction.

One of the council officers in the building next door told the community leaders that Jesse and the pastor needed to go on casting out demons because so many people were being delivered of drunkenness and diseases.

They reported that demons associated with suicide came out of a man who had tried to kill himself four times. Now he is whole. Everyone talked about the changes in the atmosphere of the community. Then he returned to his de-facto wife and was married. His witness brought large numbers to the Lord.

Back again at Weipa for meetings, the same things kept happening. A young white lady in her twenties was delivered with loud cries and healed on the second night of the meetings in Weipa, to the surprise of the aboriginals who thought only aboriginals had demons. The news spread like wildfire, and many more came for salvation, deliverance and healing.

The bus load from Wapoon north of Weipa – brought by the lady and her son who had been healed at the pastor's home previously - returned full of saved, healed and delivered people, determined to start their church in their community, which they have done.

Just as revival on Elcho Island in 1979-1980 sparked revival across Arnhem Land, and teams went out to many aboriginal communities, so this revival is touching many communities in north Queensland.

This report provides a significant closing account for this historical survey of specific impacts of the Spirit in revival. It demonstrates again the characteristics of revival and Spirit movements identified in the introduction, especially how God takes the week, poor, unknown and those who are nothing to shame the wise, humble the proud, and pull down the mighty. It demonstrates the transforming possibilities of Spirit movements for individuals, families, churches and communities.

God chose what is foolish in the world to shame the wise;
God chose what is weak in the world to shame the strong;
God chose what is low and despised in the world,
things that are not, to reduce to nothing things that are,
so that no one might boast in the presence of God.[37]

Endnotes

[1] Claudio Freidzon, 1997, *Holy Spirit, I Hunger for You,* Creation House, pp. 14-16, 47.

[2] Richard Riss, 1995, "A History of the Worldwide Awakening of 1992-1995",
http://www.grmi.org/renewal/Richard_Riss/history.html

[3] Riss, 1995.

[4] Daren Trinder, 1993, "A New Way of Living" Christian Outreach Centre, Brisbane, June.

[5] Riss, 1995.

[6] 'The Father's Blessing' is the Toronto Airport Christian Fellowship's preferred name for this revival widely reported and discussed as 'The Toronto Blessing'.

[7] John Arnott, 1995, *Keep the Fire,* Marshall Pickering, pp. 58-59.

[8] James Beverley, Professor of Theology and Ethics at Ontario Theological Seminary, summarises the voluminous reactions to the 'Toronto Blessing' ranging through five responses, that it is regarded as:

1. a renewal with prophetic and eschatological significance - a further harbinger of the Spirit's outpouring promised at the close of the age;

2. a significant renewal, as was the Azusa Street revival, but not necessarily eschatologically significant;

3. a mixed blessing, involving significant renewal but clouded with some dangerous or harmful aspects;

4. a fundamentally flawed renewal movement, fostering psychological aberrations and theological error so it should be opposed;

5. a major deception typical of eschatological warnings about a

great falling away into apostasy at the end.

The majority position, though not necessarily therefore correct, appears to be a combination of the second and third positions. It is regarded primarily as a significant renewal of hundreds of thousands of people and many thousands of churches, not necessarily an eschatological phenomenon, and mixed with a range of reactions, some of which are suspect or damaging particularly where the phenomena are idolised, imitated, or psychologically induced (Beverley, 1995, *Holy Laughter and the Toronto Blessing,* Zondervan, p.22-23).

[9] Beverley's conclusion (1995, p.162) has been amply demonstrated that "Fundamentally, neither The Toronto Blessing nor the Holy Laughter revival should be understood as something without parallel in the work of God today. Rather both realities are simply two ways among countless others that God uses to manifest his gracious and creative salvific work through Jesus Christ ... One can properly recognize every wonderful aspect of both movements without giving into temptation to elitism and self-absorption, something that manifests so often in famous renewal movements."

[10] The term 'Awakening' for this Spirit movement is used often, probably originating with Richard Riss, 1995, and his widely circulated report published on the internet.

[11] Based upon information submitted by Randy Clark, Global Awakening, 2010.

[12] Riss, 1995.

[13] Riss, 1995.

[14] Reported by Nicky Gumbel in October 1999 in Melbourne (Terry Craig, 1999, "The Alpha Campaign" in *Alive* Magazine, Issue 11, November/December, p. 7).

[15] A & J FitzGibbons, 1995, *Something Extraordinary is Happening,*.Monarch, p. 15.

[16] Awakening e-mail, 30 August, 1996.

[17] Brian Shick, 1998, "Christian Life Centre, Mt Annan", *Renewal Journal*, No. 12, pp. 17-20..

[18] Greg Beech, 1996, "Times of Refreshing", Renewal Journal, No. 7, pp. 9-11.

[19] Riss, 1995.

[20] Riss, 1995.

[21] E-mail report, June 12, 1999, by Larry Booth, Senior Pastor of the First Baptist Church in Seattle Beach, Melbourne, Florida: larbooth@juno.com

[22] Based upon information submitted by Randy Clark

[23] Riss, 1995.

[24] John Kilpatrick, 1997, When the Heavens are Brass, Revival Press, pp. ix-xiv.

[25] David Hogan, 1997, reproduced from a sermon by David Hogan in Brisbane, November 1996, condensed and reproduced in Renewal Journal, Issue 9, 1997, pp. 33-39..

[26] Information from http://members.aol.com/azusa/index.html reproduced from The Remnant International, via Asuza e-mail.

[27] Source: Awakening e-mail, April 13, 1998, written by Ken Lawson.

[28] Reported in the Mobile Register, May 10, 1997.

[29] Mobile Register, May 10, 1997.

[30] *Mobile Register*, May 10, 1997.

[31] Tommy Tenney, 1998, *The God Chasers,* Destiny Image, pp. 4-8.

[32] Adapted from Awakening e-mails.

[33] *Charisma,* July, 1998.

[34] Craig Siggins, 1998, *Renewal Journal*, Issue 11, pp. 8-9, adapted from *Alive Magazine*, No. 5, June 1998, pages 8-10, and from *Vision*, the magazine of the Australian Baptist Missionary Society, July 1998, pages 12-15.

[35] Robert McQuillan, 1998, *The Australian Evangel*, August, p. 32.

[36] Geoff Waugh, 1999, *Renewal Journal*, No. 14, pp. 39-42. This report was compiled from e-mail correspondence with Brian Pickering and personal discussion with Jesse Padayache in Brisbane.

[37] 1 Corinthians 1:27-29.

Chapter 7

Twenty-first Century
Transforming Revival ████████████████████

Revival explodes globally now. Where God's people take his Word and his promises seriously in repentance, unity and commitment, revivals of New Testament proportions blaze like wildfire across the nations of the earth.

This chapter gives some examples of current transforming revivals where whole communities and even the ecology have been totally changed.

Snapshots of Glory (George Otis Jr.)

George Otis Jr presents vivid stories of the transformation of cities and regions in the two DVDs Transformations 1 and 2, and other DVDs of The Sentinel Group. This transforming revival now spreads world wide in the twenty-first century. Otis summarises some outstanding examples, rooted in the late twentieth century, and blossoming now.[1]

> For some time now, we have been hearing reports of large-scale conversions in places like China, Argentina and Nepal. In many instances, these conversions have been attended by widespread healings, dreams

and deliverances. Confronted with these demonstrations of divine power and concern, thousands of men and women have elected to embrace the truth of the gospel. In a growing number of towns and cities, God's house is suddenly the place to be.

In some communities throughout the world, this rapid church growth has also led to dramatic socio-political transformation. Depressed economies, high crime rates and corrupt political structures are being replaced by institutional integrity, safe streets and financial prosperity. Impressed by the handiwork of the Holy Spirit, secular news agencies have begun to trumpet these stories in front-page articles and on prime-time newscasts.

Of those on file, most are located in Africa and the Americas. The size of these changed communities ranges from about 15,000 inhabitants to nearly 2 million.

Miracle in Mizoram

One of the earliest and largest transformed communities of the twentieth century is found in Mizoram, a mountainous state in northeastern India. The region's name translates as "The Land of the Highlanders." It is an apt description as a majority of the local inhabitants, known as Mizos, live in villages surrounded by timbered mountains and scenic gorges.

The flora is not entirely alpine, however, and it is not uncommon to see hills covered with bamboo, wild bananas and orchids. The Mizos are hearty agriculturists who manage to grow ample crops of rice, corn, tapioca, ginger, mustard, sugar cane, sesame and potatoes.

But it is not farming prowess that sets Mizoram's 750,000 citizens apart. Nor, for that matter, is it their Mongol stock. Rather it is the astonishing size of the national church, estimated to be between 80 and 95 percent of the current population. This achievement is all the more remarkable in view of the fact that Mizoram is sandwiched precariously between Islamic Bangladesh to the west, Buddhist Myanmar to the east and south, and the Hindu states of Assam, Manipur and Tripura to the north.

Before the arrival of Christian missionaries in the late nineteenth century, local tribes believed in a spirit called Pathan. They also liked to remove the heads of their enemies. But in just four generations Mizoram has gone from being a fierce head-hunting society to a model community – and quite possibly the most thoroughly Christian place of comparable size on earth. Certainly in India there is no other city or state that could lay claim to having no homeless people, no beggars, no starvation and 100 percent literacy.

The churches of Mizoram currently send 1,000 missionaries to surrounding regions of India and elsewhere throughout the world. Funds for this mission outreach are generated primarily through the sale of rice and firewood donated by the believers. Every time a Mizo woman cooks rice, she places a handful in a special 'missionary bowl.' This rice is then taken to the local church, where it is collected and sold at the market.

Even the non-Christian media of India have recognized Christianity as the source of Mizoram's dramatic social transformation. In 1994, Mizoram celebrated its one-hundredth year of contact with Christianity, which began with the arrival of two missionaries, William Frederick Savage and J. H. Lorraine. On the occasion of this centennial celebration, *The Telegraph* of Calcutta (February 4, 1994) declared:

Christianity's most reaching influence was the spread of education ... Christianity gave the religious a written language and left a mark on art, music, poetry, and literature. A missionary was also responsible for the abolition of traditional slavery. It would not be too much to say that Christianity was the harbinger of modernity to a Mizo society.

A less quantifiable but no less palpable testimony to the Christian transformation of Mizorarn is the transparent joy and warmth of the Mizo people. Visitors cannot fail to observe "the laughing eyes mid smiling faces," in the words of one reporter, on the faces of the children and other residents of Mizoram. And nowhere is this spirit of divine joy more evident than in the churches, where the Mizo's traditional love of music and dance has been incorporated into worship. The generosity of the people is also seen in their communal efforts to rebuild neighbours' bamboo huts destroyed by the annual monsoons.

Eighty percent of the population of Mizorarn attends church at least once a week. Congregations are so plentiful in Mizoram that, from one vantage point in the city of Izol, it is possible to count 37 churches. Most fellowships have three services on Sunday and another on Wednesday evening.

Almolonga, Guatemala

In the mid-1970s, the town of Almolonga was typical of many Mayan highland communities: idolatrous, inebriated and economically depressed. Burdened by fear and poverty, the people sought support in alcohol and a local idol named Maximon. Determined to fight back, a group of local intercessors got busy, crying out to God during evening prayer vigils. As a consequence of their partnership with the Holy Spirit, Almolonga, like Mizoram, has become one of the most thoroughly transformed communities in the world. Fully 90 percent of the town's citizens now consider themselves to be evangelical Christians. As they have repudiated ancient pacts with Mayan and syncretistic gods, their economy has begun to blossom. Churches are now the dominant feature of Almolonga's landscape and many public establishments boast of the town's new allegiance.

Although many Christian visitors comment on Almolonga's "clean" spiritual atmosphere, this is a relatively recent development. "Just twenty years ago," reports Guatemala City pastor Harold Caballeros, "the town suffered from poverty, violence and ignorance. In the mornings you would encounter many men just lying on the streets, totally drunk from the night before. And of course this drinking brought along other serious problems like domestic violence and poverty. It was a vicious cycle."

Donato Santiago, the town's aging chief of police, told me during an October 1998 interview that he and a dozen deputies patrolled the streets regularly because of escalating violence. "People were always fighting," he said. "We never had any rest." The town, despite its small population, had to build four jails to contain the worst offenders. "They were always full," Santiago remembers. "We often had to bus overflow prisoners to Quetzaltenango." There was disrespect toward women and neglect of the family.

Pastor Mariano Riscajché one of the key leaders of Almolonga's spiritual turnaround, remembers, "I was raised in misery. My father sometimes drank for forty to fifty consecutive days. We never had a big meal, only a little tortilla with a small glass of coffee. My parents spent what little money they had on alcohol."

In an effort to ease their misery, many townspeople made pacts with local deities like Maximon (a wooden idol rechristened San Simon by Catholic syncretists), and the patron of death, Pascual Bailón. The latter, according to Riscajché, "is a spirit of death whose skeletal image was once housed in a chapel behind the Catholic church. Many people went to him when they wanted to kill someone through witchcraft." The equally potent Maximon controlled people through money and alcohol. "He's not just a wooden mask," Riscajché insists, "but a powerful spiritual strong-man." The deities were supported by well-financed priesthoods known as confradías.

During these dark days the gospel did not fare well. Outside evangelists were commonly chased away with sticks or rocks, while small local house churches were similarly stoned. On one occasion six men shoved a gun barrel down the throat of Mariano Riscajché. As they proceeded to pull the trigger, he silently petitioned the Lord for protection. When the hammer fell, there was no action. A second click. Still no discharge.

In August 1974, Riscajché led a small group of believers into a series of prayer vigils that lasted from 7 p.m. to midnight. Although prayer dominated the meetings, these vanguard intercessors also took time to speak declarations of freedom over the town. Riscajché remembers that God filled them with faith. "We started praying, 'Lord, it's not possible that we could be so insignificant when your Word says we are heads and not tails.'"

In the months that followed, the power of God delivered many men possessed by demons associated with Maximon and Pascual Bailón. Among the more notable of these was a Maximon cult leader named José Albino Tazej. Stripped of their power and customers, the confradías of Maximon made a decision to remove the sanctuary of Maximon to the city of Zunil.

At this same time, God was healing many desperately diseased people. Some of these hearings led many to commit their lives to Christ (including that of Madano's sister-in-law Teresa, who was actually raised from the dead after succumbing to complications associated with a botched caesarean section).

This wave of conversions has continued to this day. By late 1998 there were nearly two dozen evangelical churches in this Mayan town of 19,000, and at least three or four of them had more than 1,000 members. Mariano Riscajché's El Calvario Church seats 1,200 and is nearly always packed. Church leaders include several men who, in earlier years, were notorious for stoning believers.

Nor has the move of God in Almolonga been limited to church growth. Take a walk through the town's commercial district and you will encounter ubiquitous evidence of transformed lives and social institutions. On one street you can visit a drug-store called 'The Blessing of the Lord.' On another you can shop at 'The Angels' store. Feeling hungry? Just zip into 'Paradise Chicken,' 'Jireh' bakery or the 'Vineyard of the Lord' beverage kiosk. Need building advice? Check out 'Little Israel Hardware' or 'El Shaddai' metal fabrication. Feet hurt from shopping? Just take them to the 'Jordan' mineral baths for a good soak.

For 20 years the town's crime rate has declined steadily. In 1994, the last of Almolonga's four jails was closed. The remodelled building is now called the 'Hall of Honour' and is used for municipal ceremonies and weddings. Leaning against the door, police chief Donato Santiago offered a knowing grin. "It's pretty uneventful around here," he said.

Even the town's agricultural base has come to life. "It is a glorious thing," exclaims a beaming Caballeros. "Almolonga's fields have become so fertile they yield three harvests per year." In fact, some farmers I talked to reported their normal 60-day growing cycle on certain vegetables has been cut to 25. Whereas before they would export four truckloads of produce per month, they are now watching as many as 40 loads a day roll out of the valley.

Nicknamed "America's Vegetable Garden,' Almolonga's produce is of biblical proportions. Walking through the local exhibition hall I saw (and filmed) five-pound beets, carrots larger than my arm and cabbages the size of oversized basketballs. Noting the dimensions of these vegetables and the town's astounding 1,000 percent increase in agricultural productivity, university researchers from the United States and other foreign countries have beat a steady path to Almolonga.

"Now," says Caballeros, "these brothers have the joy of buying big Mercedes trucks -with cash." And they waste no time in pasting their secret all over the shiny vehicles. Huge metallic stickers and mud flaps read 'The Gift of God,' 'God Is My Stronghold' and 'Go Forward in Faith.'

Some farmers are now providing employment to others by renting out land and developing fields in other towns. Along with other Christian leaders they also help new converts get out of debt.

How significant are these developments? In a 1994 headline article describing the dramatic events in Almolonga, Guatemala's premier newsmagazine *Cronica Semanal* concluded "the Evangelical Church ... constitutes the most significant force for religious change in the highlands of Guatemala since the Spanish conquest.[2]

The Umuofai of Nigeria

The Umuofai kindred are spread out in several villages situated near the town of Umuahia in Abia State in southeastern Nigeria. A major rail line links the area with Port Harcourt, about 120 kilometers to the south. Like most parts of coastal Africa, it is distinguished by dense tropical flora and killer humidity.

The interesting chapter of the Umuofai story began as recently as 1996. Two Christian brothers, Emeka and Chinedu Nwankpa, had become increasingly distressed over the spiritual condition of their people. While they did not know everything about the Umuofai kindred, or their immediate Ubakala clan, they knew enough to be concerned. Not only were there few Christians, but there was also an almost organic connection with ancestral traditions of sorcery, divination and spirit appeasement. Some even practiced the demonic art of shape-shifting.

315

Taking the burden before the Lord, the younger brother, Chinedu Nwankpa, was led into a season of spiritual mapping. After conducting a partial 80-day fast, he learned that his primary assignment (which would take the good part of a year) was to spend one day a week with clan elders investigating the roots of prevailing idolatry - including the role of the ancestors and shrines. He would seek to understand how and when the Ubakala clan entered into animistic bondage. According to older brother Emeka, a practicing lawyer and international Bible teacher, this understanding was critical. When I asked why, Emeka responded, "When a people publicly renounce their ties to false gods and philosophies, they make it exceedingly undesirable for the enemy to remain in their community."

The study was finally completed in late 1996. Taking their findings to prayer, the brothers soon felt prompted to invite kindred leaders and other interested parties to attend a special meeting. "What will be our theme?" they asked. The Master's response was quick and direct. "I want you to speak to them about idolatry."

On the day of the meeting, Emeka and Chinedu arrived unsure of what kind of crowd they would face. Would there be five or fifty? Would the people be open or hostile? What they actually encountered stunned them. The meeting place was not only filled with 300 people, but the audience also included several prominent clan leaders and witch doctors. "After I opened in prayer," Emeka recalls, "this young man preaches for exactly 42 minutes. He brings a clear gospel message. He gives a biblical teaching on idolatry and tells the people exactly what it does to a community. When he has finished, he gives a direct altar call. And do you know what happens? Sixty-one adults respond, including people from lines that, for eight generations, had handled the traditional priesthood."

When the minister finished the altar call, the Nwankpa brothers were startled to see a man coming forward with the sacred skull in his hands. Here in front of them was the symbol and receptacle of the clan's ancestral power. "By the time the session ended," Emeka marvels, "eight other spiritual custodians had also come forward. If I had not been there in the flesh, I would not have believed it."

As Emeka was called forward to pray for these individuals, the Holy Spirit descended on the gathering and all the clan leaders were soundly converted. The new converts were then instructed to divide up into individual family units - most were living near the village of Mgbarrakuma - and enter a time of repentance within the family. This took another hour and twenty minutes. During this time people were under deep conviction, many rolling on the ground, weeping. "I had to persuade some of them to get up," Emeka recalls.

After leading this corporate repentance, Emeka heard the Lord say, 'It is now time to renounce the covenants made by and for this community over the last 300 years." Following the example of Zechariah 12:10-13:2, the Nwankpas led this second-phase renunciation. "We were just about to get up," Emeka remembers, "and the Lord spoke to me again. I mean He had it all written out. He said, 'It is now time to go and deal with the different shrines.' So I asked the people, 'Now that we have renounced the old ways, what are these shrines doing here?' And without a moment's hesitation they replied, 'We need to get rid of them!'"

Having publicly renounced the covenants their ancestors had made with the powers of darkness, the entire community proceeded to nine village shrines. The three chief priests came out with their walking sticks. It was tradition that they should go first. Nobody else had the authority to take such a drastic action. So the people stood, the young men following the elders and the women remaining behind in the village square. Lowering his glasses, Emeka says, "You cannot appreciate how this affected me personally. Try to understand that 1 am looking at my own chief. I am looking at generations of men that I have known, people who have not spoken to my father for thirty years, people with all kinds of problems. They are now born-again!"

One of these priests, an elder named Odogwu-ogu, stood before the shrine of a particular spirit called Amadi. He was the oldest living representative of the ancestral priesthood. Suddenly he began to talk to the spirits. He said, "Amadi, I want you to listen carefully to what 1 am saying. You were there in the village square this morning. You heard what happened." He then made an announcement that Emeka will never forget.

Listen, Amadi, the people who own the land have arrived to tell you that they have just made a new covenant with the God of heaven. Therefore all the previous covenants you have made with our ancient fathers are now void. The elders told me to take care of you and I have done that all these years. But today I have left you, and so it is time for you to return to wherever you came from. I have also given my life to Jesus Christ, and from now on, my hands and feet are no longer here.

As he does this, he jumps sideways, lifts his hands and shouts, "Hallelujah!"

"With tears in my eyes," Emeka says, reliving the moment, "I stepped up to anoint this shrine and pray. Every token and fetish was taken out. And then we went through eight more shrines, gathering all the sacred objects and piling them high.

"Gathering again back in the square I said, 'Those who have fetishes in your homes, bring them out because God is visiting here today. Don't let Him pass you by.' At this, one of the priests got up and brought out a pot with seven openings. He said to the people, 'There is poison enough to kill everybody here in that little pot. There is a horn of an extinct animal, the bile of a tiger and the venom of a viper mixed together.' He warned the young men, 'Don't touch it. Carry it on a pole because it is usually suspended in the shrine.' This was piled in the square along with all the ancestral   skulls." Soon other heads of households brought various ritual objects-including idols, totems and fetishes-for public burning.   Many of these items had been handed down over ten generations.

Emeka then read a passage from Jeremiah 10 that judges the spirits associated with these artifacts. Reminding the powers that the people had rejected them, he said, "You spirits that did not make the heavens and the earth in the day of your visitation, it is time for you to leave this place." The people then set the piled objects on fire. They ignited with such speed and intensity that the villagers took it as a sign that God had been waiting for this to happen for many years. When the fire subsided, Emeka and his brother prayed for individual needs and prophetically clothed the priests with new spiritual garments. Altogether the people spent nine hours in intense, strategic-level spiritual warfare.

Emeka recalls that when it was over, "You could feel the atmosphere in the community change. Something beyond revival had broken out." Two young ministers recently filled the traditional Anglican church with about 4,000 youth. And in the middle of the message, demons were reportedly flying out the door! Having renounced old covenants, the Umuofai kindred have made a collective decision that nobody will ever return to animism. "Today," Emeka says, "everybody goes to church. There is also a formal Bible study going on, and the women have a prayer team that my mother conducts. Others gather to pray after completing their communal sweeping."

In terms of political and economic development, good things have begun to happen but not as dramatically as in Almolonga. Still, there is evidence that God has touched the land here much like He has in the highlands of Guatemala. Shortly after the public repentance, several villagers discovered their plots were permeated with saleable minerals. One of these individuals was Emeka's own mother, a godly woman whose property has turned up deposits of valuable ceramic clay.

Hemet, California

For years this searing valley in southern California was known as a pastor's graveyard. Riddled with disunity, local churches were either stagnant or in serious decline. In one case, street prostitutes actually transformed a church rooftop into an outdoor bordello. The entire community had, in the words of pastor Bob Beckett, "a kind of a nasty spiritual feeling to it."

The Hemet Valley was fast becoming a cult haven. "We had the Moonies and Mormons. We had the 'Sheep People,' a cult that claimed Christ but dealt in drugs. The Church of Scientology set up a state-of-the-art multimedia studio called Golden Era, and the Maharishi Mahesh Yogi purchased a property to teach people how to find enlightenment." The latter, according to Beckett, included a 360-acre juvenile facility where students were given instruction in upper-level transcendental meditation. "We're not talking about simply feeling good; we're talking about techniques whereby people can actually leave their bodies."

These discoveries got Beckett to wondering why the Maharishi would purchase property in this relatively obscure valley and why it would be located in proximity to the Scientologists and the spiritually active Soboba Indian reservation. Sensing something sinister might be lurking beneath the town's glazed exterior, Beckett took out a map and started marking locations where there was identifiable spiritual activity."

The deeper this rookie pastor looked, the less he liked what he was seeing. It seemed the valley, in addition to hosting a nest of cults, was also a notable centre of witchcraft.

Nor were cults the only pre-existing problem. Neighborhood youth gangs had plagued the Hemet suburb of San Jacinto for more than a century. When pastor Gordon Houston arrived in 1986 the situation was extremely volatile. His church, San Jacinto Assembly, sits on the very street that has long hosted the town's notorious First Street Gang. "These were kids whose dads and grandfathers had preceded them in the gang. The lifestyle had been handed down through the generations."

"We were one of the first school districts that had to implement a school dress code to avoid gang attire. It was a big problem. There were a lot of weapons on campus and kids were being attacked regularly. The gangs were tied into one of the largest drug production centres in Riverside County."

It turns out the sleepy Hemet Valley was also the methamphetamine manufacturing capital of the West Coast. One former cooker I spoke to in June 1998 (we'll call him Sonny) told me the area hosted at least nine major production laboratories. The dry climate, remote location and 'friendly' law enforcement combined to make it an ideal setup. "It was quite amazing," Sonny told me. "I actually had law officers transport dope for me in their police cruisers. That's the way it used to be here."

The spiritual turnaround for Hemet did not come easily. Neither the Beckerts nor the Houstons were early Valley enthusiasts. "I just didn't want to be there," Bob recalls with emphasis. "For the first several years, my wife and 1 had our emotional bags packed all the time. We couldn't wait for the day that God would call us out of this valley."

The Houstons didn't unpack their bags to begin with. We drove down the street, took one look at the church and said, "No thank you." We didn't even stop to put in a resumé." It would be three years before the Houstons were persuaded to return to the Hemet Valley. "God asked if we would be willing to spend the rest of our lives in this valley. He couldn't have asked a worse question. How could I spend the rest of my life in a place 1 didn't love, didn't care for and didn't want to be a part of?"

Yet God persevered and the Becketts eventually surrendered to His will. "Once we made this pact, Susan and I fell in love with the community. It might sound a little melodramatic, but I actually went out and purchased a cemetery plot. I said, "Unless Jesus comes back, this is my land. I'm starting and ending my commitment right here." Well, God saw that and began to dispense powerful revelation. I still had my research, but it was no longer just information. It was information that was important to me. It was information I had purchased; it belonged to me."

Now that the Beckets had covenanted to stay in the community, God started to fill in the gaps of their understanding. He began by leading Bob to a book containing an accurate history of the San Jacinto mountains that border Hemet and of the Cahuilla Nation that are descendants of the region's original inhabitants. "As I read through this book I discovered the native peoples believed the ruling spirit of the region was called Tahquitz. He was thought to be exceedingly powerful, occasionally malevolent, associated with the great bear, and headquartered in the mountains. Putting the book down, I sensed the Lord saying, "Find Tahquitz on your map!"

"When I did so, I was shocked to find that our prayer meeting 15 years earlier was held in a cabin located at the base of a one-thousand-foot solid rock spire called Tahquitz peak! I also began to understand that the bear hide God had showed me was linked to the spirit of Tahquitz. The fact that it was stretched out over the community was a reminder of the control this centuries-old demonic strongman wielded, a control that was fuelled then, and now, by the choices of local inhabitants. At that point I knew God had been leading us."

Bob explained that community intercessors began using spiritual mapping to focus on issues and select meaningful targets. Seeing the challenge helped them become spiritually and mentally engaged. With real targets and timelines they could actually watch the answers to their prayers.

The facts speak for themselves. Cult membership, once a serious threat, has now sunk to less than 0.3 percent of the population. The Scientologists have yet to be evicted from their perch at the edge of town, but many other groups are long gone. The transcendental meditation training centre was literally burned out. Shortly after praying for their removal, a brushfire started in the mountains on the west side of the valley. It burned along the top of the ridge and then arced down like a finger to incinerate the Maharishi's facility. Leaving adjacent properties unsinged, the flames burned back up the mountain and were eventually extinguished.

The drug business, according to Sonny, has dropped by as much as 75 percent. Gone, too, is the official corruption that was once its fellow traveller. "There was a time when you could walk into any police department around here and look at your files or secure an escort for your drug shipment. The people watching your back were wearing badges. Man, has that changed. If you're breaking the law today, the police are out to get ya. And prayer is the biggest reason. The Christians out here took a multimillion-dollar drug operation and made it run off with its tail between its legs."

Gangs are another success story. Not long ago a leader of the First Street Gang burst down the centre aisle of Gordon Houston's church (San Jacinto Assembly) during the morning worship service. "I'm in the middle of my message," Gordon laughs, "and here comes this guy, all tattooed up, heading right for the platform. I had no idea what he was thinking. When he gets to the front, he looks up and says, "I want to get saved right now!" This incident, and this young man, represented the first fruit of what God would do in the gang community. Over the next several weeks, the entire First Street family came to the Lord. After this, word circulated that our church was off limits. 'You don't tag this church with graffiti; you don't mess with it in any way.' Instead, gang members began raking our leaves and repainting walls that had been vandalized." More recently, residents of the violent gang house across from San Jacinto Assembly moved out. Then, as church members watched, they bulldozed the notorious facility.

Gang members are not the only people getting saved in Hemet Valley. A recent survey revealed that Sunday morning church attendance now stands at about 14 percent - double what it was just a decade ago. During one 18-month stretch, San Jacinto Assembly altar workers saw more than 600 people give their hearts to Christ. Another prayer-oriented church has grown 300 percent in twelve months.

The individual stories are stirring. Sonny, the former drug manufacturer, was apprehended by the Holy Spirit en route to a murder. Driving to meet his intended victim he felt something take control of the steering wheel. He wound up in the parking lot of Bob Beckett's Dwelling Place Church. It was about 8 o'clock in the morning and a men's meeting had just gotten underway. "Before I got out of the car," Sonny says ruefully, "I looked at the silenced pistol laying on the seat. I remember thinking, 'Oh my God, what am I doing.' So I covered it with a blanket and walked into this prayer meeting. As soon as I did that, it was all over. People are praying around me and I hear this man speak out: 'Somebody was about to murder someone today.' Man, my eyeballs just about popped out of my head. But that was the beginning of my journey home. It took a long time, but I've never experienced more joy in my life."

As of the late 1990s, Hemet also boasted a professing mayor, police chief, fire chief and city manager. If this were not impressive enough, Beckett reckons that one could add about 30 percent of the local law enforcement officers and an exceptional number of high school teachers, coaches and principals. In fact, for the past several years nearly 85 percent of all school district staff candidates have been Christians.

And what of the Valley's infamous church infighting? "Now we are a wall of living stones," Beekett declares proudly. "Instead of competing, we are swapping pulpits. You have Baptists in Pentecostal pulpits and vice versa. You have Lutherans with Episcopalians. The Christian community has become a fabric instead of loose yarn."

Houston adds that valley churches are also brought together by quarterly concerts of prayer and citywide prayer revivals where speaking assignments are rotated among area pastors.

One fellowship is so committed to raising the profile of Jesus Christ in the valley that they have pledged into another church's building program. To Bob Beckett it all makes sense. "It's about building people, not building a church. In fact, it is not even a church growth issue, it is a kingdom growth issue. It's about seeing our communities transformed by the power of the Holy Spirit."

Cali, Columbia

For years Colombia has been the world's biggest exporter of cocaine, sending between 700 hundred and 1,000 tons a year to the United States and Europe alone.[3] The Cali cartel, which controlled up to 70 percent of this trade, has been called the largest, richest and most well-organized criminal organization in history. Employing a combination of bribery and threats, it wielded a malignant power that corrupted individuals and institutions alike.

Randy and Marcy MacMillan, co-pastors of the Communidad Christiana de Fe, have labored in Cali for more than 20 years. At least 10 of these have been spent in the shadow of the city's infamous drug lords.

"These people were paranoid," Randy recalls. "They were exporting 500 million dollars worth of cocaine a month, and it led to constant worries about sabotage and betrayal. They had a lot to lose."

For this reason, the cartel haciendas were appointed like small cities. Within their walls it was possible to find everything from airstrips and helicopter landing pads to indoor bowling alleys and miniature soccer stadiums. Many also contained an array of gift boutiques, nightclubs and restaurants.

Whenever the compound gates swung open, it was to disgorge convoys of shiny black Mercedes automobiles. As they snaked their way through the city's congested streets, all other traffic would pull to the side of the road. Drivers who defied this etiquette did so at their own risk. Many were blocked and summarily shot. As many as 15 people a day were killed in such a manner. "You didn't want to be at the same stoplight with them," Randy summarized.

Journalists had a particularly difficult time. They were either reporting on human carnage – car bombs were going off like popcorn - or they were becoming targets themselves. Television news anchor Adriana Vivas said that many journalists were killed for denouncing what the Mafia was doing in Colombia and Cali. "Important political decisions were being manipulated by drug money. It touched everything, absolutely everything."[4]

By the early 1990s, Cali had become one of the most thoroughly corrupt cities in the world. Cartel interests controlled virtually every major institution - including banks, businesses, politicians and law enforcement.

Like everything else in Cali, the church was in disarray. Evangelicals were few and did not much care for each other. "In those days," Rosevelt Muriel recalls sadly, "the pastors' association consisted of an old box of files that nobody wanted. Every pastor was working on his own; no one wanted to join together."

When pastor-evangelists Julio and Ruth Ruibal came to Cali in 1978, they were dismayed at the pervasive darkness in the city. "There was no unity between the churches," Ruth explained. Even Julio was put off by his colleagues and pulled out of the already weak ministerial association.

Ruth relates that during a season of fasting the Lord spoke to Julio saying, "You don't have the right to be offended. You need to forgive." So going back to the pastors, one by one, Julio made things right. They could not afford to walk in disunity - not when their city faced such overwhelming challenges.

Randy and Marcy MacMillan were among the first to join the Ruibals in intercession. "We just asked the Lord to show us how to pray," Marcy remembers. And He did. For the next several months they focused on the meagre appetite within the church for prayer, unity and holiness. Realizing these are the very things that attract the presence of God, they petitioned the Lord to stimulate a renewed spiritual hunger, especially in the city's ministers.

As their prayers began to take effect, a small group of pastors proposed assembling their congregations for an evening of joint worship and prayer. The idea was to lease the city's civic auditorium, the Colisco El Pueblo, and spend the night in prayer and repentance. They would solicit God's active participation in their stand against the drug cartels and their unseen spiritual masters.

Roping off most of the seating area, the pastors planned for a few thousand people. And even this, in the minds of many, was overly optimistic. "We heard it all," said Rosevelt Muriel. "People told us, 'It can't be done,' 'No one will come,' 'Pastors won't give their support.' But we decided to move forward and trust God with the results."

When the event was finally held in May 1995, the nay-sayers and even some of the organizers were dumb-founded. Instead of the expected modest turnout, more than 25,000 people filed into the civic audito-rium - nearly half of the city's evangelical population at the time! At one point, Muriel remembers, "The mayor mounted the platform and proclaimed, 'Cali belongs to Jesus Christ.' Well, when we heard those words, we were energized." Giving themselves to intense prayer, the crowd remained until 6 o'clock the next morning. The city's famous all-night prayer vigil - the 'vigilia' - had been born.

Forty-eight hours after the event, the daily newspa-per, *El Pais*, headlined, "No Homicides!" For the first time in as long as anybody in the city could remember, a 24-hour period had passed without a single person being killed. In a nation cursed with the highest homi-cide rate in the world, this was a newsworthy develop-ment. Corruption also took a major hit when, over the next four months, 900 cartel-linked officers were fired from the metropolitan police force.

In the month of June, this sense of anticipation was heightened when several intercessors reported dreams in which angelic forces apprehended leaders of the Cali drug cartel. "Within six weeks of this vi-sion," MacMillan recalls, "the Colombian government declared all-out war against the drug lords." Sweeping military operations were launched against cartel assets in several parts of the country. The 6,500 elite commandos dispatched to Cali arrived with explicit orders to round up seven individuals suspected as the top leaders of the cartel.

"Cali was buzzing with helicopters," Randy remembers. "The airport was closed and there were police roadblocks at every entry point into the city. You couldn't go anywhere without proving who you were."[5]

(Suspicions that the drug lords were consulting spirit mediums) were confirmed when the federalés dragnet picked up Jorge Eliecer Rodriguez at the fortune-telling parlour of Madame Marlene Ballesteros, the famous 'Pythoness of Cali". By August, only three months after God's word to the intercessors, Colombian authorities had captured all seven targeted cartel leaders.

Clearly stung by these assaults on his power base, the enemy lashed out against the city's intercessors. At the top of his hit list was Pastor Julio Ceasar Ruibal, a man whose disciplined fasting and unwavering faith was seriously eroding his manoeuvring room.

On December 13, 1995, Julio rode into the city with his daughter Sarah and a driver. Late for a pastors' meeting at the Presbyterian Church, he motioned to his driver to pull over. "He told us to drop him off," Sarah recounts, "and that was the last time I saw him."

Outside the church, a hit man was waiting in ambush. Drawing a concealed handgun, the assassin pumped two bullets into Julio's brain at point-blank range.

331

"I was waiting for him to arrive at the meeting," Roosevelt remembers. "At two o'clock in the afternoon I received a phone call. The man said, 'They just killed Julio.' I said, 'What? How can they kill a pastor?' I rushed over, thinking that perhaps he had just been hurt. But when I arrived on the scene, he was motionless. Julio, the noisy one, the active one, the man who just never sat still, was just lying there like a baby."

"The first thing I saw was a pool of crimson blood," Ruth recalls. "And the verse that came to me was Psalm 116:15: 'Precious in the sight of the Lord is the death of his saints.' Sitting down next to Julio's body, I knew I was on holy ground."

Julio Ruibal was killed on the sixth day of a fast aimed at strengthening the unity of Cali's fledgling church. He knew that even though progress had been made in this area, it had not gone far enough. He knew that unity is a fragile thing. What he could not have guessed is that the fruit of his fast would be made manifest at his own funeral.

In shock, and struggling to understand God's purposes in this tragedy, 1,500 people gathered at Julio's funeral. They included many pastors that had not spoken to each other in months. When the memorial concluded these men drew aside and said, "Brothers, let us covenant to walk in unity from this day forward. Let Julio's blood be the glue that binds us together in the Holy Spirit."

It worked! Today this covenant of unity has been signed by some 200 pastors and serves as the backbone of the city's high profile prayer vigils. With Julio's example in their hearts, they have subordinated their own agendas to a larger, common vision for the city.

Emboldened by their spiritual momentum, Cali's church leaders now hold all-night prayer rallies every 90 days. Enthusiasm is so high that these glorious events have been moved to the largest venue in the city, the 55,000-seat Pascual Guerrero soccer stadium. Happily (or unhappily as the case may be), the demand for seats continues to exceed supply.

As the kingdom of God descended upon Cali, a new openness to the gospel could be felt at all levels of society - including the educated and wealthy. One man, Gustavo Jaramillo, a wealthy businessman and former mayor, told me, "It is easy to speak to upper-class people about Jesus. They are respectful and interested." Raul Grajales, another successful Cali businessman, adds that the gospel is now seen as practical rather than religious. As a consequence, he says, "Many high-level people have come to the feet of Jesus."

Explosive church growth is one of the visible consequences of the open heavens over Cali. Ask pastors to define their strategy and they respond, "We don't have time to plan. We're too busy pulling the nets into the boat." And the numbers are expanding. In early 1998, I visited one fellowship, the Christian Centre of Love and Faith, where attendance has risen to nearly 35,000. What is more, their stratospheric growth rate is being fuelled entirely by new converts. Despite the facility's cavernous size (it's a former Costco warehouse), they are still forced to hold seven Sunday services. As I watched the huge sanctuary fill up, I blurted the standard Western question: "What is your secret?" Without hesitating, a church staff member pointed to a 24-hour prayer room immediately behind the platform. "That's our secret,' he replied.

My driver, Carlos Reynoso (not his real name), himself a former drug dealer, put it this way: "There is a hunger for God everywhere. You can see it on the buses, on the streets and in the cafes. Anywhere you go people are ready to talk." Even casual street evangelists are reporting multiple daily conversions - nearly all the result of arbitrary encounters.

Although danger still lurks in this city of 1.9 million, God is now viewed as a viable protector. When Cali police deactivated a large, 174-kilo car bomb in the populous San Nicolis area in November 1996, many noted that the incident came just 24 hours after 55,000 Christians held their third *vigilia*. Even *El Pais* headlined: "Thanks to God, It Didn't Explode."[6]

Cali's prayer warriors were gratified, but far from finished. The following month church officials, disturbed by the growing debauchery associated with the city's *Feria*, a year-end festival accompanied by 10 days of bull fighting and blowout partying, developed plans to hold public worship and evangelism rallies.

"When we approached the city about this," Marcy recalls, "God gave us great favour. The city secretary not only granted us rent-free use of the 22,000-scat velodrome (cycling arena), but he also threw in free advertising, security and sound support. We were stunned!" The only thing the authorities required was that the churches pray for the mayor, the city and the citizens.

Once underway, the street witnessing and rallies brought in a bounty of souls. But an even bigger surprise came during the final service which, according to Marcy, emphasized the Holy Spirit "reigning over" and "raining down upon" the city of Cali. As the crowd sang, it began to sprinkle outside, an exceedingly rare occurrence in the month of December. "Within moments," Marcy recalls, "the city was inundated by torrential tropical rain. It didn't let up for 24 hours; and for the first time in recent memory, *Feria* events had to be cancelled!"

On the evening of April 9, 1998, I had the distinct privilege of attending a citywide prayer vigil in Cali's Pascual Guerrero stadium. Arriving at the stadium 90 minutes early, I found it was already a full house. I could feel my hair stand on end as I walked onto the infield to tape a report for CBN News. In the stands, 50,000 exuberant worshipers stood ready to catch the Holy Spirit's fire. An additional 15,000 'latecomers' were turned away at the coliseum gate. Undaunted, they formed an impromptu praise march that circled the stadium for hours.

Worship teams from various churches were stationed at 15-metre intervals around the running track. Dancers dressed in beautiful white and purple outfits interpreted the music with graceful motions accentuated by banners, tambourines and sleeve streamers. Both they and their city had been delivered of a great burden. In such circumstances one does not celebrate like a Presbyterian, a Baptist or a Pentecostal; one celebrates like a person who has been liberated!

"What you're seeing tonight in this stadium is a miracle," declared visiting Bogota pastor Colin Crawford. "A few years ago it would have been impossible for Evangelicals to gather like this." Indeed, this city that has long carried a reputation as an exporter of death is now looked upon as a model of community transformation. It has moved into the business of exporting hope.

High up in the stadium press booth somebody grabbed my arm. Nodding in the direction of a casually dressed man at the broadcast counter he whispered, "That man is the most famous sports announcer in Columbia. He does all the big soccer championships." Securing a quick introduction, I learned that Rafael Araújo Gámez is also a newborn Christian. As he looked out over the fervent crowd, I asked if he had ever seen anything comparable in this stadium. Like Mario, he began to weep. "Never," he said with a trembling chin. "Not ever."

At 2:30 in the morning, my cameraman and I headed for the stadium tunnel to catch a ride to the airport. It was a tentative departure. At the front gate crowds still trying to get in looked at us like we were crazy. I could almost read their minds. *Where are you going? Why are you leaving the presence of God?* They were tough questions to answer.

As we prepared to enter our vehicle a roar rose up from the stadium. Listening closely, we could hear the people chanting, in English, *"Lift Jesus up, lift Jesus up."* The words seemed to echo across the entire city. I had to pinch myself. Wasn't it just 36 months ago that people were calling this place a violent, corrupt hell-hole? A city whose ministerial alliance consisted of a box of files that nobody wanted?

In late 1998, Cali's mayor and city council approached the ministerial alliance, with an offer to manage a citywide campaign to strengthen the family. The offer, which has subsequently been accepted, gives the

Christians full operational freedom and no financial obligation. The government has agreed to open the soccer stadium, sports arena and velodrome to any seminar or prayer event that will minister to broken families.

Global Phenomenon

As remarkable as the preceding accounts are, they represent but a fraction of the case studies that could be presented. Several others are worth mentioning in brief.

Kiambu, Kenya

Topping this list is Kiambu, Kenya, one-time ministry graveyard located 14 kilometres northwest of Nairobi. In the late 1980s, after years of profligate alcohol abuse, untamed violence and grinding poverty, the Spirit of the Lord was summoned to Kiambu by a handful of intercessors operating out of a grocery store basement known as the "Kiambu Prayer Cave."

According to Kenyan pastor Thomas Muthee, the real breakthrough came when believers won a high profile power encounter with a local witch named Mama Jane. Whereas people used to be afraid to go out at night, they now enjoy one of the lowest crime rates in the country. Rape and murder are virtually unheard of. The economy has also started to grow. And new buildings are sprouting up all over town.

In February, 1999, pastor Muthee celebrated their ninth anniversary in Kiambu. Through research and spiritual warfare, they have seen their church grow to 5,000 members - a remarkable development in a city that had never before seen a congregation of more than 90 people. And other community fellowships are growing as well. "There is no doubt," Thomas declares, "that prayer broke the power of witchcraft over this city. Everyone in the community now has a high respect for us. They know that God's power chased Mama Jane from town" (26).

Vitória da Conquiste, Brazil

The city of Vitória da Conquiste (Victory of the Conquest) in Brazil's Bahia state, has likewise, experienced a powerful move of God since the mid 1990s. As with other transformed communities, the recovery is largely from extreme poverty, violence and corruption.

Vitória da Conquiste was also a place where pastors spent more pulpit time demeaning their ministerial colleagues than preaching the Word. Desperate to see a breakthrough, local intercessors went to prayer. Within a matter of weeks conviction fell upon the church leaders. In late 1996, they gathered to wash one another's feet in a spirit of repentance. When they approached the community's senior pastor - a man who had been among the most critical - he refused to allow his colleagues to wash his feet. Saying he was not worthy of such treatment, he instead lay prostrate on the ground and invited the others to place the soles of their shoes on his body while he begged their forgiveness. Today the pastors of Vitória da Conquiste are united in their desire for a full visitation of the Holy Spirit (27).

In addition to lifting long-standing spiritual oppression over the city, this action has also led to substantial church growth. Many congregations have recently gone to multiple services. Furthermore, voters in

1997 elected the son of evangelical parents to serve as mayor. Crime has dropped precipitously, and the economy has rebounded on the strength of record coffee exports and significant investments by the Northeast Bank.

San Nicolás, Argentina

Ed Silvoso of Harvest Evangelism International reports similar developments in San Nicolás, Argentina, an economically depressed community that for years saw churches split and pastors die in tragic circumstances. According to Silvoso, this dark mantle came in with a local shrine to the Queen of Heaven that annually attracts 1.5 million pilgrims.

More recently, pastors have repented for the sin of the church and launched prayer walks throughout the community. They have spoken peace over every home, school, business and police station and concentrated intercession over 10 "dark spots" associated with witchcraft, gangs, prostitution and drug addiction. The pastors have also made appointments with leading political, media and religious (Catholic) officials to repent for neglecting and sometimes cursing them.

As a result of these actions the Catholic bishop is preaching Christ and coming to pastors' prayer meetings. The mayor has created a space for pastors to pray in city hall. The local newspaper has printed Christian literature. The radio station has begun to refer call-in problems to a pastoral chaplaincy service. The TV station invites pastors onto live talk shows to pray for the people. In short, the whole climate in San Nicolás has changed.

Villages, cities, countries

In other parts of the world God has been at work in *villages* (Navapur, India; Serawak, Malaysia [Selakau people]; and the North American Arctic) in *urban neighbourhoods* (Guatemala City; Sao Paulo, Brazil; Resistencia, Argentina; Guayaquil, Ecuador) and even in *countries* (Uganda). The United States has witnessed God's special touch in places as far-flung as New York City (Times Square); Modesto, California; and Pensacola, Florida.

Early in my ministry I never thought of investigating transformed communities. I was too preoccupied with other things. In recent days, however, I have become persuaded that something extraordinary is unfolding across the earth. It is, I have come to realize, an expression of the full measure of the kingdom of God. Finding examples of this phenomenon has become my life. And the journey has taken me to the furthest corners of the earth.

Transforming Revival in the South Pacific

Transforming revival is now spreading through large numbers of villages and communities in the South Pacific, as elsewhere in the world. Pastors from Papua New Guinea, the Solomon Islands, Vanuatu and Fiji tell the amazing and inspiring story.

Teams of pastors and intercessors now travel in the islands to lead whole communities in repentance and unity. Many of them use a process they call **Healing the Land (HTL).** This involved at least a week of teaching, prayer, confession, reconciliation, and renouncing the idolatry and witchcraft which is common in village communities.[7]

Papua New Guinea

Papua New Guinea lies directly north of eastern Australia. Tribal people with over 700 different languages inhabit its coastal lowlands and towering highland ranges. Rev Walo Ani and his wife Namana describe community transformation through revival and Healing the Land (HTL) on the south coast of Papua New Guinea.

Karawa Village

It was a very exciting week in August 2006 where we saw the Lord move mightily in the lives of the village elders, chiefs, church leaders and the people. A group of dedicated young people's prayer ministry team started praying and fasting from 1st of July for the HTL Process. We witnessed repentance, forgiveness and reconciliations between family and clan members, and between individuals.

The Lord went ahead and prepared the hearts of people in every home as we visited. They were ready to confess their sins and ask for forgiveness from each other and reconcile. In some homes, members of families gave their hearts to the Lord. Visitation of homes took two days. On the third morning, after the dedication of the elements of salt, oil and water, the village elders and chiefs publicly repented as they identified with sins of their forebears; and each of them publicly gave their clans to the Lord.

Three dinghies and a big canoe with people all went in different directions up several rivers and along the nearby coast to anoint specific places for cleansing that had been defiled through deaths and killings in the past.

That night there was a time of public confession and renouncement of things that were a hindrance in the lives of the people around a huge bonfire. It was a solemn night; the presence of the Lord was so powerful that people were coming forward and burning their witchcraft and charms publicly. No one could hold back, even the deacons and church elders, village elders, women and young people were all coming forward. Young people started confessing their sins and renouncing and burning drugs, cigarettes and things that were hindering their lives from following Christ.

A young man, who had murdered another young man about 11 years ago, came forward and publicly confessed his sin and asked for forgiveness from the family of the murdered man. That was a big thing; there was a pause and we waited and prayed for someone from the other side to respond. Only the Lord could do this.

The younger brother of the man who was killed came out finally, and offered forgiveness. We could hear crying among the people; it was a moving moment where God just took control. Mothers, brothers and members of both extended families became reconciled in front of the whole village. We could sense the release upon both families and village. It was an awesome time; the meeting went on into the early hours of the next morning. At the end of all this at about 2:00 am the pastor stood up and said the prayer to invite Jesus into the community.

The village is not the same; you can sense the release and freedom of Christ in the lives of the people. The Holy Spirit is still moving in people's lives and they are coming to their pastor for prayer. Recently, a young man surrendered two guns to the pastor. News of what God has done and is still doing has spread to neighbouring villages. God birthed a new thing in our area and I believe that many more villages will see the transforming power of God because they are hungry and desperate to see change in their communities.

There were a lot of testimonies arising seven months after the HTL Process. Two water wells which had a salty taste were anointed with oil and now have good fresh water in them. One of the rivers that was anointed and prayed for now has fresh water instead of salty water half way up the river.

Alukuni, one of the villages which experienced their pigs being stolen by the Karawa young people over the years, testified that since HTL in Karawa none of their pigs had been stolen so far. Righteousness is rising up in the village.

The king tides in January to March usually caused floods in the middle of Karawa village dividing the village in two. After the HTL Process last August, the 2007 king tides have not caused any flooding. Praise the Lord!

A barren woman conceived after one of the visitation teams dealt with the generational curses holding her in bondage for sixteen years. Nine months after the Karawa HTL Process she gave birth to a beautiful baby boy named Simon.

There is abundance of fruit and garden food and two harvests of fruit on the orange trees have been observed so far.

A hunger for prayer has risen among the young people. Straight after the HTL Process young people from one of the clans started a prayer group which is still going on. Two other clans started prayer groups after a lot of struggle to get going over the years. The HTL team was the main support behind "Kids Games" which were held December 2006 in the neighbouring village of Keapara.

The studies were on Joseph and when they came to the section on forgiveness the Lord moved in a powerful way and revival started among the children. They stood and asked for forgiveness from their parents. There was crying and reconciliation between children and parents. The Lord is arresting the hearts of the young, the old and the children and there is no holding back.

Karawa is still experiencing the blessings of God with abundance of crabs, fish and garden produce. The economic life of the village is growing stronger.

One of the things prayed for was good education for their children, especially the smaller ones who do elementary schooling and did not have proper classrooms. Nine months after the HTL Process, Karawa which was the second last on the list of applications for school funding, was brought up to second priority and their application was approved. A semi-trailer loaded with building materials for two classrooms worth K75,000 (Kina, about AU$35,000) arrived in the village. The classrooms have now been built and the children are using them. Only the Lord could have done this.

Makirupu Village

Makirupu is about 2 hours drive east of Port Moresby, with a population of about 600. The United Church was the established church there and CRC and AOG have also planted churches there in recent years which caused a lot of offences between families.

In March 2007, we had eight days for the HTL Process, two teaching sessions in the mornings and one at night. From 5:30 pm for four days the prayer team did house to house visitation of all of the 126 homes in the village. The HTL team of seven and the prayer team all fasted and prayed for those eight days. The teaching was done in the language people understood very well. The Lord moved in a mighty way convicting people of land disputes, immorality and fornication, fear of witchcraft and sorcery (fear was at its peak when the HTL Process began), lies, gambling, stealing, marriage problems, witchcraft, sorcery and charms and many other issues. Miracles of healing started from day one; people who were deaf began to hear, their ears were healed.

From research I had done we discovered that the mission land was defiled by three previous pastors who had ministered in the village and who had committed adultery and fornication in the last 30 years, the last one about 18 months ago. This involved the last pastor and a young girl in the church behind the pulpit areas in the church building. That pastor was suspended from ministry. There was a court case between the family of the young girl (who defended her saying she was innocent) and the deacons of the church. There was actual physical fighting as well. This case involved the whole village; almost all the young people

left the church. Because of this, the life and attendance of the services were affected. The life of the
church was slowly dying away. This issue was never
resolved properly; it was like a dark shadow hanging
over the whole village. Our first focus of prayer would
be the cleansing of the mission land.

On the second night of prayer we had a time of identification repentance and the current pastor came forward and repented on behalf of the three former pastors of adultery and fornication. Something happened
in the heavenlies. A deacon came forward and repented on behalf of the deacons, followed by a women's
leader all repenting of the same sin and their involvement in it. More people came out and confessed.

The presence of the Lord was very heavy in the church.
I asked if there was anyone to repent on behalf of the
young people and the young girl who had committed fornication and adultery with the last pastor came
forward, trembling and crying, confessing, repenting
and asking for forgiveness from God and the whole
village. The people were amazed at what God was
doing. Only He could do that.

The girl who had denied outright what she had done
18 months ago was arrested by God's presence and
could not hide any more. A Sunday School representative came forward and repented and asked for
forgiveness. A former deacon could not hold back.
He came forward and confessed that he had been the
messenger boy for the pastor and the girl and he said
sorry to the Lord for denying Him.

Because of this incident 18 months ago, all the young
people had left the church but when the air was

cleared, the next day all the young people came and the church building was full to capacity. The fear of the Lord entered the hearts of the people. That same night the anointing elements were mixed and the mission land was anointed, cleansed and rededicated to God. It was an awesome time.

The AOG pastor also asked for forgiveness from the United Church for leaving the church and causing division. He and his wife and all his church members were part of the prayer warrior team right from day one of the Process. A couple of days later the CRC members started joining us and by the end of the Process all three churches were united to see change in the community. The prayer warrior team grew from 7 to 40. Praise God!

The next day news of what had happened had reached everyone in the village and the nearby villages and more people came for the meetings. They were hungry to hear the Word of the Lord. The next few days people were seeing signs and wonders, something they had never experienced before. Revival had started and the fear of God came upon the people. Also on the third day the village chief invited Jesus into the community.

On the last day the whole village gathered at the spot where the village was started some five or six generations ago. Anointing oil was mixed and all the chiefs and village elders were anointed and reinstated. After that, groups of people and prayer team took oil to certain places previously defiled because of bloodshed in the past on garden land. They anointed these places while deacons took oil to the boundaries of the village and the beach and dedicated the land back to God.

After lunch everyone came back to the village and started a bonfire. Church deacons and leaders were the first ones to come forward with confessions of adultery, immorality and witchcraft. Families with land disputes came out and reconciled with people they had taken to court. Young people came out with charms and magic and burnt them in the fire. A mother came out with her ten year old daughter and confessed she had handed down her sorcery and magic to her and said she was sorry, asking for forgiveness from God. Both were prayed for. Husbands and wives reconciled, artefacts of magic and idolatry were burnt. God was doing His cleaning up in the lives of the people.

The next day we had a time of celebration and you could see the release and freedom in people's lives; singing was coming from their hearts and joy was bubbling over. The Lord had again touched people's hearts and His presence was so evident that the people did not want to stop celebrating, although it was getting dark and there was no light.

The land and the people are being healed. The day after the Process a couple of men went crabbing and caught bigger and more crabs than usual. A week later a lady went to her garden to find that the bad weed which had been a problem to most gardens had started to wither and die. She went back to the village and told everyone. The fear that had gripped the hearts of the people had also been broken in prayer and now women are going to their gardens on their own – something they could not do before. A few days after the HTL Process, men began to go fishing and to their surprise they were catching more and bigger fish than before.

There has been a case of instant healing of a patient with a stroke after the AOG pastor and his wife shared with her family about Roots and Foundations and how curses come into lives. The whole family confessed, repented and reconciled with each other. The pastor's wife had some of the oil that was mixed in the village the week before and began anointing the lady while they prayed. To their surprise, she was healed instantly. She began to speak and eat on her own. The pastor said he had never experienced anything like this before. The presence of the Lord was so great they all started worshipping Him and time was not an issue any more. Praise God for this miracle!

During the Process, the pastors of the AOG, the United Church and an Elder of the CRC church, standing on behalf of the pastor, all repented of all the offences and misunderstandings between them in the past. So now the three churches have decided to have a combined service once a month in the middle of the village. The young people from all three churches are already having combined prayer meetings and they are in the process of building a big shelter in the middle of the village for the combined church services.

A couple of months after the HTL Process a security firm from the city turned up in the village and recruited all the unemployed 'rascal' young men who had been stealing and causing problems. These young men had been stealing pigs and other things and then reselling them in the city. One of them could not fit into city life so he went back to the village. He stole a pig and when his family found out they chased him out of the village. He went to stay with relatives in another village and in the process found the Lord there!

The villagers reported there has not been any stealing since the men were employed. There has also been increase in their garden produce, fruit and nut trees. The people are able to see their own produce come to maturity and sell it, whereas in the past it would have been stolen.

Makirupu and one of the nearby villages are known for getting floods during heavy rains. One month before we got there, it had been raining heavily but the Lord has kept the floods away. It surely is amazing!

Kalo Village

Kalo is the village where in 1881 four Cook Island missionaries and their families were killed. The killings were led by the chief of one of the clans. Since the killings this particular clan has been under a curse and the whole village is also affected by it. The leaders and the people of this clan know that they are under a curse and they are desperate to be freed from it. There have been unexplained deaths, not many of their children go beyond high school; those that go to work in towns don't last long and they lose their jobs.

The outcome of the talks is that the leaders of this clan called all their families together, from far and near to come and start the repentance and reconciliation Process. This was supported by the pastor and all the Church and clan leaders of Kalo. It was a moving occasion and the leaders agreed to proceed with the HTL Process and a bigger reconciliation event with the relatives of the Cook Island missionaries present in the near future.

Every year at their Church anniversary the Kalo people used put on the play of the landing of the Cook Island missionaries and their killings but straight after putting on this play, someone always died. They cannot explain it and they don't put it on any more. After talks with Walo, they have decided to do the play again but this time including a time of repentance, forgiveness and reconciliation after the play.

Healing the Land involved community repentance, reconciliation and rededication of all the people to God, along with acknowledging our stewardship under God for the land and the sea. This commitment continues to spread throughout the South Pacific islands, especially in Fiji, Vanuatu, Papua New Guinea and also the Solomon Islands.

Solomon Islands

Many revival movements continue to spread throughout the villages of the South Pacific, as in the Solomon Islands, an archipelago of almost 1,000 islands, scattered west of Papua New Guinea to Vanuatu. Leaders of revival movements in the Solomon Islands often take that fire to other South Pacific nations as well.

2003 - April: Western District

The Lord poured out his Spirit in fresh and surprising ways in New Georgia in the Western District of the Solomon Islands in 2003, and touched many churches in the capital Honiara with strong moves of the Holy Spirit. God's Spirit moved powerfully especially on youth and children. This included many conversions, many filled with the Spirit, many having visions and revelations. Churches began to grow with new vigor.

Ethnic tension (civil war) raged for two years to 2002 with rebels armed with guns causing widespread problems and the economy failing with the wages of many police, teachers and administrators unpaid. In spite of this, and perhaps because of it, the Holy Spirit moved strongly in the Solomon Islands.

An anointed pastor from Papua New Guinea spoke at an Easter Camp in 2003 attended by many youth leaders from the Western Solomons. Those leaders returned on fire. The weekend following Easter, from the end of April, 2003, youth and children in the huge, scenic Marovo Lagoon area were filled with the Spirit, with many lives transformed.

Revival began with the Spirit moving on youth and children in village churches. They had extended worship in revival songs, many visions and revelations and lives being changed with strong love for the Lord. Children and youth began meeting daily from 5 p.m. for hours of praise, worship and testimonies. A police officer reported reduced crimes and said that former rebels were attending daily worship and prayer meetings.

Revival continued to spread throughout the region. Revival movements brought moral change and built stronger communities in villages in the Solomon Islands, including these lasting developments:

1. Higher moral standards. People involved in the revival quit crime and drunkenness, and promoted good behaviour and co-operation.

2. Christians who once kept their Christianity inside churches and meetings talked more freely about their lifestyle in the community and among friends.

3. Revival groups, especially youth, enjoyed working together in unity and community, including a stronger emphasis on helping others in the community.

4. Families were strengthened in the revival. Parents spent more time with their youth and children to encourage and help them, often leading them in Bible readings and family prayers.

5. Many new gifts and ministries were used by more people than before, including revelations and healing. Even children received revelations or words of knowledge about hidden magic artefacts or ginger plants related to spirit power, and removed them.

6. Churches grew. Many church buildings in the Marovo Lagoon have been pulled down to be replaced by much bigger buildings to fit in the crowds. Offerings and community support have increased.

7. Unity. Increasingly Christians unite in reconciliation for revival meetings, prayer and service to the community.

A team of law students from the University of the South Pacific CF in Port Vila, Vanuatu, visited Honiara and the Western Solomon Islands in mid 2003. Sir Peter and Lady Margaret Kenilorea hosted the team in Honiara. Sir Peter was the first Prime Minster of the independent Solomon Islands, and then the Speaker in the Parliament.

Dr Ronald Ziru, then administrator of the United Church Hospital in Munda in the western islands hosted the team there, which included his son Calvin. The team had to follow Jesus' instructions about taking nothing extra on mission because the airline left behind all their checked luggage in Port Vila! They found it at Honiara after their return from the western islands.

The team first experienced the revival on an island near Munda. Two weeks previously, early in July, revival started there with the Spirit poured out on children and youth, so they just wanted to worship and pray for hours. They meet every night from around 5.30 p.m., and wanted to go late every night! The team encouraged the children to see school as a mission field, to pray with their friends there, and learn well so they could serve God better.

At Seghe and in the Marovo Lagoon the revival had spread since Easter. Some adults became involved, also repenting and seeking more of the Holy Spirit. Many outpourings and gifts of the Spirit emerged, including the following:

Transformed lives - Many youths that the police used to check on because of alcohol and drug abuse became sober and on fire for God attending daily worship and prayer meetings. A man who rarely went to church led the youth singing group at Seghe. Adults publicly reconciled after years of old rifts or strife.

Long worship - This included prophetic words or actions and visions. About 200 youth and children led worship at both Sunday services with 1,000 attending in Patutiva village where the revival began. They sang revival songs and choruses accompanied by their youth band.

Visions - Children saw visions of Jesus (smiling at worship, weeping at hard hearts), angels, hell (with relatives sitting close to a lake of fire, so the children warned them). Some saw Jesus with a foot in heaven and a foot on earth, like Mt 28:18 - "All authority in heaven and on earth has been given to me." One boy preached (prophesied) for 1½ hours, Spirit-led.

Revelations - especially 'words of knowledge' about hidden things, including magic artefacts and good luck charms. Children showed parents where they hid these things! If other adults did that there would be anger and feuds, but they accept it from their children. One boy said that a man accused of stealing a chain saw (and sacked) was innocent as he claimed, and gave the name of the culprit, by word of knowledge. The accused man returned to work.

Spiritual Gifts – teaching sessions discussed traditional and revival worship, deliverance, discernment of spirits, gifts of the Spirit, understanding and interpreting visions, tongues, healing, Spirit-led worship and preaching, and leadership in revival. Many young people became leaders moving strongly in many spiritual gifts.

These revival effects continued to spread throughout the Solomon Islands.

2006 - June: Guadalcanal Mountains

Revival in the Guadalcanal Mountains, the main island in the Solomon Islands, started at the Bubunuhu Christian Community High School on Monday, July 10, 2006, on their first night back from holidays. They took teams of students to the villages to sing, testify, and pray for people, especially youth. Many gifts of the Spirit were new to them - prophecies, healings, tongues, and revelations (e.g., about where magic items were hidden).

South Seas Evangelical Church (SSEC) pastors Joab Anea (chaplain at the high school) and Jonny Chuicu (chaplain at the Taylor Rural and Vocational Training Centre) the led revival teams. Joab reported on this revival:

> We held our prayer in the evening. The Spirit of the Lord came upon all of us like a mighty wind on us. Students fell on the ground. I prayed over them and we were all praying for each other. The students had many gifts and saw visions. The students who received spiritual gifts found that the Lord showed them

the hidden magic. So we prayed about them and also destroyed them with the power of God the Holy Spirit. The students who joined in that night were speaking and crying in the presence of God and repenting.

We also heard God calling us to bring revival to the nearby local churches. The Lord rescues and re-leased many people in this time of revival. This was the first time the Lord moved mightily in us.

Pastor Jonny Chuicu teaches Biblical Studies and dis-cipleship at the Taylor Rural and Vocational Training Centre. He teaches about the gifts of the Holy Spirit, and is using the book: Understanding Our Need of Re-vival, by Ian Malins.

Some of the people (who are all students) have gifts of praying and intercession, worship, healing, preaching, and teaching.

Another revival ministry team of 22 visited the Solomon Is-lands for a month, in November-December 2006, most com-ing from Pentecost Island, Vanuatu, on their first internation-al mission. The rest came from Brisbane – an international group of Bible College students (from Holland, England, Ko-rea, and Grant Shaw who grew up in China) plus Jesse Pa-dayachee, an Indian healing evangelist originally from South Africa, now in Brisbane, who joined the team for the last week. Jerry Waqainabete and his wife Pam (nee Kenilorea), participated in Honiara. Rev Gideon Tuke, a United Church minister, organized the visit.

In the Solomon Islands the revival team of 15 from Vanu-atu and 6 from Brisbane visited villages in the Guadalcanal Mountains, three hours drive and seven hours trekking from Honiara, and held revival meetings in November 2006 especially to encourage revival leaders. They walked up mountain tracks to where revival was spreading, especially among youth. Now those young people have teams going to the villages to sing, testify, and pray for people. Many gifts of the Spirit are new to them. The team prayed for the sick and for anointing and filling with the Spirit. They prayed both in the meetings and in the villages.

2006 - December: Choiseul Island

Gideon, Grant and Geoff participated for five days in December, 2006, at the National Christian Youth Convention (NCYC) in the north-west at Choiseul Island - 2 hours flight from Honiara. Around 1500 youth gathered from across the nation, many arriving by outboard motor canoes. The group coming from Simbo Island in two canoes ran into trouble when their outboard motors failed. Two of their young men swam from noon for nine hours in rough seas to reach land and get help for their stranded friends.

The Friday night convention meeting saw a huge response as Grant challenged them to be fully committed to God. Most of the youth came out immediately so there were hundreds to pray for. The anointed worship team led the crowd in "He touched me" for nearly half an hour as prayer continued for them, including many wanting healing.

Here is Grant's description of that youth crusade night:

> We were invited to speak for their huge night rally. Geoff began and God moved on the young people in a special way. Then he handed it over to me at about half way and I gave some words of knowledge for healing. They came forward and we prayed for them most of them fell under the Spirit's power and all of

them testified that all the pain left their body. After that I continued to speak for a bit and then gave an altar call for any youth who choose to give their lives fully to Jesus, no turning back!

Most of a thousand youth came forward, some ran to the altar, some crying! There was an amazing outpouring of the Spirit and because there were so many people Geoff and I split up and started laying hands on as many people as we could. People were falling under the power everywhere (some testified later to having visions). There were bodies all over the field (some people landing on top of each other). Then I did a general healing prayer and asked them to put their hand on the place where they had pain. After we prayed people began to come forward sharing testimonies of how the pain had left their bodies and they were completely healed! The meeting stretched on late into the night with more healing and many more people getting deep touches.

It was one of the most amazing nights. I was deeply touched and feel like I have left a part of my self in Choiseul. God did an amazing thing that night with the young people and I really believe that he is raising some of them up to be mighty leaders in Revival.

A young man healed that night returned to his nearby village and prayed for his sick mother and brother. Both were healed immediately. He told about that the next morning at the convention, adding that he had never done that before.

The delegation from Karika, in the Shortland Islands further west, returned home the following Monday. The next night they led a meeting where the Spirit of God moved in revival. Many were filled with the Spirit, had visions, were healed, and discovered many spiritual gifts including discerning spirits and tongues. That revival has continued, and spread in the Shortland Islands.

Vanuatu

Vanuatu's 80 islands stretch between the Solomon Islands in the west to the Fiji islands in the east. It has seen many revival movements.

2002 - April: Port Vila

The Lord moved in a surprising way at the Christian Fellowship (CF) in the School of Law in Port Vila, Vanuatu's capital, on Saturday night, April 6, the weekend after Easter 2002. The university's CF held an outreach meeting on the lawn and steps of the grassy university square near the main lecture buildings, school administration and library. God moved strongly there that night.

Romulo Nayacalevu, then President of the Law School Christian Fellowship reported:

> The speaker was the Upper Room Church pastor, Jotham Napat who is also the director of Meteorology here in Vanuatu. The night was filled with the awesome power of the Lord and we had the Upper Room church ministry who provided music with their instruments. With our typical Pacific Island setting of bush and nature all around us, we had dances, drama, and testified in an open environment, letting the wind carry the message of salvation to the bushes and the darkened areas. That worked because most of those that came to the altar call were people hiding or listening in these areas. The Lord was on the road of destiny with many people that night.

Unusual lightning hovered around in the sky that night, and as soon as the prayer teams had finished praying with those who rushed forward at the altar call, the tropical rain pelted down on that open field area.

God poured out his Spirit on many lives, including Jerry Waqainabete and Simon Kofe. Both of them played rugby in the popular university team and enjoyed drinking and the night club scene. Both changed dramatically. Many of their friends said it would not last. It did.

Later, Jerry became prayer convenor at the CF and Simon its president. The very active CF at the School of Law regularly organised outreaches in the town and at the university. About one third of the 120 students in the four year law course attended the weekly CF meeting on Friday nights. A core group prayed together regularly, including daily prayer at 6 a.m., and organised evangelism events. Many were filled with the Spirit and began to experience spiritual gifts in their lives in new ways.

A team of eleven from their CF visited Australia for a month in November-December 2002 involved in outreach and revival meetings in many denominations and as well as in visiting home prayer groups. They drove 6,000 kilometres in a 12-seater van, including a trip from Brisbane to Sydney and back to visit Hillsong.

The team prayed for hundreds of people in various churches and home groups. They led worship at the daily 6 a.m. prayer group at Kenmore Baptist Church in Brisbane. That followed their own 5 a.m. daily prayer meeting in the house provided miraculously for them.

Philip and Dhamika George from Sri Lanka bought that rental house with no money and made it freely available. They had befriended a back-packer stranger who advised them to buy a rental property because Brisbane house prices then began to increase rapidly in value. They had no spare money but their new friend loaned them a deposit of $10,000, interest free, to get a bank loan and buy the house. They sold the house two years later for $90,000 profit, returned the deposit loan, and used the profits for Kingdom purposes especially in mission.

The law students from the CF grew strong in faith. Jerry, one of the students from Fiji, returned home for Christmas vacation after the visit to Australia, and prayed for over 70 sick people in his village, seeing many miraculous healings. His transformed life challenged the village because he had been converted at CF after a wild time as a youth in the village. The following December vacation, 2004, Jerry led revival in his village. He prayed early every morning in the Methodist Church. Eventually some children and then some of the youth joined him early each morning. By 2005, he had 50 young people involved, evangelising, praying for the sick, casting out spirits, and encouraging revival. By 2009, Jerry was a lawyer and pastor of a church in Suva and had planted a new church in his village as well.

Simon, returned to his island of Tuvalu, also transformed at university through CF. He witnessed to his relatives and friends all through the vacation in December-January, bringing many of them to the Lord. He led a team of youth involved in Youth Alive meetings, and prayed with the leaders each morning from 4 a.m. Simon became President of the Christian Fellowship at the Law School from October 2003 for a year.

2003 - May: Pentecost Island

In May 2003, a team from the CF flew to Pentecost Island in Vanuatu for a weekend of outreach meetings on South Pentecost. The national Vanuatu Churches of Christ Bible College, at Banmatmat, stands near the site of the first Christian martyrdom there.

> Tomas Tumtum had been an indentured worker on cane farms in Queensland, Australia. He was converted there and returned around 1901 to his village on South Pentecost with a new young disciple from a neighbouring island. They arrived when the village was tabu (taboo) because a baby had died a few days earlier, so no one was allowed near the village. Ancient tradition dictated that anyone breaking tabu must be killed, so they were going to kill Tomas, but his friend Lulkon asked Tomas to tell them to kill him instead so that Tomas could evangelise his own people. Just before he was clubbed to death at a sacred mele palm tree, he read from John 3:16, then closed his eyes and prayed for them.

Tomas became the pioneer of the church in South Pentecost, establishing many Churches of Christ there.

God opened a wide door on Pentecost Island (1 Cor 16:8-9). Chief Willie Bebe invited the team and hosted them at his bungalows on South Pentecost island. The weekend with the CF team brought new unity among the competing village churches. The Sunday night service went from 6-11 p.m., although it had been 'closed' three times after 10 p.m., with a closing prayer, then later on a closing song, and then later on a closing announcement. People just kept singing and coming for prayer.

Another team of four students from the law school CF returned to South Pentecost in June 2003 for 12 days of meetings in many villages. Again, the Spirit of God moved strongly. Leaders repented publicly of divisions and criticisms. Then youth began repenting of backsliding or unbelief. A great-grand-daughter of the pioneer Tomas Tumtum gave her life to God in the village near his grave at the Bible College.

Evening rallies were held in four villages of South Pentecost each evening from 6 p.m. for 12 days, with teaching sessions on the Holy Spirit held in the main village church for a week. The team experienced a strong leading of the Spirit in the worship, drama, action songs with Pacific dance movements, and preaching and praying for people.

Mathias, a young man who repented deeply with over 15 minutes of tearful sobbing later became a worship leader in revival meetings.

> When he was leading and speaking at a revival meeting at the national Bible College on South Pentecost island, a huge supernatural fire blazed in the hills directly opposite the Bible College chapel in 2005, but no bush was burned. It was seen as a sign of God's Spirit moving there.

Pentecost Bible College

By 2004, the Churches of Christ national Bible College at Banmatmat on Pentecost Island became a centre for revival teaching. Pastor Lewis Wari and his wife Marilyn hosted these gatherings at the Bible College, and later on Lewis spoke at many island churches as the President of the Churches of Christ. Lewis had been a leader in strong revival movements on South Pentecost as a young pastor from 1980-81. An older pastor evangelist, Wilson, also led many revival meetings there and on other islands in the 1980s and 1990s. Again from in March 1995 the Spirit of God moved powerfully in South Pentecost in meetings led by Pastor Lewis and Youth Evangelist Rolanson Tor.

Leaders' seminars and youth conventions at the Bible College focused on revival. The college hosted regular courses and seminars on revival for a month at a time, each day beginning with prayer together from 6 a.m., and even earlier from 4:30 a.m. in the youth convention in December, 2004, as God's Spirit moved on the youth leaders in that area.

Morning sessions continued from 8 a.m. to noon, with teaching and ministry. As the Spirit moved on the group, they continued to repent and seek God for further anointing and impartation of the Spirit in their lives. Afternoon sessions featured sharing and testimonies of what God is doing. Each evening became a revival meeting at the Bible College with worship, sharing, preaching, and powerful times of ministry to everyone seeking prayer.

Every weekend the team from the college led revival meetings in village churches. Many of these went late as the Spirit moved on the people with deep repentance, reconciliation, forgiveness, and prayer for healing and empowering.

Another law student team from Port Vila, led by Seini Puamau, Vice President of the CF, had a strong impact at the High School on South Pentecost Island with big responses at all meetings. Almost the whole residential school of 300 responded for prayer at the final service on Sunday night October 17, 2004, after a powerful testimony from Joanna Kenilorea. The High School principal, Silas Buli, prayed for years from 4 a.m. each morning for the school and nation with some of his staff.

The church arranged for more revival teaching at their national Bible College for church leaders. Teams from the college held mission meetings simultaneously in seven different villages. Every village saw strong responses, including a team that held their meeting in the chief's meeting house of their village, and the first to respond was a fellow from the 'custom' traditional heathen village called Bunlap.

Those Bible College sessions seemed like preparation for further revival. Every session led into ministry. Repentance went deep. Prayer began early in the mornings, and went late into the nights.

Chief Willie Bebe, host of most revival teams, asked for a team to come to pray over his home and tourist bungalows. Infestation by magic concerned him. So a prophetic and deliverance team of about six local intercessors prayed there. Mathias reported this way:

> The deliverance ministry group left the college by boat and when they arrived at the Bungalows they prayed together. After they prayed together they divided into two groups.
>
> There is one person in each of these two groups that has a gift from the Lord that the Holy Spirit reveals where the witchcraft powers are, such as bones from dead babies or stones. These witchcraft powers are always found in the ground outside the houses or sometimes in the houses. So when the Holy Spirit reveals to that person the right spot where the witchcraft power is, then they have to dig it up with a spade. When they dug it out from the soil they prayed over it and bound the power of that witchcraft in the name of Jesus. Then they claimed the blood of Jesus in that place.

Something very important when joining the deliverance group is that everyone in the group must be fully committed to the Lord and must be strong in their faith because sometimes the witchcraft power can affect the ones that are not really committed and do not have faith.

After they finished the deliverance ministry they came together again and gave praise to the Lord in singing and prayer. Then they closed with a Benediction.

Village evangelism teams from South Pentecost continue to witness in the villages, and visit other islands. Six people from these teams came to Brisbane and were then part of 15 from Pentecost Island on mission in the Solomon Islands in 2006.

Pentecost on Pentecost

Grant Shaw accompanied Geoff Waugh to Pentecost Island in Vanuatu in September-October 2006. Grant grew up with missionary parents, saw many persecutions and miracles, and had his dad recounting miraculous answers to prayer as a daily routine. They often needed to pray for miracles, and miracles happened. From 14 years old Grant participated in mission teams travelling internationally in Asia. Then he attended a youth camp at Toronto Airport Christian Fellowship which has had revival since 1994. He then worked there as an associate youth pastor for 18 months before studying at Bible College in Brisbane, and then became the youth pastor at a Christian Outreach Centre church in north Brisbane. So he is used to revival - all his life! In Vanuatu he had clear words of knowledge, and saw people healed daily in meetings and in the villages. That inspired and challenged everyone.

Raised from the dead

In Port Vila, Grant and Geoff attended the Sunday service at Upper Room church. That night the pastors were away in Tanna Island on mission so the remaining leaders felt God sent these two Australian visitors to preach that night! Great warning! It was fantastic, with strong worship and waves of prayer ministry for healing and anointing.

At sharing time in the service Leah Waqa, a nurse, told how she had been on duty that week when parents brought in their young daughter who had been badly hit in a car accident, and showed no signs of life. The monitor registered zero – no pulse. Leah felt unusual boldness, so commanded the girl to live, and prayed for her for an hour, mostly in tongues, and after an hour the monitor started beeping and the girl recovered.

The mission trip continued on South Pentecost once more, based in the village of Panlimsi. The Spirit moved strongly in all the meetings. Repentance. Reconciliations. Confessions. Anointing. Healings every day. The healings included Pastor Rolanson's young son able to hear clearly after being partially deaf from birth. Rolanson leads evangelism teams, and helped lead this mission.

South Pentecost attracts tourists with its land diving, men jumping from high towers with vines attached to their ankles – the genesis of bungy jumping! Grant prayed for a jumper who had hurt his neck, and the neck crackled back into place. That young man and his father prayed there on the village track to receive Christ. Grant prayed in the village for a son of the paramount chief of South Pentecost from Bunlap, a heathen village. He was healed from a painful groin and his father then invited the team to come to his village to pray for the sick. No white people had ever been invited there to minister previously.

The team, including the two Australians, trekked for a week into mountain villages. They literally obeyed Luke 10 – going with no extra shirt, no sandals, and no money. The trek began with a five hour walk across the island to Ranwas on the eastern side. Mathias led worship, with strong moves of the Spirit touching everyone in many times prayer times. At one point the preacher spat on the dirt floor, making mud to show what Jesus did once. Marilyn Wari, wife of the President of the Churches of Christ, then jumped up asking for prayer for her eyes. Later she testified that the Lord told her to do that, and then she found she could read her small Bible without glasses.

Glory in a remote village

The team trekked through the 'custom' heathen village (where the paramount chief lived), and prayed for more sick people. Some had pain leave immediately, and people there became more open to the gospel. Then the team trekked for seven hours to Ponra, a remote village further north.
Revival meetings erupted there! The Spirit just took over. Visions. Revelations. Reconciliations. Healings. People drunk in the Spirit. Many resting on the floor getting blessed in various ways. When they heard about healing through 'mud in the eye' at Ranwas some came straight out asking for mud packs also!

One of the girls in the team had a vision of the village youth there paddling in a pure sea, crystal clear. They were like that - so pure. Not polluted at all by TV, videos, DVDs, movies, magazines, worldliness. Their lives were so clean and holy. Just pure love for the Lord, especially among the young.

Angels singing filled the air about 3 a.m. It sounded as though the village church was packed. The harmonies in high descant declared "For You are great and You do wondrous things.

You are God alone" and then harmonies, without words until words again for "I will praise You O Lord my God with all my heart, and I will glorify Your name for evermore" with long, long harmonies on "forever more." Just worship.

The team stayed two extra days there - everyone received prayer, and many people surrendered to the Lord both morning and night. Everyone repented, as the Spirit moved on everyone.

Grant's legs, cut and sore from the long trek, saved the team from the long trek back. The villagers arranged a boat ride back around the island from the east to the west for the team's return. Revival meetings continued back at the host village, Panlimsi, led mainly in worship by Mathias, with Pastor Rolanson organising things. Also at two other villages the Spirit moved powerfully as the team ministered, with much reconciliation and dancing in worship.

Some people in the host village heard angels singing there also. At first they too thought it was the church full of people but the harmonies were more wonderful than we can sing.

The two Australians returned full of joy on the one hour flight to Vila after a strong final worship service at the host village on the last Sunday morning, and reported to the Upper Room Church in Port Vila on Sunday evening. Again the Spirit moved so strongly the pastor didn't need to use his message. More words of knowledge. More healings. More anointing in the Spirit, and many resting in the Spirit, soaking in grace.

The Upper Room church has seen strong touches of God in the islands, especially Tanna Island. They planted churches there in 'custom' villages, invited by the chiefs because the chiefs have seen their people healed and transformed. During missions there in 2006, many young boys asked to be 'ordained' as evangelists in the power of the Spirit. They returned to their villages and many of those young boys established churches as they spoke, told Bible stories, and sang original songs inspired by the Spirit.

All through these islands of Vanuatu revival continues to spread, not only transforming individuals and churches but also whole communities. The Healing the Land teams report on some of that below.

Healing the Land (HTL)

Pastors Walo Ani and Harry Tura tell how revival transformed whole communities in Vanuatu, including healing of the land.[8]

Hog Harbour, Espiritu Santo

The island was named Espiritu Santo because that is the island where over 400 years ago in May 1606 Ferdinand de Quiros named the lands from there to the South Pole the Great Southland of the Holy Spirit. It had a huge American military base there in World War II. James Michener was based there and included descriptions of it in his book, Tales of the South Pacific.

Pastor Walo Ani describes how God moved in the whole Hog Harbour community in the north east of Espiritu Santo island in Vanuatu.

After hearing about the Healing the Land stories of Fiji, Pastor Tali from Hog Harbour Presbyterian Church invited the Luganville Ministers Fraternal to run a week of HTL meetings in Hog Harbour village.

In April 2006, the Fraternal, under the leadership of Pastor Raynold Bori, conducted protocol discussions with the Hog Harbour community leaders and explained to them what the

Process involves. In May 2006, six pastors from Luganville did the HTL Process and God's presence came on the people that week.

Here are some of the stories of Healing the Land in a village of 800 people:

- Married couples were reconciled.

- Schools of big fish came to the shores during the reconciliation.

- A three year old conflict, bloodshed and tribal fighting that could not be stopped by the police, ended with reconciliation.

- The presence of the Lord came down on the village.

- In June of 2006, 12 pastors from the Luganville Fraternal were invited by the Litzlitz village on Malekula Island to do the HTL Process there. These pastors spent three weeks teaching and doing the Process during which many instances of reconciliation and corporate repentance were witnessed. Village chiefs and the people committed their community to God.

  One year later the President of Vanuatu re-covenanted the Nation to God on the island of Espiritu Santo.

Litzlitz Village, Malekula Island

Pastor Harry Tura, an indigenous pastor of the Apostolic Church in Vanuatu, adds his comments about transforming revival on the island of Malekula in Vanuatu. Malekula is a large island just south of Espiritu Santo Island.

I wish to indicate to you what God is doing now in Vanuatu these days as answers to your prayers, and ask that you continue to pray for us.

I went to Litzlitz village community on the island of Malekula on Sunday, June 4, 2006, and the Transformation activities started on the same day. The study activities and the process of healing the land closed on the following Sunday, June 11. The presence of the Lord was so real and manifested and many miracles were seen such a people healed, dried brooks turned to running streams of water, fish and other sea creatures came back to the sea shores in great number and even the garden crops came alive again and produced great harvests.

Pastor Walo Ani adds his observations. He joined a team of pastors from Luganville (Vanuatu's second largest town) on Espiritu Santo island in visiting Malekula Island:

In June of 2006, 12 pastors from the Luganville Fraternal were invited by the Litzlitz village on Malekula Island to do the HTL Process there. These pastors spent three weeks teaching and doing the Process during which many instances of reconciliation and corporate repentance were witnessed. Village chiefs and the people committed their community to God. Miracles happened three days after the HTL Process:

• The poison fish that usually killed or made people sick became edible and tasty again.

• The snails that were destroying gardens all died suddenly and didn't return.

• As a sign of God's transforming work a coconut tree in the village which naturally bore orange or red coconuts started bearing bunches of green coconuts side by side with the red ones.

- A spring gushed out from a dried river bed and the river started flowing again after the anointing oil was poured on it when people prayed and repented of all the sins of defilement over the area.

  - A kindergarten was established in the village one week after the HTL Process took place.

  - Crops are now blessed and growing well in their gardens.

One year later the President of Vanuatu re-covenanted the nation to God on the island of Espiritu Santo.

Vilakalak Village, West Ambae Island

Pastor Harru Tura continues his story of transforming revival in Vanuatu as he experienced it on Ambae Island. Ambae Island can be seen to the east from Espiritu Santo Island on clear days.

On Tuesday June 20, 2006, I flew to Ambae Island to join the important celebration of the Apostolic Church Inauguration Day, June 22. After the celebration I held a one-week Transformation studies and activities of healing the land at Vilakalak village community. It began on Sunday, June 25 and closed on Saturday, July 1, 2006. A lot of things had been transformed such as people's lives had been changed as they accepted Christ and were filled with the Holy Spirit for effective ministries of the Gospel of Christ.

The Shekinah glory came down to the very spot where we did the process of healing the land during the night of July 1. That great light (Shekinah glory) came down. People described it as a living person with tremendous and powerful light shining over the whole of the village community, confirming the Lord's presence at that specific village community area. On the following day people started to testify that a lot of fish and shell fish were beginning to occupy the reefs and they felt a different touch of a changed atmosphere in the village community. I flew back to Santo on Tuesday, July 4.

The lands and garden crops then started to produce for great harvests, and coconut crabs and island crabs came back in great abundance for people's daily meals these days. The people were very surprised at the look of the big sizes of coconut crabs harvested in that area. I went there a month later to see it. You can't believe it that the two big claws or arms were like my wrist when I compared them with my left wrist. That proved that the God we serve is so real and he is the owner of all the creatures.

We started the Transformation studies and activities at my church beginning on Monday, July 17, and closed on Sunday, July 23, 2006. After the Transformation studies and activities had been completed, we did the final process of healing the land on Sunday, July 23. As usual the Shekinah glory of the Lord's presence appeared the following night of Monday, July 24. The people were amazed at the scene. That confirmed that God is at work at that specific area. A lot of changes are taking place at our church base and its environment - the land, the sea, and the atmosphere above us. People experience the same blessings as the others had been through.

On Sunday, August 13, 2006, I took a flight to West Ambae again because the Walaha village community had requested me to carry out the Transformation studies and activities and healing of the lands in their area. The Transformation studies started on Monday, August 14. Again the presence of the Lord came down (Shekinah glory) on the whole village community early on Wednesday night and they all witnessed the scene the following day. They were very excited and began praising God all over the place. I took a flight back to Santo on Tuesday, August 22.

The revival is now taking place at that particular community and lives are totally changed and people turned out to be experiencing a mighty difference of atmosphere and have been transformed to people of praise and worship. All sorts of fish are coming back to the reef and garden crops came green and are now beginning to produce a great abundance of harvest at the end of this year by the look of it now. This is all the hand of the Lord who does the work which is based on the transformation key verse in 2 Chronicles 7:14, which reads: "If my people who are called by my name shall humble themselves and pray and seek my face and turn from their wicked ways, then I will hear from heaven and forgive their sins and heal their land."

Lovanualikoutu Village, West Ambae

Walo Ani and a team conducted more of the HTL Process in Vanuatu.

In 2004, Walo was invited by a pastor in West Ambae to do the HTL Process there. It wasn't until May 2007 that a small team consisting of Pastor Walo Ani, Deryck and Nancy Thomas of Toowoomba Queensland and Tom Hakwa from Lovanualikoutu village (who then worked for Telekom Vanuatu in Port Vila) flew to West

Ambae to do the HTL Process. The protocol was done by Tom some months before the team's arrival and a prayer team was already praying and fasting a month before the actual event took place. Deryck and Nancy coordinated the home visitation teams and saw many miracles of people restored to the Lord and witchcraft destroyed. The Chief said the sinner's prayer on behalf of the community one night and they all surrendered their lives to the Lord as he invited Jesus into the village.

In the morning of the last day, one of the teams was trying to pray down a stronghold in the bush when a bone fell through a hollow tree, taking them by surprise. They all jumped back but then stepped forward and dealt with it once and for all. Many taboo (sacred) places were demolished and items of witchcraft and idolatry were burnt in a bonfire as reconciliations flowed till after midnight.

Also on that morning a team of people swam out to sea with the anointing oil to worship there and dedicate the sea and reef back to God. The day after the team's departure from the village a pastor who went out spear fishing saw a large migration of fish. He in fact reportedly speared two fish together at one stage. When he reported this to the Chief there was dancing and rejoicing under the cocoa trees where the Chief and some young people had been working.

During the reconciliation when the Chief began to speak, a light shower fell from the sky. There were no clouds but only a sky full of millions of stars. Surely God was in this Process! The prayer team continues to see visions and witness miracles of more reconciliation and repentance. Harvests from sea and land have begun to be more abundant than ever before witnessed.

Fiji

The Sentinel Group's DVD Let the Seas Resound vividly describes revival transformation in troubled Fiji, a land of regular military coups. This brief update describes recent revivals in the Fiji islands, similar to revivals multiplying in the twenty-first century with significant healing of the land. Rev. Ratu (Chief) Vuniani Nakauyaca reports here on many transformed communities in Fiji,

> The most powerful events in this ongoing revival are the direct results of repentance, reconciliation and unity.

Sabeto Village

> One of the first instances of this occurred in 2002, when Chief Mataitoga of Sabeto village (between Nadi and Lautoka) had a dream from the Lord. The village had a lot of social problems as well as enmity and divisions. As a result of the dream, he called his people together to pray and fast to seek God for answers and healing. Over a period of two weeks, many of the clans spent time with the Chief to sort out their differences. They had meetings every night and God brought about reconciliation and unity in the church and village, many relationships being healed.
>
> There had only been one church in the area until the Pentecostal revival of the 1960s which spread across the cities and towns and into the rural areas during that period. Because of the rejection of the Pentecostal experience by some people, many villages had two

churches, one Methodist and one Pentecostal. This caused division between friends and family, with many people not communicating and carrying bitterness and resentment for decades.

When Ratu Mataitoga directed his people to come together as one, there was a move of the Holy Spirit with real repentance and forgiveness. Unity in the village was restored. The long term results of this action were only revealed with the passing of time. Productivity of the soil increased and long absent fish varieties returned to the reef. Mangroves that had died and disappeared have begun to grow again. The mangroves are very important for the ecology, providing shelter and breeding grounds for all kinds of fish and crabs, which were part of the staple diet of these villages.

The Healing the Land (HTL) Process, as it is now officially recognized, really started on the initiative of Pastor Vuniani Nakauyaca. For him it was a personal journey that resulted from an accumulation of various events.

The Pacific Prayer movement had a desire to see that prayer, repentance and reconciliation were carried out where necessary on location - where missionaries had been killed or where tribal conflict had taken place. These were all based on a bottom up or grass roots approach to bring healing and reconciliation.

Vuniani had visited Argentina and seen the beneficial results of reconciliation with the British over the Faulklands war. He also visited Guatemala to see the Almolonga transformation (see Transformations 1 DVD). This was a singularly dramatic community change. Jails and public bars closed, land fertility increased and crop production levels had to be seen to be believed.

What he saw brought a deeper desire in his heart to see this happen in Fiji, to give room for God to bring about community and national transformation in similar ways to what he had seen overseas. He saw the need to appropriately respond to the circumstances and use the spiritual tools available to see the nation transformed.

Nuku Village, Viti Levu

After returning to Fiji, he called some people together to seek God for solutions. They felt they should begin at Nuku, and this took place on April 1-10, 2003. Nuku is about 65 kilometres north of Suva, on the main island of Viti Levu.

The inhabitants of Nuku had been suffering feuds, infertility, mental illness and social problems for decades. The water of the stream that flowed through the village had been polluted since a day 42 years previously, the water and banks being filled with slime. At that time, children were swimming in the stream when the water suddenly turned white and they all ran for their lives. Fish died and grass died. Vuniani, as a child, was swimming in the river when this happened, so he knew the background story. It was believed that the polluted water caused blindness, infertility, madness and even death.

Vuniani and the team went up to Nuku to activate the Process. The key Scripture they went with was 2 Chronicles 7:14, "If my people, who are called by My name, will humble themselves and pray, and seek my face, and turn from their wicked ways, then I will hear from heaven, will forgive their sin and will heal their land".

They had two weeks of prayer meetings, the Methodist, Assemblies of God and Seventh Day Adventist churches being represented. They spent time studying Bible references on defilement and Healing the Land. This lead them to repent and confess their sins and the sins of their forefathers, in the same way as Nehemiah did. These included killing and cannibalism, idolatry, witchcraft, bloodshed, and immorality.

They went to the high places in the area to cleanse them of the sinful acts that had taken place there. The elders confessed sins of their forefathers. Reconciliation first took place within families, then clans and finally within the tribe. The chief of the area led a corporate prayer of repentance with the whole tribe.

On the third day of the Process, some women came running and shouting into the village, announcing that the water in the stream had become pure again. It is still pure today.

Nuku village had been heavily populated, but because of feuds and disputes, people were chased out or just left and went to live in other villages. Deputations were sent out to these to apologise for the past offences. A matanigasau (traditional apology) was sent to two villages, inviting the people to return if they wished.

The whole community now counts themselves as very blessed. The productivity of the land has increased. The stream water is pure and since that time shrimps and fish have returned to the waters. The fertility of the banks and agriculture has radically improved. Some people have even reported that the water has demonstrated healing properties.

Nabitu Village, East of Nausori

What occurred in this village was very much a follow on from what was happening around the country at the time. There was a split in the tribe and there were a lot of unresolved issues. During a business meeting in the local church, which was situated right in the middle of the village, a fist fight broke out. There was always a heaviness in the village, like a hovering dark cloud. This affected people negatively and there were not a lot of jobs available.

On the advice of chiefs, the people came together on their own initiative for a time of corporate repentance. A lay preacher in the Methodist Church facilitated the Process. There was instantly a change in the atmosphere. The heaviness that had been there had lifted and everyone could feel it. The division in the church was healed.

The lesson learned from there is that Satan's hold over people and places is tenuous to say the least. It only takes one man to lead many into forgiveness and healing. Satan has to leave, along with the oppression and curses.

Vunibau, Serua Island, at the Navua River

The HTL Process in this place was scheduled over a 14 day period. During the Process the mixture of elements was poured out onto the sand on the beach. Later that day, an elderly lady and her son went fishing on the beach. They cast the net out but when they tried to haul it back in, it seemed to be stuck. They thought that perhaps it had been caught on a stump or rock, but they found that the net was actually so full of fish that they could not pull it in.

They started walking back to the village to tell everyone, and the lady was following her son walking along the beach. Wherever his footprints were in the sand a red liquid appeared. As she walked in his footsteps she was healed of migraine, knee ailments and severe back pain, all of which she had suffered for many years. This healing has been permanent. As soon as they returned to the village she told the whole community what had happened.

All the people rushed down to the beach to see this phenomenon, including the HTL team that was still there at the time. To their amazement, right on the spot where the elements had been poured onto the sand, there was blood coming out of the sand and flowing into the sea. A backslidden Catholic man gave his life to the Lord on the spot. Photos were taken. Vuniani was called from Suva (about an hour away) and he also witnessed the blood coming out of the sand. This actually happened twice.

It was understood to be a confirming sign from the Lord that He was at work in the reconciliation and healing Process: 1 John 5:6-7, "There are three that bear witness on earth, the Spirit, the water and the blood." This was similar to the miracle of the healing of the waters in Nuku, which was also recognized as a sign of God's cleansing and healing that was taking place amongst the people. God is authenticating what he is doing.

At Vunibau many other signs quickly followed. Large fish returned to their fishing grounds. On one occasion, considerable quantities of prawns came ashore so that people could just pick them up. Crabs and lobsters have also returned, and they have been able to sell the large lobsters for up to $25-$30 each.

After this sign of the blood, Pastor Vuniani recalled the scripture in Acts 2:19 where the Lord had spoken through the prophet Joel that *"I will grant wonders (signs) in the sky above, and signs on the earth below, blood, and fire and vapour (pillars) of smoke"* (NASB). He wondered what would come next after the sign of the blood and felt that the next sign would be fire.

Nataliera, Nailevu North

In Nataliera village there were four churches. There was no communication between their members, affecting even closely related families within the village. Traditional witchcraft was still being practised and there were about eight sorcerers there. In addition, there had been many more deaths than would be normal.

After forgiveness and reconciliation, the members of these four churches would meet every Wednesday for prayer and fasting. On the first Sunday of every month, the four congregations would combine for one large gathering. An Eco Lodge, previously closed, is now prospering after the HTL Process.

For many years the fishing on the reef had become lean. Large fish were very scarce and for many years the catch had only ever comprised "bait fish" – the very small ones. Much of the coral reef was dead and what was left seemed to be dying.

After reconciliation, on two separate occasions fire was seen to fall from the sky onto the reef. After this, large fish returned in abundance. The coral is now regenerating and new growth can be seen in abundance.

When stormy weather strikes and the boats can't go out, the women pray and large fish swim in close to the shore and become trapped in a small pond so that the women are able to just wade in and catch them. When women from neighbouring villages heard of this, they tried praying for the same provision, but without the same result.

Draubuta, Navosa Highlands, north of Sigatoka

Vuniani's son, Savanaca, was working with two teams in the highlands. While they were there, pillars of smoke descended on the villages. This was seen by many neighbouring villagers who described it as thick bloodstained smoke. This sign was seen at almost exactly the same time as fire was seen to fall on the reef at Nataliera.

In this area there were many marijuana plantations. The Nadroga council had been trying to prevent the plantings. During the HTL Process, a deputation of marijuana growers approached the team and asked what the Government would do for them if they destroyed their crops. They had a list of demands which they presented to the team.

The marijuana crop was large, and estimated to be worth about $11 million. There were 9 growers involved. The team leaders told the farmers that it was their choice, that they should obey God and trust him for their livelihood, without any promises from anyone to do anything for them. If they could not, then they should not participate in the Healing Process.

By the time the Process had finished, the people had destroyed the crop as part of the reconciliation Process. After the HTL ministry, a total of 13,864 plants were uprooted and burnt by the growers themselves. There were 6,000 seedlings as well.

These are a few of the many miraculous events that have occurred in Fiji since 2001. Every week, more such events are happening as the forgiveness, reconciliation and HTL processes are being experienced.

The theme text of the Healing the Land process and transforming revival still applies powerfully today: *If my people who are called by my name will humble themselves and pray and seek my face and turn from their wicked ways, then I will hear from heaven, and will forgive their sin and heal their land.*[9]

Endnotes

[1] Edited from George Otis Jr., 1999, Informed Intercession, Renew, pp.15-53, reproduced with permission of Gospel Light publications, Ventura, California, USA, first in Renewal Journal, No. 17, 2001, pp. 4-30.

[2] Mario Roberto Morales, "La Quiebra de Maximon," Cronica Semanal, June 24-30, 1994, pp. 17,19,20. In English the headline reads 'The Defeat of Maximon.'

[3] This is based on estimates developed by the U.S. Drug Enforcement Administration. Colombia is also a major producer of marijuana and heroin. See 'Colombia Police Raid Farm, Seize 8 Tons of Pure Cocaine,' Seattle Times, October 16, 1994.

[4] Documenting the dimensions of Colombia's national savagery, Bogota's leading newspaper, El Tiempo, cited 15,000 murders during the first six months of 1993. This gave Colombia, with a population of 32 million people, the dubious distinction of having the highest homicide rate in the World.

[5] This unique group was comprised of Colombian police, army personnel and contra guerrillas. The June 1995 campaign also included systematic neighbourhood searches. To insure maximum surprise, the unannounced raids would typically occur at four a.m. "Altogether," MacMillan reported, "The cartel owned about 12,000 properties in the city. These included apartment buildings they had constructed with drug profits. The first two floors would often have occupied flats and security guards to make them look normal, while higher-level rooms were filled with rare art, gold and other valuables. Some of the apartment rooms were filled with stacks of 100-dollar bills that had been wrapped in plastic bags and covered with mothballs. Hot off American streets, this money was waiting to be counted, deposited or shipped out of the country."

The authorities also found underground vaults in the fields behind some of the big haciendas. Lifting up concrete blocks, they discovered stairwells descending into secret rooms that contained up to 9 million dollars in cash. This was so-called 'throw-away' money. Serious funds were laundered through banks or pumped into 'legitimate' businesses. To facilitate wire transfers, the cartel had purchased a chain of financial institutions in Colombia called the Workers Bank.

[6] "Gracias a Dios No Explotó," El Pais, Cali, November 6, 1996; "En Cali   Desactivan Un 'Carrobomba,' El.Pais, Cali, November 6, 1996.

[7] Reports here by Vuniani Nakauyaca and Walo Ani are edited from Vuniani Nakauyaca and Walo Ani, 2007, A Manual for Healing the Land, Toowoomba City Church, Australia, pp.77-91.

[8] Reports by Harry Tura are reproduced from his prayer letters.

[9] 2 Chronicles 7:14. Further details of many revivals in the South Pacific are included with photographs in Geoff Waugh, 2010, South Pacific Revivals.

Geoff Waugh

Conclusion

Specific impacts of the Holy Spirit's anointing (Luke 4:18) and empowering (Acts1:8) occur repeatedly in revivals from Pentecost to now.

Revival history demonstrates how the light shines in the darkness, and the darkness has never overcome it (John 1:5). Often revivals intervened when it seemed that darkness triumphed and evil abounded. Grace (charis) abounded much more (Romans 5:20). God continually poured out his Spirit especially in gracious response to the earnest, persistent, believing, repentant prayers of his people.

From that initial outpouring at Pentecost until now revivals are controversial, disturbing and confusing. They often look better from a distance in time and space. They may look and sound very messy close up. Revivals in the history books or in Africa sound wonderful! Revivals in your own backyard can be a headache.

Noisy outbursts of strange behaviour such as speaking in tongues may cause huge crowds to come and see what is going on, even before any preaching begins (Acts 2:6). Preachers may have to explain that they and their friends are not drunk as everyone thinks they are (Acts 2:15). Hundreds or thousands of brand new Christians may suddenly invade your church with all the problems and possibilities they bring (Acts 2:41). People in authority may object violently to these disturbing developments, especially if they involve healing in Jesus' name without any doctor present, and thousands more believing in Jesus without even a New Testament to guide them (Acts 4:14). Those are the messy and wonderful problems typical of revival.

This book briefly surveyed a little of that story from the evangelical revivals in the eighteenth century to the current revivals of the last few decades. Revivals still burst into flame in spite of rampant unbelief and the spread of evil or persecution. Flashpoints of revival include Africa, Latin America, China, Korea, and the Pacific where hundreds of millions have become Christian in a few decades.

It is an astounding story. A small community of Moravians prayed around the clock in 'hourly intercessions' for a century and sent out missionaries while Whitefield, Wesley, Edwards and others fanned the flames of the Great Awakening. Revival ignited further missionary zeal in the nineteenth century when Finney, Moody and others led widespread revivals as hundreds of thousands cried out to God in prayer. The awesome Welsh revival early in the twentieth century ignited revival fires around the world and ushered in a century of repeated outbursts of revival with hundreds of millions turning from darkness to light.

Revival historian Edwin Orr described these awakenings following the Great Awakening of 1727-1745 as the Second Awakening of 1790-1830 (The Eager Feet, fired with missionary commitment), the Third Awakening of 1858-60 (The

Fervent Prayer, spread through countless prayer groups) and the Worldwide Awakening from 1900 (The Flaming Tongue, spreading the word around the globe).

The twentieth century saw further movements of revival and renewal with the amazing growth of the church globally. The Pentecostal rediscovery of New Testament ministry in the power of the Holy Spirit ignited revival fires across the world.

Following the dark days of two world wars evangelists and revivalists such as Billy Graham, Oral Roberts, T. L. and Daisy Osborn and others gained global exposure from 1947-1948. Another outpouring of revival and renewal surged through the seventies with revivals in Canada, the Jesus People movement in America, charismatic renewal in the churches, and a fresh outpouring of mission and evangelism in developing nations which launched people such as Reinhard Bonnke, Yonggi Cho, and many more in leading hundreds of thousands to the Lord and establishing massive churches and ministries. The nineties continued to see an acceleration of revival including the spread of revival from countries such as Argentina and from local communities such as Pensacola.

Accounts such as the ones in this book raise other awkward questions. How much is of God? How much is just human reaction to the Spirit of God? How much is mere excitement and enthusiasm? How much is hysteria? How much is crowd manipulation? How much is demonic?

The answers to such questions can fall into two equally dangerous and opposite extremes. On one hand we may think it is all of God alone, when in fact there are always many human reactions and even demonic attacks mixed in with powerful revivals. On the other hand we may dismiss it all as emotional hype, psychological reactions and/or sociological developments, when in fact God has brought people from death to life and from darkness to light in huge numbers, permanently affecting their eternal destiny.

When the religious and political leaders in Jerusalem faced similar dilemmas, especially the boldness of uneducated and ordinary people with a flaming zeal for the Jesus those leaders had killed, they were not happy (Acts 4:13-21). In fact, they wanted to kill those revivalists as they had killed Jesus. However, one of their more insightful leaders reminded them that they may end up fighting against God a rather unequal match (Acts 5:33-39).

May God grant us the faith to believe in our great God who is able and willing to do far more than anything we could ever ask or imagine (Ephesians 3:20-21), the hope that shines in a dark world where we desperately need God's grace to abound in revival (Romans 5:20-21), and the love to serve and bless one another as Jesus demands of us and as he himself loves us (John 13:34-35).

You and I can humble ourselves, and pray, and seek God's face, and turn from our wicked ways. God promises to hear from heaven, forgive our sin and heal the land (2 Chronicles 7:14).

Flashpoints of revival ignited the early church and they turned their world upside down (Acts 17:6). Fire fell again and again in revivals, and still does. We need people full of faith, vision, wisdom, love and the fire of the Holy Spirit as we live for God in our moment in history.

Other books by Geoff Waugh

See renewaljournal.com and amazon.com for details and reviews.

South Pacific Revivals: community and ecological transformation. Revivals in the Solomon Islands, Papua New Guinea, Vanuatu and Fiji.

Living in the Spirit: The Holy Spirit and the Christian Life. Personal and group studies on the Holy Spirit.

Looking to Jesus: Journey into Renewal and Revival. Autobiography of 70 years including revival ministry and mission.

Light on the Mountains: pioneer mission in Papua New Guinea. Beginnings of the Australian Baptist Mission in Papua New Guinea.

Church on Fire: renewal and revival in Australia. Renewal and revival reports including Aboriginal revival.

Discovering Aslan: High King above all kings in Narnia. Exploring the Story within the stories of The Chronicles of Narnia.

other products from globalawakening

In "There Is More," Randy lays a solid biblical foundation for a theology of impartation, and takes a historical look at impartation and visitation of the Lord in the Church. This is combined with personal testimonies of people who have received an impartation throughout the world and what the impact has been in their lives. You are taken on journey throughout the world to see for yourself the lasting fruit that is taking place in the harvest field - particularly in Mozambique. This release of power is not only about phenomena of the Holy Spirit, it is about its ultimate effect on evangelism and missions. Your heart will be stirred for more as you read this book.

"This is the book that Randy Clark was born to write."
- Bill Johnson

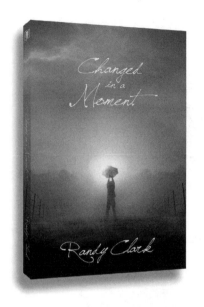

Changed in a Moment
Randy Clark

"Changed In a Moment shares new stories that demonstrate to believers that God is still doing today what He was doing more than 15 years ago. I remain amazed at the power of God to radically change a person's life in a matter of seconds. Join me as we seek to understand the profoundness of being "changed in a moment" by God.

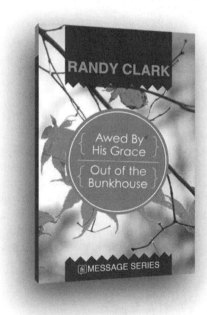

Awed by His Grace/Out of the Bunkhouse
Randy Clark

In this booklet, Randy shares with us much of his personal journey, being awed by His grace. Then he reinforces our understanding that coming into relationship with God is so much more than just being forgiven. Our prayer is that each of you will learn to grow in showing that same grace to others, that they might truly experience the Father's heart through us.

globalawakening

For a schedule of upcoming events and conferences, or to purchase other products from Global Awakening, please visit our website at:

http://www.globalawakening.com